D0868805

CRIMINAL CONVERSATIONS

Criminal Conversations is an anthology of the work of Tony Parker who has been the most outstanding interviewer of criminals since the Second World War. Described as the 'Mayhew of his times', his work spans the 1960s to the 1990s and he speaks intimately to all kinds of offenders – inadequates, professional criminals, sex offenders, frauds and false pretence merchants. His work is both timely and timeless.

This collection of Tony Parker's work, selected by him shortly before his death in 1996, provides the very essence of his quite distinctive contribution. The Introduction by Professor Terence Morris, who knew Tony Parker for nearly forty years, provides both an appreciation of and the context for his work. The book is then divided into six major parts:

- 'Inadequates' – the stage army of offenders who keep returning to prison
- 'Villainy: a way of life' – on professional criminals
- 'Some answers to a question' – what should a judge do with you?
- 'Nonces' – on sex offenders
- 'Frauds and false pretence merchants'
- 'At death's door' – those sentenced to death or to life imprisonment for murder

In the final section, some of Tony Parker's prescriptions for interviewing are set out and Lyn Smith concludes with some reflections on his methodology.

Keith Soothill is Professor of Social Research in the Department of Applied Social Science at Lancaster University.

CRIMINAL CONVERSATIONS

An anthology of the work of
Tony Parker

Edited by Keith Soothill
Introduction by Terence Morris

London and New York

CROWOOD COLLEGE LIBRARY
FARMVILLE, VIRGINIA 23901

HV
6945
.C75
1999

First published 1999
by Routledge
11 New Fetter Lane, London EC4P 4EE

Simultaneously published in the USA and Canada
by Routledge
29 West 35th Street, New York, NY 10001

© 1999 Tim Parker, except final chapter, 'Only listen...',
© 1999 Lyn Smith
Introduction © 1999 Terence Morris

Typeset in Bembo by Routledge
Printed and bound in Great Britain by TJ International Ltd,
Padstow, Cornwall

All rights reserved. No part of this book may be reprinted
or reproduced or utilised in any form or by any electronic,
mechanical, or other means, now known or hereafter
invented, including photocopying and recording, or in any
information storage or retrieval system, without permission in
writing from the publishers.

British Library Cataloguing in Publication Data
A catalogue record for this book is available from the British Library

Library of Congress Cataloging in Publication Data
Criminal Conversations: an anthology of the work of Tony Parker/
edited by Keith Soothill: Introduction by Terence Morris.
Principally interviews confined to the words of the persons
interviewed.
1. Criminals – Great Britain – Case studies.
2. Criminals – Great Britain – Interviews.
3. Prisoners – Great Britain – Case studies.
4. Prisoners – Great Britain – Interviews.
5. Criminal psychology – Great Britain – Case studies.
I. Parker, Tony. II. Soothill, Keith.
HV6945.C75 1999   98-42332
364.3'0941–dc21   CIP

ISBN 0–415–19739–2 (hbk)
ISBN 0–415–19740–6 (pbk)

LONGWOOD COLLEGE LIBRARY
FARMVILLE, VIRGINIA 23901

CONTENTS

LONGWOOD LIBRARY

1000325028

CONTENTS

PREFACE

The origin of this book is straightforward. When I saw an obituary of Tony Parker in a newspaper in 1996, I was saddened. I did not know Tony, but I recognised it was the end of an era. There would be no more new books from Tony Parker.

The world seems to divide between those who have read some of his work and those who may not even know of his name. The former group includes a considerable range of people. I have had the experience of seeing Tony's books quite unexpectedly on a variety of bookshelves. He has made an entry into many people's lives. However, I also recognised the reality that future, even current, generations of students and others could not experience the intimate quality of his work, for the majority of his books are out of print.

A few months after his death I wrote to his last publisher, who informed me that Tony had been planning an anthology. He knew that he was dying. Richard Johnson of HarperCollins suggested that I contacted Tony's widow, Margery. One sometimes hears of the problems of contacting dead authors' relatives who fail to co-operate. Margery, and later Tim – Tony's son – have been marvellous in assisting me to complete this anthology. They have helped in so many ways, both in terms of being generally supportive and in helping me with specific background information.

Margery found the draft of an outline proposal for an anthology. It was quite remarkable that Tony had chosen to concentrate on his 'criminal canon'. Roughly half his books are based on interviews with criminals and others connected with the criminal justice system, such as governors and prison officers. His other books focus on a considerable range of topics, but the overall theme of his work can perhaps be summarised as being about social exclusion in its various guises. He was concerned with all people living at the margins of society. However, I was delighted that Tony had in mind a 'criminal anthology', for these are the books which I regard as special. Perhaps they were also special for him, in the sense that he started with interviewing criminals and he will always be most closely associated with this body of work.

Margery provided me with the set of books on which Tony had been working. The project – without a title – had moved some way forward, for extracts were marked up in the books and some sketchy notes were sometimes found in the margins. I quickly made a decision that I would try to construct an anthology which would represent as close as I could get to what Tony wanted. My editing role started when I realised that Tony had identified more and sometimes longer extracts than could be included in this book. So I had to choose. I hope Tony would have been pleased with the outcome.

I only met Tony once. This was when he was waiting to see my wife's boss, Neville Vincent, who was then Secretary of the Central Council of Probation Committees. He was described to me as an author, so out of curiosity I bought one of his books, *The Unknown Citizen*. It was a revelation.

The Unknown Citizen relates to Tony Parker's conversations with 'Charlie Smith'. Charlie is a man, repeatedly in trouble, repeatedly in court, repeatedly in prison. As Tony Parker explains, we cannot seem to help people like Charlie or check them in their ways, but we tend to fall back eventually simply on punishment either in anger or despair. In his conversations, Tony Parker listens and speaks very little. He regarded himself as 'a blackboard for people to write on'. As a consequence, Charlie's own story comes across vividly. The book provides insights into how we sometimes simply fail to understand each other. I can still remember how Tony Parker asked Charlie whether he had seen the prison welfare officer, meaning had the officer dealt with his problems. Charlie tells Tony that he had seen the welfare officer crossing the prison yard last week. One learns that middle-class persons go and see people, while prisoners like Charlie wait to be called. This part of the book made a lasting impact on me, but it was not an extract which Tony chose to include. This anthology has other gems which Tony has chosen.

In the Introduction, Professor Terence Morris usefully locates Tony Parker within the criminological tradition. He explains how Tony's work has in some ways been overlooked and neglected. Terry was my doctoral supervisor in the 1960s, and until recently I was not aware that he knew Tony Parker so well and for so long. Perhaps we all failed to acknowledge his importance in a concerted way during his lifetime. However, I suppose it was not easy. After all, Tony Parker was by all accounts a modest man who was himself a wonderful misfit in the criminological world. In the concluding section of this book, the focus is on his methodology. He rarely wrote of his technique which he had moulded over the years. However, he made a short list of points which he sent to those who enquired. Lyn Smith, who planned to write a book with Tony Parker on his methodology, provides some important insights.

Tony Parker probably made more of an impact on the real world than any academic criminologist, but he recognised towards the end of his life that he had not really changed things. Sir Stephen Tumim, the former Chief Inspector of Prisons, once called Tony Parker 'the Mayhew of our times'. In my view, everyone of 'our times' continues to need to read Tony Parker's conversations. They are both timeless and timely as many of the issues he implicitly raises remain with us.

Keith Soothill
August 1998

ACKNOWLEDGEMENTS

Everyone contacted has been most enthusiastic about this project which highlights Tony Parker's work. He is remembered most warmly. However, in particular, I wish to thank Margery Parker, Tony's widow, who has been extremely supportive from the outset, together with Tim Parker, Tony's son, who has been very helpful in various ways. In terms of sorting out permissions etc., Tim and myself are most grateful to Gill Coleridge in particular and to Richard Johnson for his support and interest. Finally, I wish to thank all those at Routledge involved in the publication of this book.

Keith Soothill

counted nothing human indifferent to him.[1] And he knew, as Hillaire Belloc had once thoughtfully observed, that

> of all the creatures that move and breathe upon the earth, we
> of mankind are the fullest of sorrow[2]

As a Prison Visitor he would have been given a copy of *Voluntary Workers: Regulations and Advice*, a minuscule booklet bearing a Prison Commission document number of 1023 and a printer's mark of 16 November 1946. He would have been:

> requested to read them very carefully, and at all times to regard
> the strict observance thereof as is applicable to (his) own
> work as a necessary condition of the continuance of that
> work.

Of prisoners he would have read further that:

> A healthier outlook on life and human society, and a sense
> of responsibility towards fellow citizens, can best be devel-
> oped in the quickening mind and the sounder physique
> which result from making the day's work, both of hand and
> brain, as strenuous and as interesting as possible. To this end
> the prisoner receives simple but sufficient food....An object
> of equal importance is that of creating and sustaining mental
> activity, and arousing interests which will drive out of his
> mind the range of selfish and sordid ideas by which it has
> too often been occupied, and prove an abiding gain for the
> prisoner's future life.

So, Prison Visitors had the task of introducing a balanced perspec-tive into the lives of these wretched convicts, lessening their selfishness and seeking to rouse in them some idea of their obliga-tions to their fellow citizens. Avoiding such controversial issues as politics and religion – the first with its potential challenge to the existing social order and the second being the fiefdom of the prison chaplain who was employed for the purpose – the Prison Visitor was

---

1 Terence, *c.* 190–159 BC: 'Homo sum; humani nil alienum puto' (I am a man; I count nothing indifferent to me).
2 Belloc, Hillaire (1925) *The Cruise of the Nona*, Constable & Co., p. 347.

the embodiment of what remained of the original Pennsylvania system of penal reform. Presented with the values of an orthodox world by an individual whom the prisoner would come to trust and regard as his natural social superior, he would begin first to question and then to reject those pursuits of a short-run, hedonistic character which, though they might have landed him in prison, were largely all he had learned in the disprivileged social world from which he came.

If such language and objectives seem archaic, almost to the point of sounding like the script of some Sunday-night costume drama, it is necessary to travel back to that period immediately after the Second World War in order to place Tony and his work in perspective. This was a time when the social sciences were still sceptically regarded and when criminology, generally believed to be the science of detecting crime and capturing criminals, remained suspect as being something emanating from the Continent – that place so often cut off by fog in the Channel. The Prison Commissioners had, certainly since the early 1920s, pursued humane and constructive policies, shot through with compassionate Christianity in general and greatly influenced by Quaker values in particular, which were aimed at the protection of society through the reformation of the criminal. But that was not a view universally held. Among many lawyers and most judges there was a contention that anyone who sought to explain crime – save in terms of the moral turpitude or weakness of the offender – was seeking only to excuse it.

The most powerful players in the criminal justice system of the 1950s – the judges and magistrates, the police and the legal profession – were sceptical if not openly hostile to anything which challenged the view of human (and by inclusion, criminal) nature as based on other than a variant of eighteenth-century rationalism that held that men naturally sought pleasure and avoided pain. Those who chose crime did so for the pleasures that it brought and needed, therefore, to experience the pain of punishment. The cure for crime in individuals, and its prevention generally, lay in the application of that rationalist approach. In the context of a neo-Hegelian penal philosophy it was argued that not only did the offender deserve to be punished but, that since it was in his best moral interest, it was also his *right*; and more than that; the punishment of crime should be of such a character that it would deter both the individual from re-offending and others from considering the very prospect of it for the first time. And all this while, the dark shadow of capital punishment loomed over the entire criminal justice system. Combined with a law of homicide that owed almost everything to the common law, and its interpretation by a range of judges from Coke in the seventeenth century to Goddard in the twentieth, injustices resulted that ranged from a failure by Home Secretaries to exercise mercy to wrongful conviction whether on account of the evidence or the summing up at the end of the trial.

There was yet another shadow that loomed darkly over the criminal justice system, not of a law but a lawyer, in the person of Rayner Goddard, Lord Chief Justice of England. From his appointment in 1946 to his retirement in 1958 he exerted a powerfully dominant influence that was felt not only in the conduct of criminal trials but especially in the Court of Criminal Appeal, as it was then known. Since 1917 he had held successively the Recorderships of Poole, Bath and Plymouth, until 1932 when he was elevated to the King's Bench Division. Goddard seldom concealed his dislike of the criminal or his distrust of those whom he perceived as 'excusing' criminal behaviour. In 1952, by now aged 76, he presided over the trial of Craig and Bentley for the murder of PC Miles in the course of a commercial burglary. Craig, who fired the fatal shot, was too young to hang. The mentally retarded Bentley, by that time in custody, having held to have said 'Let him have it, Chris!', was hanged on 28 January 1953 aged 19. But as a result of progress in law reform in the shape of the Criminal Cases Review Committee, it was in his own court that Bentley's conviction was to be overturned on 30 July 1998 and he, Goddard the judge, to be condemned not to death, but to the indelible obloquy which history must attach to the unjust judge. In his partisan summing up to the jury, his language was not that of a judge but an advocate.[3]

Thus at the time when Tony Parker was doing his first work among convicted criminals there were a variety of forces at work, in society in general and within the criminal justice system, that could produce a bewildering pattern of inconsistency and unpredictability. The judiciary, at all levels, reflected the stern unbending approach personified

---

3   The Lord Chief Justice, Lord Bingham, delivering the judgment of the Court of Appeal (Criminal Division) in R. *v* Bentley was widely reported in the press: 'It is with genuine diffidence that the members of this court direct criticism towards a trial judge widely recognised as one of the outstanding judges of this century. But we cannot escape the duty of decision. In our judgment the summing up in this case was such as to deny the appellant that fair trial which is the birthright of every British citizen.' It might be said of Goddard, as of Jeffreys in the seventeenth century, that at his best he was an outstanding lawyer but at his worst a truly terrible judge.

by the Lord Chief Justice. The pattern of sentencing, though it did not produce the very long sentences with which we are presently familiar, did include capital punishment. And while the Prison Commissioners were committed to liberal and constructive policies, prisons were old and insanitary[4] and discipline maintained by such sanctions as solitary confinement, bread and water diet and, at the order of the Visiting Magistrates, the birch and the cat o' nine tails.

Those who sought to improve the lot of offenders, though transparently sincere in their concern were, nevertheless, often bound by the constraints of class and culture. In Denis Mitchell's 1956 film of Strangeways – the first ever made inside a British prison – we see the formal approach of the committee of the local Discharged Prisoners' Aid Society and, no less, the hats of the women members worn as naturally at that meeting as when having afternoon tea in a Manchester department store. The approach to working with offenders was still informed by the best of Victorian philosophy; it was generously Christian; it sought to rehabilitate, to save the sinner and reserve condemnation for the sin. But it was an approach characterised by a commitment to social orthodoxy and, insofar as it was coloured by any criminological theory, reflected the kind of liberal positivism that had become deeply entrenched in the profession of social welfare both in Britain and North America.

The idea of the criminal being 'different', a modern-day savage, possessed of little if any nobility, needing to be civilised, was deeply entrenched. While liberal reformers assumed civilisation to be possible through kindness and example, those sceptical of that approach placed more reliance on control. Like badly behaved dogs, recalcitrant horses or the slaves of earlier times, there was nothing like punishment to demonstrate to the criminal classes in particular and the lower orders in general, that it was not for them to challenge but to obey.

The decade of the 1960s, often identified (largely inaccurately) as an age of promiscuous hedonism, witnessed a number of profound changes both in the intellectual approach to the phenomena of crime and deviance and the shape of the criminal justice system itself. The new deviancy theory and later the New Criminology were to ensure that those academic orthodoxies that had been based upon various

---

4 Apart from Camp Hill (1912) and Everthorpe (1957) (though modelled on the Wormwood Scrubs of 1865) no new prisons had been built since Victorian times. Cell sanitation was by chamber pot.

forms of positivism were finally, and largely fatally, challenged. A combination of labelling theory – imported from North America – and the activation of a hitherto disregarded political perspective transformed the academic criminological landscape. Not only was crime to be understood as a social construct rather than an intrinsic quality of behaviour; it was to be seen as a label selectively applied in the context of social control, to the powerless by the powerful. These were the years in which Marx was to be read and Gramsci's notebooks to be discovered, and the connections between traditional positivism and European fascism illuminated. At last it began to be understood that those who legislate have done so for centuries in the context of self-interest; that the dominant concerns of the criminal law for the protection of property are rooted in its unequal distribution in society, and that the evidence of history is that the grosser the inequalities, the more fearful are the consequences for those who infringe its protecting laws.

The 1960s produced many substantial and overdue reforms, not least the abolition of capital punishment. Among the least recognised, since its effects have been of the 'slow release' variety, was the fundamental reform of the magistracy, both with regard to their appointment and the introduction of compulsory basic and continuous refresher training. Of the enthusiasms of that period, little discernible remains save that paradoxically, while the quality of higher judiciary is now of an order that would have seemed impossible forty years ago, the penal system has slid inexorably backwards towards having a carceral rather than a rehabilitative priority.

What, the reader may ask, has this to do with Tony Parker and his work? In one sense, no more than being some account of the times through which he lived and in which his work was done. But in another, a great deal, since he was the chronicler of so many lives that were shaped by those various forces which affect the complex phenomena of social control. To understand the rationale of his work and its impact, one must understand something of the man. Not an academic in the conventional sense, he had many lines into the world of academe. Not a political figure, he had his connections and his antennae were finely tuned. His work was that of an ethnographer, initially of those deviants at the very margins of society and later of those, though not pejoratively identified as deviant, who nevertheless found themselves in situations outwith the mainstream. He saw, but above all he listened and in so doing enabled the often inarticulate – and those to whom no one had ever troubled to listen – to speak for themselves.

He began with criminals, and it may be that it was this part of his work which will be best remembered; certainly, it cannot fail to withstand the test of time. When Henry Mayhew began collecting his vignettes of life on the streets of mid-Victorian London he was working against the grain of contemporary social inquiry; the gifted amateurs of the Statistical Society of London preferred to rely upon numbers and tabulations, which they duly analysed to produce theories about crime and delinquency and were able to avoid the sights and smells of deviancy in the flesh. For Mayhew it was otherwise, perhaps because the instincts of the journalist were strong in him. When Tony Parker was beginning his work with a tape recorder, the conventional criminologist fell to his task with a questionnaire. His subject, generally captive and readily produced from a sample of inmates who were often only too willing to vary the boredom of their prison lives by donating an hour of idleness to some 'college type', would be interrogated, often with what the technical literature described by the somewhat unfortunate term 'subsidiary probes'. While the unstructured interview was not unknown, it was often frowned on as giving methodological hostages to fortune. How could it be replicated for purposes of comparison? What guarantee would there be that the data were representative?

When Tony sat down and started his tape recorder the methodology was altogether simpler; he listened and the machine recorded. What was more important was *technique*, for the most dependable recording machines of the 1950s and 1960s tended to be intrusively large and relied upon reels of magnetic tape that had to be carefully wound on to spools. The interviewee would almost always be seeing a recording machine for the first time, and it could be as unsettling as the great plate cameras with which the Victorians captured their images of compliant − and often naked − savagery. It was for the subject to determine the agenda. Some, encouraged by this newly acquired autonomy, pronounced philosophically. In *The Courage of his Convictions*, Robert Allerton famously produces a variation on the Brechtian assertion that property is theft. When the bank is robbed, says Allerton, the manager does not write to every customer saying, 'Our branch has been robbed of so many thousands of pounds and I am sorry to say that the enclosed statement indicates how many of them were yours.' Corporate wealth, notwithstanding that it may be inclusive of individual wealth, is not vulnerable in the same way.

Allerton was, of course, reiterating what many a juvenile delinquent had asserted to many a policeman and probation officer: that to steal from an individual, especially one who was visibly poor, was unacceptable while a theft from a department store was a theft from no one. Or, as it was once put to me about a theft from Woolworths: 'That Barbara Hutton's a millionairess. She won't miss it!' In *The Courage of his Convictions*, we savour some sense of the criminal as the defiantly radical critic of the *status quo*; the voice of the criminal who is not supposed to be critical but to accept that rich men in their castles and poor men at their gates are where they are by a supervening divine ordinance which it is not their privilege to question.

In 1965, before feminist criminology had acquired an existence, let alone academic legitimacy, Tony published *Five Women*, a poignantly moving account of what the penal system had managed to achieve in the lives of five women who had been to prison and a sixth, a 17-year-old, who had emerged from borstal. Re-reading it after more than thirty years, one is tempted simply to observe *plus ça change, toujours la même chose*; but the book does more than provide a benchmark against which contemporary penal practice may be measured. It recounts, in a style oddly reminiscent of that anger which resonates through Zola's *Germinal*, the oppression of these hapless women, not merely in terms of their class but additionally their gender, by those habituated to the exercise of power. Here, too, in *Five Women* the horror of child abuse is presented not clinically, but almost poetically and all the more powerfully for that. Sixty-year-old Janie Preston – with eighteen convictions and more than twelve years of prison behind her – had been sentenced by Judge Neville Laski at Liverpool Assizes to eight years' preventive detention: she had stolen £55.

> A stout ugly unhappy old woman, she put her hands down dejectedly on the edge of the table…put her face down on her hands, and wept. Bitterly and unceasingly, she poured out her Lancashire accented threnody; unhesitatingly, because she could tell me about it, I'd understand her, I'd know what it was like, because I had a Lancashire accent too…[5]

His empathy with Janie enabled Tony to hear of a private shame which she had carried for nearly fifty years. The extracts in this book of Janie's story capture a painful but memorable account of a personal trouble which has emerged as an important public issue in the last two decades. However, the sadness of the individuals involved is rarely

5   Parker, T. (1965) *Five Women*, London: Hutchinson, pp. 147–8.

resolved: 'She wants to be left alone and if a prison cell is the only place she can have solitude, she does not very much mind.'[6]

In 1965 appeared *The Plough Boy*, an account of the trial and conviction of Michael John Davies for the murder of 17-year-old John Beckley in a gang fight near Clapham Common in the summer of 1953. Davies had been sentenced to death and spent 92 days in the death cell, the longest period for any prisoner in modern times. He was 20 years old. He was to serve seven years of the life sentence to which the death penalty was commuted. Tony sought to get the thoughts of the trial judge, Mr Justice Hilbery, long after the trial was over. He had joined in the questioning of witnesses or interrupted with comments a total of 243 times: 54 times in the evidence of Davies himself and nine times in the course of the final speech for the defence, all in the course of four days. At the first the judge failed to respond; then, getting another letter from Tony, invited him to lunch. Tony wrote that it might be thought churlish if he were to accept a lunch when he had written a book so critical of the trial over which the judge had presided, so could he come *after* lunch? The judge changed his mind, thinking it perhaps unwise or even improper, that they should meet. *Res ipsa loquitur*, as a lawyer might say.

Sex offenders, con-men, the inmates of Grendon psychiatric prison; all are caught in the sweep of his ever sharply focussed observation of the human condition. Latterly, his interest shifted to lighthouse keepers, professional soldiers, to the people of a small American town and to those who had to endure the bombs and sectarian bitterness that have disfigured the face of Ireland for the last quarter of a century. In no enterprise upon which he ventured, in nothing that he wrote, did he ever seek to disguise that which was surely the thing which burned most fiercely within him: a compassion for humankind. For all his astonishing skills in gathering what social scientists would call data, no one could call him an academic. The nearest his work approached that would be by comparison with the best of the Chicago School of the 1920s where Robert Park sent his students into the streets and bars of the city to discover the sociological facts. And Park remained at heart the newspaperman he had originally been. Tony was altogether too passionate, too sensitive to injustice and hypocrisy, ever to compromise with them; too much aware of pain, of sorrow, of loneliness, of humiliation, of cruelty and of injustice, ever to be able to stand wholly apart from the subjects of his inquiry.

6   ibid., p. 169.

For him the people who gave him their time were not like moths to be examined under the glass; if they resembled *lepidoptera* at all, it was as creatures held gently in his hand until in the spreading of their wings their special beauty was revealed.

This book must of necessity contain but a sample of Tony's work; more than a simple tasting but less than an entire feasting. His mark is upon it all as surely as the hand of any artist is set indelibly upon his work, no matter what the material in which it is done. These were the things he was called upon to do but in this, his vocation, we may discern a blending of those elements that Durkheim had once distinguished from each other; the sacred and the profane. In his portrayal of the human condition, shot through with injustice and pain and, so often, that lack of love which is among the chief sources of bleakness in this life, he depicts those profanities that are ultimately corrosive of the human spirit. But alongside them are the transcendent glimpses of that longing for perfection, the desire to love as well as to be loved and the manifestations of altruism that lift mankind above the mire of self-interest.

His was, as those who knew him well would confirm, a deeply spiritual nature, notwithstanding that he endured many of the uncertainties that most of us experience from time to time. One writer who had a powerful influence upon him was John Donne, poet, divine and a seventeenth-century Dean of St Paul's. In his *Devotions upon Emergent Occasions and severall steps in my Sicknes*[7] Donne writes:

> No man is so little, in respect of the greatest man, as the greatest in respect of God, for here, in that we have not so much as a measure to try it by; proportion is no measure for infinity. He that hath no more of this world but a grave; he that hath his grave but lent him until a better man, or another man must be buried in the same grave, he that hath no grave but a dunghill, he that hath no more earth than that which he carries, but that which he is, he is not that earth which he is, but even in that is another's slave; hath as much proportion to God as if all David's worthies and all

---

7   Donne, John (1626) *Devotions upon Emergent Occasions and severall steps in my Sicknes*, The Third Edition, London. Two years before his death, after I had given a public lecture, as Tony and I parted company he smiled and gave me a small packet which he said contained 'After Eights'. Opening the packet the next day I found it to contain this volume, still in the better part of its seventeenth-century binding. A note simply said, 'As a token of our long years of friendship.'

the world's monarchs and all imaginations, giants, were knea-
ded and incorporated into one and as though that one were
the survivor of all the sons of men to whom God had given
the world.

Part I

INADEQUATES

The terms actually used to describe the stage army of offenders who keep returning to prison after continually failing to cope in the outside world may change in each generation, but their characteristics do not. Tony Parker was most unusual in having the interest, patience and ability to listen to these men and women who had no doubt been frequently questioned by persons in authority as they journeyed through the criminal justice system over the years. However, persons in authority rarely have the time or technique to elicit a full answer. In contrast, Tony could encourage them in a remarkable way to tell the story of their lives.

Their accounts provide an insight into another world for most of us. However, it is not one world but a variety of other worlds that these persons have inhabited. When Tony met them either in prison or soon after their release, their prospects seemed grim. Indeed, prison was now where they seemed to belong.

The psychologist who spoke about Charlie Smith effectively indicates why these accounts are something more than voyeurism: 'The more we increase people's understanding of men like Charlie and show that what they are now is largely the result of their life's experience, the less condemnatory and the more constructive society's reaction to them may, I hope, become.'

IN THE COOLER[1]

Kendon Prender

His cell was up on the sixth floor of the courthouse. In its end wall there was a square of wire-meshed glass out of reach ten feet up, and from the entrance there was nothing to be seen through the bars of the heavy metal sliding door except the white-painted brickwork of the corridor outside it. A burly young man with long gingery hair and pale blue eyes, wearing orange dungarees, he sat on his bunk with his legs stretched out in front of him. His voice was a quiet flat drawl.

—Well no sir I do not come from around these parts at all, that's right no I do not. My home town in Elgin, that's 30 miles south of Baxter, right on the Tipton County line. That's my home town where I was born and where my Ma and Pa are, but I guess now it's two years or more since I been down that way. I don't have much to do with my folks and they don't have much to do with me, and that way we get along pretty good. My Pa he's a drinking man and I'm kind of a drinking man too you could say: we have some awful fights if we get together when we've both been drinking, so most often we try and keep ourselves apart. That way no one gets hurt and my Ma she don't get to cry.

Well sir I have two brothers and one sister: I'm 24 and I'm the oldest one of us. As far as I could tell you I'm the only one's been in any kind of trouble, least not the last time I heard. And my Pa no, he's not been in no trouble, he's a regular hard-working man is my Pa. I sure don't know what's different about me, and I can tell you I wish sometimes I did. Then I'd maybe know what to do about it, only the

---

1 *A Place Called Bird* (1990) London: Pan Books, pp. 208–15.

15

way I'm heading right now it's getting to be just one thing after the other, and that's sure worrying me some.

This last time that judge gave it to me straight, she said I was lucky it was only going to be 12 months here in the County Jail, and maybe I wouldn't have to do all of it if I behaved myself. She said next time she was going to send me on in front of the District judge and he'd give me a heavier sentence for sure. Drunk driving she said was something she regarded as real serious, specially this being my third time in court here for it: but 12 months, I think that was real heavy of her. I had in mind more like she'd give me maybe 6 months, or 6 and 6 months suspended, something of that order. To tell you the truth I was kind of surprised about it because I'd not been in front of her before. When I saw her I thought she was a real pretty judge with nice-looking legs: but there you are, that didn't make no difference when it came the time to sentence me. Kind of makes you think about these things, something like that does: makes you think the next time you go drunk driving, don't do it around Auburn County, else you've got big trouble for yourself.

I don't know that I can make a good job of piecing my life story together for you, but I'd sure be happy to give it a try. Only I'll have to think some first, just give me a minute to think some first and kind of get it in order OK? Well I'm 24 years of age for a start, did I tell you that? Yeah well that's what I am, 24. And I have two brothers and a sister, did I tell you that too? I did, yeah.... You know maybe if you could ask me some questions or something that might help some.

Went to school, yeah I sure did. I went to Junior School and to High School both, that was in Overland. My Dad, he worked for a trucking company and Overland was where we lived. It was later on that we went to Elgin after my Dad and my Ma split up and got divorced: the guy there I call my Pa, he's the man married my Ma after her and my Dad were divorced. Sure, I liked going to school but I never got good grades and stuff and so I didn't go to school that much, I'd sooner stay home or run around with the other guys. We didn't have gangs so much, just groups of guys running around. What did we do, well we didn't do very much of anything, I'd say chiefly we smoked: smoked marijuana chiefly I'd say, yeah. I'd say I started using like most kids do, around 11 or 12 somewhere there: the usual age but not younger than that: I guess I was different from most kids a bit, because after I started I didn't stop. No sir I never have stopped, I still use now when I'm out. I kind of like it you know, it gives you a nice feeling: I've never had heroin or cocaine, I think those things are harmful to you, but I sure do like to smoke marijuana. I had a girl friend once, now she was all the time shooting and wanting me to as well, but I just didn't go along with that. That stuff can give you bad health and all sorts: I do, I keep right away from it. What I chiefly like when I smoke is it relaxes you and makes you amiable towards folk: it gives you a kick but it's a kick into relaxation, which is sort of good. You talk to anyone who smokes, they'll tell you the same.

Let's see now, my family: well I'd say they were an average family, that's about all there is to say. I think my Ma was kind of unhappy most times and my Pa was unhappy some of the time, I'd put it like that. He drank a lot: I wouldn't say he was an alcoholic but he was going that way if you know how I mean. A very silent man most of the time, he didn't talk much to anyone, not to me nor to my brothers and my sister. Me and one brother, we have the same father: then the other brother and my sister, they were his children that he had with my Ma. I think I've got that right, I'm pretty sure it was that way. Only you kind of forget: when you're young and you all live together you don't take too much notice of that kind of thing.

Well yessir that is right: from somewhere around twelve on, I didn't spend too much of my time home, no I did not. I spent my time with my friends, and mostly we lived in different places on our own that we found, like kids do. Places with no one in them, empty buildings, garages, places of that sort. We never did nothing very bad, like I said we were just running around. Well yes, I dabbled in a little stealing, yes I did. But nothing great, I was mostly into breaking into workshops and garages and stealing tools – things of that sort. I never stole nothing there wasn't somebody wanting it, no stealing for the sake of stealing, I didn't do that. You could get a good set of tools for an auto mechanic, and you could sell that for a good price that'd give you enough to keep yourself living for a while: then you went out and stole something else if you didn't have money. But stealing just because something was lying around, whether you really needed it or not, well that was something else. You could get caught for stealing something, and you'd get into trouble for that, and you hadn't had a need for it anyway: I could never see the sense in that.

Yes I did, I got caught a time or two. Then it was mostly you got fined, so you had to go steal something else to get the money you needed for the fine. You had to pay the fine off before you could settle down again. Or they'd send you to the Juvenile Probation Officer and he'd tell you you were to go to school and go back to your folks to live, which you'd maybe have to do for a while. That way I'd sometimes have it where it could be a whole week in school, and living with my folks: but then everyone kind of stopped bothering you anymore.

I guess I was first sent away it must have been when I was 14 or 15, something like that. They sent me to a big school in Topeka that was for bad boys. If you add it all up, I'd say I was there it must have been close on one year all told. That was because of the system they had. They had I think it was nine levels, or maybe eight: you started at number one, where you were locked up and you couldn't do sport or swimming or nothing. Then after some weeks, if you'd done OK there you went up to level two, which was where you could watch the TV at night until eight o'clock. Level three you could go outside the building and walk around the place: and level four, level five, you went on up like that. Only if you did something wrong, they put you back down level one and you had to start over. I guess the highest I got was level five or six, somewhere around there.

They had school lessons, yes a bit of schooling yeah: but mostly the emphasis was on exercise, physical fitness, gymnasium: climbing ladders, hanging on a rope with one hand you mustn't fall off else they threw a bucket of water over you, stuff like that. The thing was to show them you were a pretty tough sort of a person, whatever they could throw at you, you could take it and not let them think they could break you down. You didn't learn much except things from the other guys who were there, about ways of breaking doors, taking automobiles and ways to steal most anything there was. Like a sort of college education for you in crime. That was what I mostly learned there.

Then after I'd got out from there I got caught again, and this time they sent me to another place, I think that one was in Kansas City Kansas. That was more of a prison sort of a place, they kept me there six months I think it was. That time it was for drugs, they said I was a dealer. But I never, I wasn't no dealer, that was wrong. I might sometime let a friend have something, but I was never in it in the way of business. It wasn't too bad that place as a matter of fact: they mostly just left you alone.

Then what happened…oh yeah I had this steady girl and times were good for a while, yeah. Around then I was 17 and she was 18: she didn't use drugs at all, her thing was drink and I moved off drugs onto drink myself. We used to go out in the country driving around, with maybe a few cans of beer and a bottle of bourbon or so, and we had ourselves a real good time. Her and me we used to work together real good: we'd go in a filling station for some gas, and one or other of us would catch the attendant's attention and the other one take a few things. Our method was if it was moveable and common and saleable, we'd take it and dispose of it some place down the line. We worked like that in stores too. The important thing was not to keep it very long: they always say for every person ready to steal something, there's three more that won't take the risk themselves but are waiting to buy it from you, and I'd say myself that was about right.

I can't recall for you that girl's name, Dawn, Doreen I think it was some name like that. She was a sweet girl though and together we were real good, I do remember that.

What I was getting into then was drinking alcohol, and I started getting arrested then for DWI. That's driving while intoxicated, it's called. The first few times I did OK, I said I had a drink problem and I needed help. So then they put you on a detox programme. Usually that's say 30 days in a unit: alcohol counsellors give you talks and you talk about your problems in a group, and you get some sessions where you talk with the doctor on your own. Sometimes in some of them folk from outside come along, people from Alcoholics Anonymous who've had problems with drinking themselves: they tell you what are the signs to look out for when you're outside, if you want it you can have what they call antabuse tablets to take when you go out. Everything you want to help you, they provide it for you: I reckon they do a pretty good job at it those people, they surely do.

Oh no, sure it worked: it worked with me every time, four or five times, things was just fine. One programme I got, it was 45 days in the unit plus I think it was another two months afterwards as an outpatient three times a week. It took me off alcohol, that was what, three, three and one half months? It worked real good. But it was always the same problem for me, when I finished the programme I'd take a drink because I thought I'd learned how to handle it, and in maybe two days or sometimes three I'd be drunk again. And then I'd go driving and they'd arrest me again for DWI. If they don't have anything else against you, usually they put you back on another programme again. I used to get good reports from my programmes, about how I'd been co-operative with them and it looked like I'd succeeded, and they thought it was worth for me to try again.

Then sometime around there was the only time I was in serious trouble. It was for a robbery I done, only this one was serious. There was this guy I knew and I needed money real bad: I asked him if he'd loan me some but he wouldn't. He was a neighbour of my Ma and Pa's, and he knew my Pa would pay him the money back if he wanted it. I think it wasn't much I was asking him for, only 200 dollars or so. But he said he wasn't going to give it to me. And I needed it real bad. He had a dry clean business, the type where you put coins in machines and operate it yourself, and at night he used to go get the money out of them and bring it home in a box. So one night I waited for him at the street corner near where he lived, and I had a stocking over my head. I didn't have a weapon, nothing like that: I just ran at him and pushed him over and took the box with the money and ran off. I guess the stocking was too thin or something, because he recognised me. I'd gotten the money hidden in a garage some place, so when the Sheriff's Department people came around I told them I knew nothing about it. I said it couldn't have been me that done it, I was way way away over the other side of the country that night at my girl's place. She backed me on that. But I was pretty dumb myself: they kept on asking me questions and things, and they promised me if I told them the truth, and where the money was so they could go get it back, they'd give me a break and nothing serious would happen to me. They went on that way all the way through a whole day. And so in the end because they kept making me these promises and telling me to trust them, all they wanted to do was help me, so that was it, finally I said yes and told them everything they wanted to know. I really buried myself and I got what I deserved, I surely did. They gave me nine months in gaol with one half of it suspended. Next time around I'll not be as dumb as that, I'll not believe what people tell me about how they're going to help me, no sir I will not.

You could say it was quite a light sentence for something like that, yes I suppose you could. Only if the guy'd lent me the money you could say too I wouldn't have done it. And he didn't have very much in the box, only 100 dollars, something like that. This guy when he came to court and they asked him, he said he knew my Pa and we were neighbours, he didn't think I was bad but more foolish: that's what his words were, something like that. He said I'd learned my lesson. I think that was right myself: the lesson I learned from it was something like that's not really for me, and I'm not really for it. I'm not successful at those kind of things.

Well, I guess what I'd like most is for to get out of here: it's sure awful boring being locked up here all the time in the cooler. Where are we, level four or five is it? I'm the only prisoner they got here, and I'd like someone to talk to once in a while: it gets like you feel some night they might all go home and forget they've left you in here. I have three meals a day: the food is things like hamburger, potatoes, chicken, beans or corn. I don't know where it comes from.

Someone brings it along that corridor to me, I guess they send out for it from the Sheriff's office. They don't let me out for exercise: there's nowhere for me to go to have exercise, I just walk up and down the floor here about ten minutes once an hour, something like that.

No, I don't have no visits, it's too far for my Ma or Pa to come here from right the other side of the state. I have a girl writes to me once in a while, but she's not been to see me yet. Some place here there's a library I think, they send books in for me to read. Mostly westerns is what I like best, one of the clerks from the office here, she asked me what I liked and that's what I told her so that's what I get.

They might let me out soon, I mean before the end of my time: they do that if you've behaved yourself good. I couldn't exactly say when that would be, because I don't know exactly when it is now. Sometimes the Sheriff comes along to ask me how I'm doing, and he loans me his newspaper to look at: I don't know just when the last one was so that's why I'm not sure of the date and things. The way I see it, it don't matter a lot right now to me though.

Well what I do mostly in the day is I set here and wait for the time to pass. Sometimes I do yes, I try to think to myself why I'm like I am and what the cause of it is, but I never have the answers. So far I've not had a lot of success in my life, but I don't think it's because I'm stupid or nothing like that. I think the chief thing is I'm a loner. What I mean by that is I never seem to get very close with anyone, and no one gets close with me, not girls or anyone. The people I've liked best were the people I've done my drinking with: we've always gotten along OK. To answer your question straight, I guess that's because they seem to take me as I am. No sir, I've never met no one I could say who'd given me good advice: lots of folks have given me advice, I mean I've had advice from most everyone I've known including myself, but somehow it just doesn't seem to count. Last time, right there in the courtroom here, a guy came up to me and asked why didn't I try and see if God could turn my life around for me, ask God if he could run my life better for me than I could myself. I don't know what he meant properly, maybe praying and things like that. I thought maybe I might give that a try sometime.

Yessir it's sure been nice for me talking to you too, and yes I'd appreciate that, I really would, if you would send me something in. They don't let me have drink and I don't smoke, but maybe some hair shampoo or a packet of cookies would be good, something like that. No it don't matter what sort of cookies, I'd like it if you were to surprise me with what sort: any kind except chocolate chip, I don't like them, that would be great, I'd appreciate that.

A LIFE STORY[1]

Charlie Smith

Year	Age	
1913	Born	
1914	1	
1915	2	
1916	3	Father and mother died.
1917	4	In Cottage Homes.
1918	5	ditto
1919	6	In first orphanage.
1920	7	ditto
1921	8	With first foster-parent.
1922	9	With second foster-parent.
1923	10	ditto
1924	11	With third foster-parent.
1925	12	ditto
1926	13	In second orphanage.
1927	14	ditto
1928	15	ditto
1929	16	ditto
1930	17	Tailor's apprentice. Living in digs.
1931	18	Left tailor. Living with sister.
1932	19	Signed on for seven years in Army.
1933	20	In Army.
1934	21	ditto
1935	22	Sailed for India. Contracted pneumonia.
1936	23	In India.
1937	24	Went to China.

1 *The Unknown Citizen* (1963) London, Hutchinson, pp. 162–3.

1938	25	In China.
1939	26	Signed on for further five years in Army.
1940	27	Went to North Africa, then Syria.
1941	28	Ill with nephritis.
1942	29	Sent back to England.
1943	30	First prison sentence: one month.
1944	31	Married. Discharged from Army.
1945	32	Working as a tailor.
1946	33	Started own business. Marriage broken.
1947	34	Second prison sentence: six, six, and six months concurrent.
1948	35	Third prison sentence: twelve months.
1949	36	Divorced. Fourth prison sentence: three years.
1950	37	In prison.
1951	38	Fifth prison sentence: eighteen months.
1952	39	Sixth prison sentence: three years plus one concurrent.
1953	40	In prison.
1954	41	ditto
1955	42	Seventh prison sentence: seven years' preventive detention.
1956	43	In prison.
1957	44	ditto
1958	45	ditto
1959	46	ditto
1960	47	ditto
1961	48	Eighth prison sentence: ten years' preventive detention.

An essay by Charlie Smith[2]

(Write about what you hope, what you wish, and what you think…)

I hope first that I can keep in the same frame of mind that I have been since I started my present job.

I hope that someone will know that I appreciated what was done for me by people when I came out.

---

2 *The Unknown Citizen* (1963) London: Hutchinson, pp. 164–5.

23

I hope the World's Political Leaders dont plunge the world into a atomic war.

I hope the younger generation will be sportminded instead of scooter and pop music mad.

I hope the Govt. will realise that the sex side of life in Britain is a disgrace and will bring out new laws to protect young people from its disgrace.

I hope that the book will be a great success not in the commercial sense but in the sense that it will be beneficial to young people who are on the threshold of life after school.

I hope that all these things will come to pass and if I live long enough I can say to myself well you did help even if it was just by hoping.

Being an orphan since 3 yrs old I often wish that I had a mother and father so that I could have the normal upbringing to have enabled me to take my place in life as a normal human being.

I wish I could settle down to things such as a job and home for yrs instead of weeks or months at a time.

I wish I could banish the thought that people are looking at me or that if I say something to a stranger that I will say the wrong thing.

I wish that my sister Margaret and my brother Sam could have been brought up together in a natural way so that we could speak freely to each other instead of being tongue tied when we meet.

I wish I had taken the advice given me by so many people especially the advice that Margaret and Alf tried to give me.

Last of all I wish my memory was as it used to be because it causes me to make all sorts of blunders and embarrasses me at times so much that I lose interest instantly in what I was doing or saying.

The things that go through my mind not only amaze me sometimes but often make me think Im not all there for instance I will try & explain. I will go to bed which is the place I do all my, to me, serious thinking and go over all the things Ive done that day & then I start thinking of what I will do in the future all sorts of things go through my mind such as − will I be able to stick this job for long what is there at the end of it for me if I stay on until Im 70 yrs old & then when Ive sorted it all out and made my mind up to try my best to stick in and try to make it my last job before retiring on pension the awful thought comes into my head will they find out about my past & of course this sets my mind on other things like what I would do if I did get found out to have a criminal past. This is the time of think-ing I dont like it frightens me and if I dwell on it too long I know that

I will be miserable next day so I shut my mind to worldly things then think of my religion. This I think is the happy time of the day I know I sleep better when I form mental pictures of Christs childhood & the stories I remember from the Bible in fact without these things to think about I would be lost.

Conversation with a psychologist[3]

There is no possibility of presenting to a court any kind of defensible argument about Charlie Smith's actions being anything to do with limited intelligence.[4] His handicaps – and they are severe – are not intellectual but emotional.

Is he the sort of person sometimes described as an inadequate psychopath?

That term is loosely applied, and I would prefer to avoid it, first because of the difficulty of defining it precisely and so obtaining general agreement as to its use; and secondly because it is too frequently used in diagnosis as a kind of 'writing off'. Charlie does show many of the symptoms usually accepted as typical of the psychopath – inability to learn from experience or be deterred by punishment, lack of affectionate regard for others, disregard of moral standards with little apparent sense of guilt, short-sighted impulses directed towards obtaining immediate satisfaction, episodic emotional outbursts with alternating phases of dependence and independence, and little or no foresight. But these are also characteristic of people with deep-rooted neuroses, and of those who have suffered severe and lasting emotional deprivation.

He is an inadequate and unstable person, apparently dependent on others but subject to no one. As a child his only security lay in the unreal world of orderly and impersonal institutional life, and his Army service provided merely an extension of this. Since then, imprisonment has reinforced his superficial adaptation to life in an institution, and as each failure to cope with freedom resulted in further incarceration, his past experience became emphasized and confirmed, reducing to a minimum his chances of making a life for himself in the ordinary world. 'Outside' was difficult and dangerous, 'inside' was relatively safe.

It's possible that if his marriage had been successful he might have

---

3 *The Unknown Citizen* (1963) London: Hutchinson, pp. 147–9.
4 Tested with the Terman-Merrill revision of the Binet Scale, he has an IQ of 106, which is average.

achieved a measure of adjustment, for then at least he would have been living in the community with someone who did accept him. But it is not difficult to understand his inability to form permanent or lasting ties when one looks at the series of broken relationships which persisted throughout his childhood. Even his brief and spasmodic contacts with foster-parents all ended unsatisfactorily. So his present situation is a development of his past history; the pattern of constantly changing situation, job, and address repeats that of his childhood, with its deprivation, change, and rejection.

I do not think he could last for long as a free man if he were left entirely to his own devices. One of the main dilemmas which will always face anyone who tries to help him is that he appears unable to live outside some kind of supportive community, but at the same time finds it almost impossible to adjust to the requirements, however minimal, of any kind of 'voluntary' community which is available to protect him. It may well be, in fact, that a lonely, shifting existence in a succession of temporary lodgings is the only way which he can live at present.

Even under these conditions he is not an easy person to help. He makes very little emotional contact with anybody who tries to help him, and will always look to them mainly as sources of financial assistance. Expressions of concern for his welfare have no more real value for him than threats of punishment from those who try to frighten him into changing his ways. Aggravating though this is, there is no immediately satisfactory solution.

Could he be helped by treatment?

He *could* be helped – but it is doubtful if the free psychiatric and social services available at present could provide the frequent and intensive assistance which he needs. They already have long waiting lists of people more recognizably handicapped than Charlie, and who are more likely to respond to less intensive treatment, whereas he would require skilled attention for a long time. He is not a young man, he has practically no insight into his own emotional difficulties, and he has by now established very strong psychological defences. To get through these, and help him to face himself and his circumstances, might well cause him considerable distress, which he would find difficult to tolerate. I repeat, he would require the greatest skill and a great deal of time.

There is one further comment I would like to make. The more we increase people's understanding of men like Charlie and show that what they are now is largely the result of their life's experience, the less condemnatory and the more constructive society's reaction to them may, I hope, become.

The Unknown Citizen[5]

MAY IT PLEASE YOUR LORDSHIP. . .

On the occasions when I stand before you after pleading guilty and am asked if I have anything to say or add to a written statement, I always answer 'No'. This has now happened eight times.

We face each other across the court, you in the majestic regalia of the Law, and I in the grimy suit of crime. Behind you is society, on whose behalf you function, and which supports you in what you do. Behind me is an indefensible record, and a lifetime barren even of minor success. The gulf in sympathy and understanding between us is so vast, so deep, that communication is impossible. Yet you always ask me if I have anything to say.

There is nothing I could think of that should be said. And even if I could I would never know how to express it...

But if I could think, and if I could express myself, My Lord... What *might* I say?

The total sentences of imprisonment so far given to me amount to twenty-six years. This exceeds what I might have expected to receive had I been a traitor to my country,[6] a dangerous gangster,[7] or a murderer.[8]

'But,' your Lordship might say – and in fact has said – 'society must be protected.' Yet the sum involved in all my thefts to date is £178, and to be sentenced to twenty-six years' imprisonment for this is out of proportion to what I would probably have received if my depredations had been committed all at once and on a far greater scale.[9]

I am dealt with, my Lord, as though I were one of the toughest and most dangerous criminals in the land; for crimes that are not much more than nuisances, that I am utterly inept at committing, and which bring me benefits in no way comparable with those popularly supposed to be gained from a life of crime. Not for me any of the

---

5 *The Unknown Citizen* (1963) London: Hutchinson, pp. 154–60.
6 William John Vassall was given eighteen years for betraying Admiralty secrets.
7 Niven Scott Craig received twelve years for armed robbery.
8 Iain Hay Gordon was released after serving seven years of a life-sentence for murder.
9 Jack Taylor, a property dealer found guilty of obtaining a total of £162,000 by forged or false documents, received six years.

spuriously glamorous rewards: no planning or excitement of carrying out major coups, no extravagant living, penthouses, gambling, big cars, and lovely girls. Only the loneliness of furnished rooms, meaningless wandering in and out of pubs, and patent medicines for the pains in my stomach.

Nor is your Lordship's method of dealing with me economical to the community. It is not cheap to keep a man in prison; he has to be housed, clothed, and fed while he is there, at the taxpayers' expense. The cost of this, excluding maintenance and repair of buildings, is currently £459 16s 11d, per prisoner per year.[10] Allowing for remission on the time served, this still means that you are involving the taxpayer in a cost, for me alone, of £9,200. Would it be unreasonable to suggest that if this money has to be spent, some way of spending it might be found that would give a better return? It would almost pay the salary of one social worker engaged to do nothing else but look after me for nine years – and this would carry some hope of helping me to adjust to society, which is more than can be said for putting me in prison.

I may point out, too, that during the weeks, the months, and years that you have had me in prison, no attempt has been made at all to give me any kind of psychological treatment that might help me live more usefully when I am released. Your concern has been with protecting society – yet would it not be better protected if, while you had me, you tried to improve me? Moreover, you have had captive an example of a problem you know little about and can think of nothing to do with; but in that time you have not studied it or tried to increase your own knowledge. The years have been wasted, my Lord: there has been no more profit in them for society than there has been for me.

Imprisonment neither reforms nor deters me. It confirms and completes the destruction of my personality, and has now so conditioned me that I am almost totally incapable of living outside. A prison has become the only place in which I can exist satisfactorily, and it has become a kindness on your part to return me to it, since the strain of living outside is so painful and intense.

You use this very argument, occasionally, in support of what you are doing, saying: 'You are better off, really, in prison.' This might be acceptable if you were confining me there for life. But society is not

10 Report of the Commissioners of Prisons 1961, published 1962.

yet as cynical and despairing as that, and does not allow you to do it. That being out of the question, then, what purpose is there in experimenting with three years, with seven years, or with ten? At the end of each of those periods there is still inflicted on me the cruelty of release – a cruelty made greater by each sentence I serve, and one which I am helped to face less each time I come out. If you were to say: 'The longer your sentence, the more understanding and practical help we will give you on release', the procedure might possibly be justified. Only this is not said, or done; in fact the opposite happens. The effort made by society to help prisoners' readjustment is, in the majority of cases, in inverse proportion to the number of their convictions. It is no use blaming the after-care societies for this: the habitual offender is looked upon by everyone as being irredeemable, and time and money are regarded as being better spent on the young and the first offenders, from whom there is more hope of change.

I – the recidivist, the repeating offender, the habitual criminal, call me what you will, my Lord – I am left to get on with living, while I am outside, as best I can. So long as I do not trouble you, you ignore me – until I lay hands on your property. Then you hit me hard. You fall back, regularly and with increasing severity, on the ineffectual, irrelevant concept of deterrence... 'Three years didn't change you, we'll try seven.' 'Seven makes no impression? Let's try ten.'

Set standards I am incapable of attaining, and then punished for not attaining them...Is it surprising I regard myself as a failure before I begin to try, that I do not think it worth while to make much effort, knowing I cannot succeed?

If my mental and emotional handicaps had manifested themselves throughout my life in physical symptoms, my Lord, I would not be standing in court. I should be a wreck in a wheelchair. No one would then dream of admonishing me for my failure to live a successful life, or think it anything but a waste of breath to exhort me to pull myself together and walk like other men. There would be available for my assistance all the social ministrations of state agencies, and the charitable attentions of numerous individuals. No one would demand that I grow new, healthy limbs, and properly functioning internal organs. So long as I preserved a degree of cheerfulness, I would be admired for my fortitude and perseverance. Because I was immediately obvious as a man in need of help, people would assist me unhesitatingly and unthinkingly, believing it their duty to do so.

But because my disabilities do not show in this simple and recognizable way they draw no understanding or acceptance. I look all right from the outside, I have a head and body and arms and legs like anyone else, I can move about and I can talk. I get drunk, break into houses, steal, and run away. Obviously there cannot be anything seriously the matter with me, it can only be that I do not try. All I need, therefore, is advice pointing out the folly of my ways and, if I persist in them, punishment.

That the punishment makes no difference is irrelevant. It should work; it must be continued until it does. A doctor who repeatedly prescribed for his patients a course of treatment that denied any necessity for diagnosis of the possible cause of the sickness; that by its repetition made the sickness worse; and that showed its inefficiency by the regularity with which the patients reappeared with even worse symptoms…such a doctor would be rightly considered a dangerously inept practitioner, and would bring upon himself both the criticism of the fellow members of his profession and the anger of the public.

But those concerned with punishment and penology are allowed by society to continue like this. When pressed they defend themselves by arguing that they cannot think of an alternative. They use imprisonment, they say, as a last resort, because they cannot think what else to do. The sentence becomes a substitute for thought. If it were not possible to use it – if, for instance, the repeated sending to prison of habitual offenders were made illegal – then some alternative would *have* to be thought of. While it remains, no one needs to think very hard.

The problem should not be insoluble. After all, one similar to it faces parents when they are trying to deal with an intractable child. Whatever the child does, and whatever punishment is applied, they deal with him while still keeping him with the family and continuing to live with him. They try to adjust to him, and try to help him adjust to them. The one thing they never do, and would not think of doing, is to put him up in the attic and lock him away for a period of twenty-six years, meantime living as though he was no concern of theirs. And if they did, my Lord…the Law would punish *them*.

You cannot, you say, with all your facilities for research and your salaried experts to command – you cannot think – what to do with me. But when I use the same argument about my behaviour – that I cannot think how to alter it – this is dismissed with contempt.

Yet it is literally true. I cannot think. I have not been equipped by life for the process of mature or rational thought. I have never had the security of belonging with roots in one place, I have never had the sun of being loved for who I was. Ever since I can remember, in orphanages, foster-homes, the Army, and prison, I have had drilled into me the virtue of obedience, of doing as I was told. I have always been, and have known I was being, a problem and an encumbrance to others. Under such conditions and conditioning, how many could shake off the fetters and grow into a whole man? Some could, some have. But I am not one of them; and I wish I were.

And now it is too late. What has happened has happened. I am what I am. For me there is no release. I cannot, by thinking, gain freedom from the conditioning of my thoughts.

My mind is a confused no-man's-land of waterlogged craters and barbed wire, of collapsed dug-outs and uncharted wastes of mud: shrouded in a pall of dark, through which I flounder perpetually, frightened and alone. There are no Very lights sent up for me to steer by, no search parties ordered out to render me assistance. Only shouts from those whose feet are dry-shod, those who stand outside the morass on ground that is safe and firm: 'Go this way!' 'Go that way!' 'Pull yourself together, man, make an effort, try!' And as I blunder about, enfilading fire comes from the Law's machine-gunners whenever they spot my head...

Had I died in a war, in conditions like these, I might have been buried as The Unknown Soldier. But I live in your society like this, and I am The Unknown Citizen.

PRIVATE SHAME[1]

Janie Preston

PREVENTIVE DETENTION, in the form introduced by the 1948 Criminal Justice Act, was intended to deal with 'persistent offenders who by their age, criminal history and character, seem to be beyond correction and can be restrained only by prolonged detention'. (*Prisons and Borstals: Statement of Policy and Practice*, Home Office, 1960.) The sentence – which might be for any period between five and fourteen years, depending on how the judge was feeling – could be given only to offenders over thirty years of age who had been in prison at least twice before: and 'it is of the essence of the system that the offender is not being punished for the last offence of which he was convicted, but is confined for the protection of society and for a period which is likely to exceed any period for which he could have been imprisoned as a punishment' (ibid.).

In addition, though the motive was never publicly stated, there was also the underlying hope that fear of receiving preventive detention might deter 'professional' criminals from continuing their life of crime. Advocates of the necessity for retaining the sentence in the penal code argued that no one could tell just how many had been so deterred. But what could be seen, and seen the more clearly the longer it remained, was that it was not often being received by 'professionals': it fell most frequently on offenders with long records of petty crime, among whose many social inadequacies was their inability to avoid capture. For that type of offender it was the least condign of all punishments.

Based on false premises, ill-considered, inept in its application, costly to the community and cruel though preventive detention was, the credit (if that is the correct word) for devising it is claimed for

1 *Five Women* (1965) London: Hutchinson, pp. 143–69.

the former Director of Prisons, Sir Alexander Paterson (1884–1947) by the editor of his posthumous papers, who describes it as 'One of the theories of penology which he evolved during his career at the Home Office. He was well aware that some men are incorrigible, and believed that society should be given the maximum protection from such men.'

Paterson had written: 'There will always remain a residuum of habitual criminals who have resisted or evaded all efforts to train them for honest life. By weakness of character or wilful defiance of society's axioms they have shown themselves unfit for freedom. "Training" in their case is likely to be a misuse of the word and a waste of time. The exact period which they should spend in prison should not be determined entirely by the gravity of the offence, but by their fitness for the resumption of social life.'

(He also wrote, on another occasion: 'We should accept with caution the findings of psychologists, and rely rather on deduction from the fundamental principles we accept'; and other ideas of his were that both corporal and capital punishment were necessary, the latter on the grounds that it was more 'merciful' than imprisonment. But it was also Sir Alexander Paterson who first stated the now often-quoted dictum 'Men come to prison *as* a punishment, not *for* punishment.' He was that curious but not uncommon mixture of insight and obtuseness and humaneness and severity which a combination of Christianity, private-school education, and service in the armed forces so steadily reproduces in order that the Prison Department of the Home Office may perpetuate itself without intercourse.)

A recommendation that preventive detention should be abolished was made by a government-appointed Advisory Council on the Treatment of Offenders in its report in 1963. But the Council suggested that in place of it courts should be given power to pass longer sentences of ordinary imprisonment on persistent offenders, thus abolishing a name but making no fundamental alteration of the legal approach to the problem. Government action in 1963 gave effect to the first of these recommendations.

It remains to be seen whether judges will ever be bold enough to refrain from passing sentence of any kind of imprisonment on petty criminals already grossly institutionalised by the amount of time they have spent inside, and try instead to find some alternative treatment which might revitalise, instead of confirm the destruction of, the offender's personality. They have the power to do it.

'The Crown Courts,' wrote Judge Neville Laski in the *Liverpool*

Daily Post in 1963, 'enable the judge to be untrammelled by the calendar and to indulge to the full in pre-sentence enquiry. I can conscientiously say that I have never dealt in terms of Preventive Detention or any lengthy sentence unless I had a full personal report on the man or woman concerned, or knew them from previous unhappy contact.'

The reports to which he refers are those made by the Home Office on the convicted prisoner. Unless an after-care agency goes out of its way to offer information, they deal almost exclusively with previous offences and convictions, in order to inform the judge of the prisoner's 'suitability' (that is, *legal eligibility*) for a long sentence. When such prisoners appear in court, one of their characteristics is that they almost invariably plead 'guilty' and offer no defence; they are therefore not given legal aid and are unrepresented. On average, less than ten minutes is devoted to each case: most of this time is taken-up by Prosecuting Counsel outlining the accused's offence, followed by a police officer recounting the previous criminal history, to whom 'Just the last three convictions, officer' is the invariable instruction from the judge. The accused is asked if he has anything to say by way of explanation of his behaviour. Not unnaturally, he usually has little to contribute. He is then sentenced.

In the eyes of the Law the fact that the offender has been properly and correctly found 'guilty' is all that matters. It is assumed – unless he is so grossly mentally disturbed that even the Court Usher can diagnose it – that the reason he continues to get into trouble is because he is either wicked or weak; and that he can only be changed by being taught a lesson. If he refuses to learn the lesson, punishment must be increased until he does; and it is finally in order 'to protect society' that the persistent offender is given either preventive detention or a long term of imprisonment. It is as if a doctor were to examine every patient who comes to his surgery; pronounce them all 'ill'; and prescribe for them all the same medicine.

Women preventive detainees are much less numerous than men. In the last ten years only about fifty have served such a sentence. This is the story of one of them, Janie Preston, whose record over the past 30 years is this:

Age 18 – 2 years' probation for larceny
Age 19 – 6 months' hard labour for larceny
Age 20 – Bound over for 12 months for larceny
ditto – 12 months for larceny of £20
Age 25 – Bound over for 12 months for larceny

Age 34 – 6 months for larceny of £30
Age 35 – 4 months for larceny
Age 37 – 8 months for larceny
Age 38 – Bound over for 2 years for larceny
Age 40 – 15 months for larceny
Age 42 – 3 months for stealing a skirt
Age 44 – 6 months for stealing £3 in an hotel
Age 48 – Fined £10 for larceny
Age 49 – 6 months for larceny
Age 50 – 2 years for larceny of £20

Her next sentence was 8 years' preventive detention, after a further offence of larceny involving £55. It was given to her when she was 52, at Liverpool Assizes by Judge Neville Laski.

I first met her two years ago, on the day after she had been released from prison. There had been a change in penal administration: all preventive detainees had suddenly been given one-third remission of sentence, instead of the one-sixth which most of them until then had usually received. As a result, five women who had already served more than two-thirds of their time were unexpectedly released. Janie was one of them.

She had been inside for over six years, was unprepared for freedom, and it meant not happiness for her, but terror. She begged to be given a job, any job, inside the prison and not be turned out until her full sentence was completed, rather than have to go out into a world where she knew no one, had nowhere to live, no job, no roots, no security. The plea was useless: the regulations had been changed, and she and the four others had to be discharged immediately.

A stout ugly unhappy old woman, she put her hands down dejectedly on the edge of the table in the room we were talking in, put her face down on her hands, and wept bitterly and unceasingly, she poured out her Lancashire-accented threnody; unhesitatingly, because she could tell me about it, I'd understand her, I'd know what it was like, because I had a Lancashire accent too…

Why musta come out, why musta, can you tell me that? Why couldn'ta stay where I was? I wasn't doin' no 'arm, was a, I'd done nothin' wrong in there, I didn't ask ter come out, did a? Why couldn't they just've left me alone? I don't want to be outside, I don't want to be, I just want to be back where a belong in me cell.

I'll never pick up again outside, never a won't, not now, a can't. Not after six year in there, I'll never do it, it can't be done. In prison you're left on your own so much, you're locked up in your cell for hours and hours on end; you can't just come out and be free, you can't, it's terrible, you can't.

They give me a room last night that they'd found for me in a little boarding-house round at the back of Waterloo. They took me there and left me, they said 'You'll be all right here for tonight now Janie, it's a nice little room with clean sheets on the bed and a dressing table, you'll be all right now Janie, you'll be fine…'

After they'd gone I just lay on the bed, I just lay there and lay there, waiting for someone to come along the landing and turn the light off outside the door, like they do in prison. All today I've been asking people what time it is, even though I've got my own watch back on again. I've been touching my clothes and wondering where they've come from, because I've forgotten them; they're the ones I had on when I went in. And I've kept feeling my hat on my head to see if it's still there…

I'll never get used to it. Why have a got to? I hate outside. Why must a be pushed out all of a sudden like this, why, why?

She had no friends; nor, she said flatly on that first day, did she want any. She didn't want to have anything to do with other people, she just wanted to be left on her own. Nobody liked her, she knew that; there was nothing likeable about her, she'd always known. She was like an animal trapped in a cage of misery and loneliness, pacing up and down in it, ready to scratch and slash and spit at anyone who tried to get near the bars.

Eight months later, I met Janie again. She was by then the only surviving member of the quintet of women who had been released together. Of the others, two had died, and two had been reconvicted and sent back to prison.

How did it feel to be the only one left? Without any pretence at concern for the others, without even a moment's thought for them, she said Oh it's absolutely smashing, I'm thrilled to be the only one who's still here. And no one ever thought I'd make it did they, she said. No one thought I'd stay out – you didn't yourself, did you?

No, I said, I didn't. No said Janie, I knew you didn't: and neither did I.

She had been lucky. After a few unsuccessful attempts at work, first as a waitress and then as a shop assistant, and walking out from each job after a few days in a temper, she had been wandering round the north London streets one day when a 6d-a-week advertisement on a postcard in a glass case outside a newspaper shop caught her eye.

'Wanted: Middle-aged house-keeper to look after elderly invalid. Live in.'

The address was nearby. At the house she was welcomed by an anxious woman whose desperate concern was to find someone to look after her eighty-two-year-old father, while she and her husband went for six months on a business trip to South Africa. Two women had been tried already; they had both left after only twenty-four hours because her father swore at them.

All that would be required, she said, would be for Janie to give the old man his breakfast at nine, his dinner at twelve-thirty, and his tea at four. For the rest of the day he wanted to be left alone in his library with his books, and he went to bed at about seven o'clock every evening. There was a basement flat for the housekeeper to live in: when the old man wanted his meals he would thump on the floor with his stick. If he was ever ill, send for the doctor, who knew him well. Three pounds a week plus housekeeping money and, of course, the little flat downstairs. The two big things were, said the woman, that her father didn't like any company and wanted to be left alone: and he sometimes used very bad language.

Janie sniffed; she thought she could put up with that, she said: she'd give it a try. The only other thing was, said the woman – she hated to ask this, but she and her husband were due to sail the very next day – could Janie possibly move in that same afternoon? She thought it could be managed, said Janie: she'd have to go home to her family and explain why it was so quick but it would probably be all right. The two previous nights she had in fact spent sleeping on benches at railway stations: Victoria one, Waterloo the other. She had a total of 4d in her pocket, and her suitcase of clothing was in the left-luggage at Waterloo.

By the end of that afternoon she was in the warmth and comfort of the basement flat. It had its own kitchen, a television set in the sitting room; and upstairs the elderly recluse who had to be fed three times a day and otherwise left alone. Probably he wouldn't live long, and probably she would soon be out of the place and wandering the streets again. But in the meantime, she might as well make the most of it.

I continued to see her. The months went by, and the old man upstairs remained alive and went on thumping on the floor three times a day for his meals. In the basement flat underneath Janie sat and knitted, or watched the television. Every day she went down to the shops at the bottom of the road for the small amounts of food necessary for the two of them. Sometimes on the way home she slipped into the pub on the corner for a quick Guinness, then hurried back to prepare the next meal.

She cut out a picture of lakes and mountains in Switzerland from a magazine, and stuck it on the wall of her bed-sitting room. In time it was joined by others: a spaniel, a television announcer, the cast of 'Emergency Ward 10', and a coloured photograph of a chef's table piled high with a decorative arrangement of the ingredients needed for *bouillabaisse*. She bought a wireless and sent up a postal order for five shillings to the Radio Caroline Club; she planted two hyacinth bulbs in fibre in a bowl, and they grew. The old man's daughter and her husband returned from South Africa and decided to leave things as they were for the time being. Janie bought herself a morning tea set, slowly knitted herself a green woollen dress, then a bright purple one.

Whenever I saw her, there was really only one subject of conversation: prison. One-third of her adult life had been spent there: she had been inside so often and so long that it made up nearly the whole fabric of her personality.

She was unused to talking about herself, and uneasy about it, and would sit taut and upright on the settee, her hands clenched tightly together in her lap and her slate-grey eyes hooded and hidden behind her glasses, until she was sure she was not under attack. A big, forbidding-looking woman, with black hair, a deeply-lined face, and a thin-lipped and twisted mouth.

As time went on and we came to know each other better, it was possible gradually to reduce the confused jumble of prisons and sentences to some sort of order; even occasionally to move away from the subjects altogether, and talk instead of her life before it became such a dreary and meaningless pattern of crime and punishment and crime. But it was always difficult for both of us; her memory was fragmented and her sense of chronology defective. Sometimes only a comma between two phrases would mark the ellipsis of nearly fifty years – 'I was always terribly quick-tempered as a girl, I was punished five times on my last sentence for swearing at the officers.'

And when she talked, it was with all the directness and openness of a Lancastrian, used as a camouflage to conceal the secret and unspeakable hurt beneath.

When we met that first day after you'd come out of prison, you said you'd no friends and you didn't want any. Have you made any friends since you've come out?

38

No, not one. I haven't tried to and I'm not going to. I stay in my room here and I don't want any friends, I can do all right without them, thanks.

Have you always been like this, or did you have friends when you were younger?

Always. I told you before, I don't like people and I never have. They've not liked me either, so we're quits. Ever since being a girl I've wanted to keep myself to myself and not have nothing to do with no one. When I was younger I always had the idea I'd like to live right out of the way on top of a mountain – somewhere like in that picture I've stuck on the wall there. Or on the top of Shap Fell, somewhere like that. I've been up over Shap two or three times. Do you know it? There's a few houses up there, aren't there, and I've always felt that's where I'd like to be, up there on my own away from everybody. I often used to wish I'd been born a man instead of a woman; and then if I had I could have got a job as a long-distance lorry driver, so I could always have been moving, on and on and on, driving for ever and ever away from people.

Why?

I don't know why, I've just felt like it as long as I can remember, that's all. I don't like people: it's as simple as that.

Who have you ever liked in your life?

No one.

Your mother and father?

Not really, no. There was an officer in Durham when I was there on remand, she said to me once 'You know what's wrong with you, Preston, is that you like no one, no one likes you, and you're proud of it.' I said 'Well there's nothing wrong with that, that's just how I like it, and you can mind your own bloody business.'

You wouldn't have been allowed to answer an officer back like that in the old days when I first went in: it was much stricter than it is now. All the prisons were a lot harder then, and I think it was better in a way too, because you knew what prison was for; it was to punish you and then let you out when you'd finished, none of this trying to reform people all the time.

I was about eighteen, I think, the first time I went in. I was taken to Strangeways and put in this big room with all the little cubicles along the side of it. You had to go in one and take all your clothes off, and they gave you a rough kind of dressing-gown thing and took all your clothes away. That first time, I thought it was what prison was going to be, spending all my time in the cubicle with only this dressing-gown to wear. Then they gave you a lump of bread and some margarine and a mug of cocoa, and then they took you for your bath. After that you went and saw the doctor. In Strangeways in those days she used to make you get up on two chairs with your legs wide apart, one foot on each, and then jump off on to the floor. You had to do it three times, to make sure you weren't concealing anything.

I had hard labour – and it was hard labour too. You had to walk everywhere in single file and you weren't allowed to talk. Number 1 labour I was doing; that was outside in the prison yard. You stood in a long line down one side of some big trestle-tables with sheets of metal on them. Then the men came from the men's part of the prison, they had wheelbarrows full of rock which they tipped out on the tables for you. We had to get out the hard lumps and bash the other rocks to bits; then the bits were shovelled along to a stone slab at the end, and there they had to be ground down with other lumps of stone into a fine powder. Then you had to sweep the powder off into barrows, and wheel it over to the storerooms. I think it was sandstone, and it was made up into blocks, they were called 'Donkey stones' that people used for whitening steps with and cleaning stone floors.

I got big segs on my hands after a time, it was better when your hands were harder, then you got used to it. They were very strict in those days; we got up at half past six, tidied our cells, then went and did an hour's work till eight; then we had breakfast, then we had school till ten o'clock, then we worked till twelve, had our dinner, and worked again until four o'clock.

One time when I was in the sewing machine shop at Strangeways Manchester, one of the officers, Miss Bishop, she's retired now, she said 'Preston, do you know that old hut on the croft round the back of Deansgate? When I leave the prison service I'm going to rent that for my girls, I'm going to have a sewing factory there, and you can come and work for me.'

I wonder if she ever did? It was a good idea. She told me to enquire at the gate of the prison if I ever went up there again, to see if she'd done it. They used to call for her when I was up in my cell crying before I came out, they'd send her to see me and have a talk with me and try and get me to agree to go out, because I never wanted to go. That's what she used to say to calm me down – 'One day Preston you can come and work for me.' I expect she'll be dead by now, Miss Bishop.

They could have done with a few like her in Holloway, I didn't like that place, it wasn't a proper prison at all. PD's, CT's, YP's

[Preventive Detainees, Corrective Trainees, Young Prisoners] all mixed up together, it was horrible. And some of those young ones, Borstal girls who'd run away and been recaptured, oh they were terrible – noisy, rowdy, thought they were really tough because they were in the nick. There was only one person in Holloway I ever talked to much at all; that was the Salvation Army woman. She found out one day I'd been in the Salvation Army when I was young, so she used to come up to my cell and talk to me about it sometimes.

How old were you when you were in the Salvation Army?

I'd be about nineteen or twenty, I suppose.

How did you come to join it?

Well I didn't actually join it, I was put in one of their hostels instead of being sent to prison. I was on probation or bound over on condition I went there, something like that. I was drinking a lot at the time as usual, and they thought the Salvation Army might cure me of it, because they're all teetotal, and they have a big thing about saving people from the evils of drink, don't they? But one day I had a row with them and left. I went through every room in the place first, every coat and jacket and handbag I could find, and got about seven pounds altogether, I think.

You were doing a lot of drinking, you say, at nineteen?

I've always been a big drinker, dear, whenever I could get it. Not now, since I've come out, because being inside for so long and having to do without it I've got out of the habit. Anyway, I can't do it much while I'm living here, because there's his meals to be got. But if I ever had to leave here and start wandering again, well that's what I'd be doing all right, there's no doubt about that.

Before when I was out, I was always in the pubs, from eleven o'clock until three o'clock, and from there to a club if I could find one until six o'clock, then straight back in the pub at six o'clock until eleven. But I wouldn't let anybody else buy me a drink, I always bought my own unless I was after somebody's money.

What I mean is, if ever a chap came in the pub like some of these men do, on their own and want to get friendly with everyone, well they stand at the bar and take out a roll of notes to show they've got plenty. And then if they see a woman on her own they offer to buy her a drink, don't they? When someone like that came in, a mug ready for plucking, well I'd have him. He could buy me a drink, two drinks if he wanted – and I'd guarantee before ten minutes I'd have his money and away. It's not difficult picking men's pockets if you're a woman, usually it's them that wants to get close to you, they start pushing theirselves near you. As soon as you've got their wallet or their purse or whatever it is, 'Excuse me' you say, 'I won't be a moment' and off you go with it. They'd never think of following you because they think you're going to the toilet, don't they?

I had nearly twenty pounds off a man once, he had it all in one pound notes in his wallet. I took it out and hid it under a slab of concrete down near a railway bridge, in case the police picked me up with it while I was wandering round. I used to go back every night and get a few pounds out to spend on my beer.

Is this when you were in your twenties or thirties or forties, when was it?

That particular time would be when I was about thirty, I should think. It's a bit difficult for me to get it all in order; I've been pinching money since right back in the early days, and getting caught all the time and going to prison for it. One part of my life wasn't much different from another, that's the trouble: I don't know if you'll ever be able to sort it all out...

My mother had thirteen children and I was the eldest. She was very young when she had me, only just over sixteen. My dad was very young too, he was only about sixteen as well. He worked in the pits; I don't think he can have been much good to her because she chucked him about four years after I was born, and married a soldier from the barracks at Ardwick. There was me and my sister she had from my father, then all the others she had from my step-father. We all called him 'Dad', he was more like our real father – when he was there, which wasn't a lot, because after a bit the Great War started and he went to France. My mum was carrying on while he was away with this man and that man, oh there were dozens of them. I shouldn't think anybody ever knew who were who's children; she was awful.

I was about nine when the war started; I don't remember a lot about it except seeing soldiers everywhere and big posters with that man on with a moustache, pointing his finger out and saying, 'We want YOU'. I used to think he meant me.

We lived just outside Manchester in one of those terraced houses like you see rows and rows of in the north. Well really we lived in two of them, because next door to our house was my grandmother and grandfather's house, and my mother had so many kids some of us lived with them, including me. The sofa in the front room of my grandma's, that was my bed for as long as I can remember, I always slept there. My grandpa had the corner grocer's shop, when we were kids we used to like it when he let us help him behind the counter, weighing out pennyworths of sweets for the other kids that came in.

I think I was quite happy as a child, I know my grandmother brought us up mostly, and was rowing with my mother about these men she used to bring back to the house. I got ill once when I was young and had to go into hospital: I don't know what it was I had, but I know it meant I couldn't ever have any children when I grew up. My granny told me about it at the time, that that was what it would mean. I seemed to get the idea she was putting the blame on my mother for it somehow, though I never found out why.

When the war was over I remember my step-father coming back in his soldier's uniform, but he didn't live with us, he soon went somewhere else and there was no man living at home at all, just a lot of these 'uncles' who kept coming. One of them was a very good-looking young chap called Mike. I met him one morning in the cemetery I used to walk through on my way to school. He was sitting on a bench there. He asked me if I'd like to go to the pictures with him and I said, Yes, I would. I thought I was really grown up, didn't I, not yet thirteen and already getting a boy-friend asking me to go to the pictures with him?

But when I got home from school in the afternoon my mum was waiting for me, and she said 'I was watching you out of the upstairs back window this morning: I saw you talking to that man in the cemetery, what did he want?' I said 'It's not *that man*, it was me uncle Mike and he wants me to go to the pictures with him.' So my mum said 'Well you're not going' and I said 'Oh you're just jealous, that's all you are.' But she wouldn't let me have any more to do with him, she said I wasn't to walk through the cemetery in the mornings on my way to school either, and so that was the end of that.

Not long after, when I was about 14 I left school and went to work in the mill, and I was earning about fifteen shillings a week which was quite a lot of money in those days. My mum and my grandmother between them used to take twelve and six a week off me, so if ever I saw any money lying around at home I used to take it and hide it in a stocking inside the back of the sofa in my grand-mother's front room. My younger sister, she could always get money for spending off my mother; and she was let stay out till all hours too, she was really spoiled. I was working and yet they treated me as if I was younger than she was, always giving her things and letting her do what she liked.

One day I came home and the stocking with the money in it had gone from the back of the sofa. I couldn't say anything about it, could I, because I wasn't supposed to have the money anyway. But I saw my sister looking at me and trying not to laugh, so it was obvious who'd had it, wasn't it? I got my own back a few years later, I walked in the house one day and there was her handbag on the kitchen table, it had about four quid in it and I had that. I still laugh, I don't know if she's any idea to this day where it went.

I worked at the mill for about a year, and then I gave up because I didn't see any point in going on working for money I had to give to my mother when I got home; especially as I'd found out by then that money came a lot easier when you pinched it instead of working for it. Most people left their back doors open in the north, and you could just go in anytime you liked to people's houses. They all used to have bits of money lying about, in jam jars on shelves, in cocoa tins on the mantelpiece, places like that. I'd knock on the back door and if there was no one there, in I'd go.

What I wanted the money for, of course, was beer, because by the time I was 16 I'd developed a proper taste for it. I first had some in a pub where I'd been sent with a jug to get it for my grandpa; I drank some on the way home, then filled the jug up with water in the kitchen. I got into the habit of doing that, then I had to have some of my own, and that's how it started.

I used to walk about for days at a time, in the pubs until I'd got no more money, then off down the road going in houses until I'd got a few shillings, then on to the next pub and so on. I went to Lancaster, Fleetwood, Blackpool, New Brighton – all over the place, always filthy dirty and just wandering about stealing and drinking and sleeping rough. The tram shelters on Blackpool promenade, the Ribble bus garage at Bolton, the railway sidings at Oldham – I've slept in them all in my time, in fact I always used to say I could sleep better rough than I could in a bed.

Now and again I used to go to big houses and ask them did they want a maid? If they said Yes I'd move in, and then out again in a few days after I'd helped myself to any money they left lying around. I never took anything else but money; and as soon as I got it, straight down to the pub until it was all gone. Of course it couldn't go on, could it? Sure enough I had to get caught, and I did. All the money I'd took, and I got caught taking half-a-crown off the kitchen mantelpiece in a big house that belonged to a chief constable, of all people!

They put me on probation for that. Not that it made any difference; I went straight off to the next town and carried on drinking and stealing there. Only a few weeks went by before I was caught again in another house – and this time I was sent to prison for six month's hard labour.

When I came out, on I went again with the wandering round and the drinking straight away. I turned up at home once in the middle of the night I remember, and got into the cellar and slept on the coal. My mother came screaming and yelling at me in the morning, told me to get out and not come back no more, said I was a dirty filthy thing and she didn't want to see me ever again.

Another time I remember I got in a garage, I think it was in Rochdale or somewhere like that. I went to sleep in the back of a car, and in the morning when I woke up I stepped straight out into a big pan of dirty black oil that was on the floor. I was trying to wipe it off myself when they came and opened up the place. When they saw me they sent for the police. But I wasn't doing anything, only sleeping in the back of a car, so the police just told me to move on.

I looked like a bundle of old rags most times, you couldn't have told whether I was a boy or a girl or an old man or an old woman or what. Now and again someone would offer me a square meal and I'd say I'd sooner have the money, and as soon as I got it I was into the nearest pub. There were men of course who'd offer me money if I'd go with them, but I'd never let them anywhere near me, the dirty beasts. I used to swear at them and tell them to go off and find themselves a tart if they wanted that sort of thing. Then they'd come over all apologetic, wouldn't they, and say they were sorry, and perhaps give me ten bob because I was shouting to quieten me down. It was an easy way of getting a few bob, to let them go on until they made their improper suggestion, and then start screaming about it.

All in all, that kind of life has been the only kind of life I've ever led – wandering round, thieving, drinking, going into prison, coming out and wandering round again. There was one period in my life where if you look at my record, it shows nearly ten years that I had between the ages of twenty-five and thirty-four without any convictions. Sometimes people say, like a Judge or someone in prison who's doing welfare, 'Well Janie, you kept out of trouble once for nearly ten years, why can't you do it again?'

Yet you know in all that time I wasn't leading a different kind of life. I don't think there was one day when I mightn't have been picked-up and sent to prison, if I'd been unlucky and it'd just happened like that. It certainly wasn't that I was going straight or anything; only that I wasn't being caught.

At one time round about then, for about a year in fact, I was friendly with a police Inspector who knew me very well because he was always in and out of the pubs that I was in. He never nicked me once. I think I was too valuable to him in letting him know what was going on round the town. He told his men to lay off me altogether – so that helped as well as far as not getting into trouble with the Law was concerned, too.

I got married once. That was funny it was; well not funny it was stupid, really. I was forty-five, forty-six perhaps, and I met this middle-aged chap in a pub one night, he was telling me all his life story about how his wife had died and all the rest of it. A couple of nights later I ran into him again in a different pub. He seemed all right, he was prepared to buy beer for me without thinking he was buying me at the same time, no messing about with his hands or anything like that, and after I'd met him about six or seven times he suddenly blurted out 'What would you say if I asked you to marry me?'

I wasn't really bothered one way or the other, was I, so long as I had my beer. He'd got a nice big house nearby that he took me to see, so that was how it happened. It lasted three weeks and then he took me to court for going after him with a chopper – one of those big meat choppers it was, I used to keep it in the top of the gas oven and take it out and threaten him with it if he ever tried to put his hands on me.

I would have too, I'd have killed him if he'd come near me. I said 'I've married you for my beer money, and I don't want any of that other business.' So he took me to court and the police came back home with me afterwards, and I had to give them the chopper. Anyway I left the house soon after that, so that was the end of him. I can't stand men mauling and messing you about, their hands all over you – ugh, no thanks, they can find someone else if they want that.

The next time I was in prison after that, I'd got six months I think it was, and I got the papers from some solicitors to say he was divorcing me, so it was good riddance to bad rubbish, I was better off where I was.

Then I got two years, didn't I, what was that for? Oh it was Woolworth's, I think, following the girl round who was emptying the tills one lunch-time. She put all the money in a bag, a hold-all thing, and when she got to the office she put it down on the floor while she unlocked the door. I put my hand in and ran off with a handful of notes but they came after me and caught me. Yes, two years I got for that, that's right.

It wasn't long after I came out from that one that I got my eight years in Liverpool. I'd been out about three or four months I think, and I was in a pub one day at Southport. I asked the publican if I could use his telephone behind the bar and he said Yes. Then as I was coming away from the counter I put my hand in his till and took a lot of notes, fifty-five pounds there was altogether, and out I went. But I made the mistake of going back in the same pub again about two weeks later, and the landlord recognised me and called the police.

Judge Laski said 'How many convictions has she got altogether?' and somebody said 'Fifteen'. He said 'All for things like this?' and they said 'Yes'. He said to me 'Well, it's terrible' he said, 'really shocking. Have you got anything to say for yourself?' I said No: well there wasn't anything *to* say, was there? So he said 'We shall have to keep you apart from the public, you're a menace, there's no doubt about that. I'm going to send you to Preventative Detention for eight years.'

I thought Well, that's it then, I'm all right, I've got nothing else to worry about now for eight years. I did the first part of it in Strangeways, then they sent me down to Holloway. I had the best cell in the prison, right up on the top floor at the end of the block it was. After they'd locked me in of a summer evening, I could climb up on my chair and look out of the window, and I could see right down to the front gate, over the wall to the road opposite, and away over all the roofs right as far as King's Cross nearly, it was smashing. No one ever came up to bother you, I was right on my own completely.

Then it had to come to a finish, and I had to come out. But if *this* comes to an end, and I have to leave here and start wandering again, when I go back inside I'm going to try and get my own cell back.

Prison holds no terrors for you, does it?

Terrors? No, why should it, I don't mind being inside. Once you're in there you're safe, aren't you?

Safe from what?

Well, I mean you can't do no more harm, can you, you can't do anything else wrong in prison? I ought to have been in for life, then I'd have been really happy.

Do you think it might have made a difference to you if you'd been treated differently when you first got into trouble – if they'd persevered with your probation, perhaps?

No I don't think so. I don't see how they could have done, anyway – they had to send me to prison, didn't they?

If you did something now that you got caught for, and the Judge decided not to send you back again, how would you feel?

I'd think he'd gone potty, wouldn't I? He'd have to send me back for another very long time, he couldn't do anything else.

You don't think there's any other way of treating habitual offenders like you?

No, of course there isn't; after all, we've done wrong, haven't we, and we've got to be punished for it. Unless…oh well, they don't do it now, so what's the use.

What were you going to say?

Well, I was going to say that another thing might be to do what they did in the old days, and deport the criminals.

Do you think you ought to have been deported?

I used to, yes, when I was younger.

Where to?

Java.

Java? Why Java?

I saw some pictures of it once, years ago it was now, long before the war, in a magazine, and I thought Yes, that's where I ought to be sent to work, amongst those people.

What people were they?

It was a leper colony, it showed you pictures of them all with leprosy, their hands, their fingers, their noses. They were all disfigured, eaten away, lying on the ground. I thought if they could send me out there and I could work among people like that, that'd be the place for me.

*

Throughout our conversations over a period of more than a year, Janie's fundamental attitudes and outlook never changed. Prison was where she belonged; she wanted to be there because she couldn't stand people; no one could ever possibly like her, and so she would never like anyone else. She ought to be in prison; she deserved to be punished; she was guilty; she was bad. She said this kind of thing repeatedly, never self-pityingly but as a kind of catechism she had learned from when she was a child.

Not being a psychotherapist I felt I had no justification for probing too deeply into the subject, merely to confirm my own theories about what lay under an attitude of this kind, mixed so obviously and inextricably as it was with a profound distaste for sex. Sometimes when we were discussing motives for behaviour a frightened and hunted look would come into her eyes, her hands would begin to twine desperately together and she was never at ease until the conversation was back again on the safe lines of prison routine or the comparative virtues and failings of different governors.

Yet often equally obviously she was trying to find an opportunity to say something which was troubling her a great deal. 'You see' she would begin, 'there's one thing connected with it which I've never told anybody…Nobody knows about it, there's nobody living now who knows about it except me, all the other people who had to do with it are dead.' Then her voice would lose its strength, she would grimace, shrug, say 'Oh well I don't suppose it's got anything to do with it, really' and go on to another subject. Even on the occasion when she came out with the startlingly plain placing of herself in the leper-colony in Java, the subsequent questions and answers led rapidly away from the point again:

Have you ever wanted to work with anyone else besides lepers?

No.

Lepers are social outcasts, aren't they, or used to be. Why do you associate yourself with them?

I don't know.

Have you always felt you were a social outcast?

Yes, but I don't know why. There was an officer in Manchester once, she said to me 'There's lots of other people worse off than you, Preston, what about the starving families in Africa?' I said, 'Oh bugger them, what about the starving families in this prison, did you see what they gave us for our dinner today?' The food in there it was terrible, it really was, they used to give us potatoes that were all black and maggoty, the bread mouldy, the tea was…

When it did come at last, it came straight and without much prompting. What it must have cost her eventually to say it is beyond calculation.

Will you have another bun?

No thank you I've had three.

What's the matter, don't you like them? I made them specially for you coming because you said you liked anything with currants in.

I like them very much but –

Have another one then and do as you're told, I don't want them all to waste do I?

All right, just one. I'll never be able to eat any supper when I get home though.

Go on, you could do with eating more, you look as though you need some weight on, you smoke too much and eat too little.

Probably. Can I just ask you one or two more questions before we finish for this afternoon?

Yes, go on. Wait till you've finished your bun though, I can't tell what you say.

Right: it's true to say, isn't it, that you have never had the slightest compunction ever about stealing – you've always taken money because you felt you had a right to?

Yes.

Why did you feel that?

I don't know. I've told you about my sister taking the stocking I kept in the settee, and then getting my own back on her; but I'm not saying I always stole to get my own back on my sister or anything like that.

Why did you steal, have you any idea?

No.

Whenever you were found out, you always got into trouble for it. Did you mind being found out?

No.

I sometimes get the feeling you were almost, well almost trying to get your own back on the world, would that be true?

Yes, it would. Yes, it's true, that is.

And the older you've got, the more you've felt there was you had to get your own back for?

Yes. Why should I feel that, do you know?

Something happens when you're young, it gets exaggerated in your feelings perhaps, it's more important than you think it is, and –

No, it isn't more important than you think it is. It's the most important thing in the world, and you know it …

Well, it may be or may not be, but you –

It is. I've never said this to no one before, not in all these years and years. No one's asked me, I suppose that's why. But now we're here at it, I might as well come out with it, it can't do any harm to anyone else, they're all dead. Have another bun.

No thank you.

You remember I told you, a long time ago, about the man in the cemetery I used to meet, and how my mother wouldn't let me go out with him? Well…it wasn't quite true, I mean in the way I told it to you. Oh, she saw us all right and she said I wasn't to have anything to do with him, that was true. But it was because he was my father, that was why. She said 'He's your father and he's been in trouble with the police for interfering with girls, don't you have no more to do with him.' So I went to my grandmother and I asked her if it was true, if it *was* my father and if he *had* been in trouble for that, and she said Yes it was and yes he had, and she said 'Don't you have anything to do with him.'

It was too late. It was much much too late. I'd been going in the woods with him for weeks every day on my way home from school. Every time I'd let him do it he'd given me a bag of sweets. I hadn't known who he was, but he knew me, that was how he knew my name and everything.

He was waiting for me again that same day after school, and on the way home when we got to the path where we always turned off in to the woods I burst out crying and I wouldn't go. I said 'You're my father, aren't you, you're my father?'

He pulled back his hand and he hit me right across the face, and he said 'Don't you tell anyone about what we've been doing, do you understand? Because if you do, you could go to prison for doing it – you could go to prison, do you understand?' And he ran off down the lane and I never saw him again. I've never let a man lay a finger on me, from that day to this.

Well, I'll put these buns back in the tin again, shall I, till tomorrow?

★

She had carried it in private shame for nearly fifty years, seeking the punishment she felt she deserved, and rarely failing to find it. She is too old now to be helped much by sympathy or understanding; too old to bother much now whether she gets it. She wants to be left alone: and if a prison cell is the only place she can have solitude, she does not very much mind.

IT'S A VERY GREAT
PROBLEM[1]

Donald

He was, he assured me several times in his stumbling and anxious thick Glaswegian accent, 'no good at things like talking at all'. He had been given a small part to play in a prison once, and although he had been terrified because it opened with his being discovered alone on the stage when the curtain rose, as soon as the first of the other characters entered and the dialogue actually began, to his astonishment he had found himself immediately perfectly at ease, with a faultless memory for all the words. Looking back on it he realised that had been the only occasion in his life when he had known exactly what to say, because all his lines had been learned by heart during months of preparation and rehearsal. He knew what the other person would be going to say, what his own reply would be, what response they would make to that and so on. It was a pity, he said wistfully, that there was no script written-out for the rest of his life.

Nevertheless, when he did eventually accustom himself to sitting and chatting for a while, sometimes every other day for weeks on end, on more than one occasion he talked for over an hour without my having to interject more than an odd word. He wore his hair plastered down with water at the front, in a great loop which completely covered his forehead and swept right across his eyebrows. From time to time an errant strand fell still further, onto his nose; when it did he lifted it back delicately and nervously patted it into place again. Frequently he talked with his eyes closed, almost whispering, the palms of his hands pressed together tightly and held up in front of his lips as though he was praying.

1 *The Frying Pan* (1970) London: Hutchinson, pp. 66–73.

—Would it no be better for you, do you think, if I was to start at the beginning of my life, and tell it to you in order? My mother was a whore, you see, but first of all I'd have to tell you how it came to that situation so that you'd understand it. Right then, yes; I was born in Glasgow in 1935. We were fairly poor people I think, I was the third out of six children, I understand my father worked on the Corporation for the buses or something like that. Three boys and three girls there were, and I was the youngest of the three boys.

When the war came my father went into the Army, and he was out in the North African campaign for five years. That was when my mother became a prostitute. When I was six or seven I was all the time seeing Yankee soldiers and Canadian airmen coming to the house, people of that sort. Someone said to me once, perhaps it was because my mother was having a hard time bringing up the children, and not much money to do it on with my father being away. But as I've always understood it, in the war soldiers had their money sent to their wives for them, plus a certain sum for each child, so that the bigger the family the bigger the allowance. And besides there were lots of other soldiers' wives with families in the same position, were there not, and I know they didn't all do what she did.

Oh aye she was taking money for it, so far as I'm concerned that makes her a prostitute, she was selling her body to men. My father never knew nothing about it, and not long after he came back from the war she went into a mental hospital in Glasgow for two years with depression; she had that electric-shock treatment, the ECT. I don't think it did her any good though, she was always moping and crying round the place after she came out. My father didn't like that at all, he'd been a sergeant in the Army: he used to shout and swear at her, tell her to pull herself together, the whole home going to pieces, the dishes not washed and everything dirty and higgledly-piggledly and untidy, the children running wild, my sisters never being washed or having their hair combed. And it was true enough that was, the house was nothing but a slum.

In the finish we all moved down to Bradford in Yorkshire, the whole family of us so we could all have a new start. My father got himself a job, I think it was with a cement company. I know it was very hard work and he used to come back home every night covered from head to foot in white dust. He was a fine man, my father; I think she held him back, if it hadn't been for her he could maybe have got himself a much more decent job than something like that.

She was a bit better herself after we'd moved, it seemed she made more effort; though in Bradford my elder brother had some kind of a nervous breakdown then too, he went into the hospital there and they gave him ECT as well. The oldest one, Michael, he'd become a real tearaway by that time, he was always drinking and fighting and getting into trouble with the police; he was very big and powerfully-built, much taller than my father, no one could control him at all. He used to come back into the house late at night and terrorise us all, until one of my parents gave him the money he'd come round for, and then he'd go away.

I had a bit of schooling in Bradford, but not much, I wasn't very bright, I was always off sick with something or other: one time I had I believe it's called meningitis, would that be it, I had to spend a long time in hospital, altogether it was something like six months. When I left school at fifteen I had my first job in a shoe-shop but I couldn't do the adding-up to give the customers their right change. It only lasted a week, then I had a job as a butcher's boy, then another one delivering for a grocer's, then one working in a rag-factory; there's so many I can't remember them all, but none of them lasted very long, by the time I was nineteen I must have had twenty or thirty different jobs.

I couldn't settle, everything seemed too much for me. I decided to run away from home to Manchester and see if I couldn't settle myself down there in digs on my own. I had a job in a steel-yard in Salford, but after they'd paid me my first week's wages I went and drank it all in a pub; I was feeling so lonely and depressed, I hadn't met a single person who'd been a bit friendly towards me since I came. That same night I went back to my lodgings, and as I went through the back-kitchen I saw the landlady's purse lying there on the table; I think there was about three pounds in it which I put in my pocket and ran off out again. I wandered about the streets all night, it was raining, I could find nowhere dry to kip-down or a sleep, and in the morning I walked into the first police station I saw and gave myself up. I got probation for that.

Do you think that would be a good place to stop there, at what we might call the beginning of my criminal career? Yes OK, I'll come in again the day after tomorrow. It's funny, I didn't think I'd be able to talk when you first asked me to consider it, I thought I'd be so tongue-tied I wouldn't get out any words at all. It's not so bad though when you get used to it, is it, I've been quite a surprise to myself. Most of the time here you see, you only have to say 'Good morning' and they say to you 'What made you say that?' I find it very confusing, all the time knowing everyone's working-out the meaning of every word you say to them, just so they can put you into a little compartment marked 'psychopathic' or 'paranoic' or something like that. You get frightened to talk to anyone at all, sometimes you want to shout-out at the top of your voice 'Would you please go away and leave me alone!' But you know all the time that if you did that, they'd write down you were a raving lunatic and perhaps put you on the ghost-train to Broadmoor or one of those places. It gives you a funny feeling all the time, you're not sure whether you're in a prison or a nut-house or where you are – and often you can't make-up your own mind which is the right place for yourself either.

—I don't think I was born to be a criminal at all; when I was a little kid I always used to be very lucky at finding things – sixpences that people dropped in the street, fountain-pens, packets of foreign-stamps, bars of toffee, all sorts. I thought it was a kind of magic thing, you know the silly ideas you get when you're a kid; I thought somehow I'd been picked-out to have special good fortune. Now I think the exact opposite, that I must have been one of those chosen to have sorrow and loneliness all through my life.

I got the probation I told you of, that was when I was coming-up for twenty years old. In the last thirteen years since it's been in and out, in and out, nothing but one imprisonment after another all the time. I had a twelve months sentence, then I had a three month, then another twelve months, two lots of two years, a three years and then another three years, which is the one I'm doing now. Those were the main ones, but there's been a few three months and six months in between as well. I know I reckoned it up last year, all told I've only been actually outside a total of just under two years out of thirteen.

The offences have all been the same, breaking into houses and robbing the gas and electricity meters, stealing small amounts of cash, purses and handbags, things of that sort people had left lying around. And bits of clothing, but always women's clothing, jumpers and skirts and coats and shoes, then selling them to second-hand clothes merchants on the market-stalls. Always things to do with women, one of the doctors said to me, it meant I hated my mother and was trying to get my own back on her. I'd already told him I hated my mother anyway, because of her being a whore; and he said I should try and talk it over with her some time, but I can't ever see myself doing that. It's not the sort of thing any man would want to go and talk to his own mother about, is it? That was one of the main reasons why I left home, because I couldn't stand the thought any longer of what she'd been.

Once I had the idea I'd go as far away as I possibly could, I'd join the Foreign Legion. I had twenty pounds that I'd saved-up when I

kind of a state at all to decide'. It was true, if he'd said to me 'Here's a loaded revolver, put it up against the side of your head and pull the trigger when I count three', I would have done just that.

A fortnight later, they brought me here.

—I do get frightened when I think of going out, but not so much as I have been in the past about going out from other places. Here you do get a bit of an opportunity to talk if you want to. Not so much on the groups and the Wing Meetings, I don't like those, there's too much shouting and people swearing at each other; sometimes a whole week'll go past and there's only about three men who've done all the talking or had all the talking done about them, that's not much help to you with your own problems. But a few of the prisoners are reasonable sorts of people, one of them might come into your cell in an evening to talk over with you something about his wife, he just wants to get it off his chest and he feels better for it afterwards. Or you can go and talk to them if you want to once in a while; perhaps you ask him to lend you some crayons or a bit of paper if you feel like doing a drawing. Yes, I do do a bit of drawing, I try and do self-portrait things mostly, I seem to have got a bit of a flair for it. That's one thing I've discovered about myself since I came here, I find it very soothing to draw.

The officers on the staff too, some of them are quite decent men; I think they're mostly a cut above the sort you get usually in prisons. If you're quiet and well-behaved they treat you more as an ordinary human being; they'll even stop and have a chat with you if they haven't got anything urgent to do. And the doctors are all right as well, only they come and go rather a lot; you never seem to have much chance to get to know them; then with each new one you've got to start right back at the beginning again. The one I'm under now, I hardly ever see him unless I'm sick, he'll prescribe medicine for me but that's about all. Most of them like you to rely on your group and talk about things you want to discuss there; then whoever's in charge of the group will report back to the doctor; I suppose he's keeping an eye on your case and would send for you if there was anything special he felt he ought to talk to you about. I'm not quite sure who is my doctor at the moment, there seem to have been a lot of changes in the past six months.

Most of all when I go out, if I could really choose I'd like to live by myself on a little island off the coast of Scotland somewhere, with just enough food to eat and a little hut; and I'd like to try and draw the sky and the sea all the time and things like that. Or a lot more self-portraits of me in different situations, with different scenery for backgrounds. Yes, if you'd like to have one, I'll do one specially for you while you're here, and I'll give it you before you go. Aye, I will, I'd be glad to.

*

Fourteen inches by eleven inches, grey cartridge-paper entirely covered with smudged whorls of deep olive-green and darkest navy-blue crayoning; in the foreground the face in brown, nostrils dilated and the eyes glancing slightly sideways, looking straight out from the slightly-turned head; the hair flattened down over the forehead and curved across above the eyebrows. Distant and high-up, in the back-ground thickly-barred windows of a prison cell, and through them a faint shaft of light falling across the gloom onto the other predominant feature besides the face; a shadowy outline of a large brass-handled coffin, with a flaring smouldering crucifix on its lid.

Harriet Martineau wrote in 1838:

> The first principle in the management of the guilty seems to me to be to treat them as men and women; which they were before they were guilty, and will be when they are no longer so; and which they are in the midst of it all. Their humanity is the principal thing about them; their guilt is a temporary state.... When the keeper watches a hundred men herded together in virtue of the one common characteristic of their being criminals, the guilt becomes the prominent circumstance and there is an end of the brotherly faith in each, to which each must mainly owe his cure.
>
> Harriet Martineau (1802–76)[1]

1 Quoted in *The Unknown Citizen* (1963) London: Hutchinson, p. 12.

Part II

VILLAINY:
A WAY OF LIFE

The contrast between the accounts in Part I of persons being buffeted by life's experiences and the life stories of the three professional criminals featured here could not be more dramatic. Robert, Archie and Hank all reckon they had come to see crime as a way of life, as an occupation, as a career, as a profession. However, to say they had *chosen* this route is tempting but probably misleading. Nevertheless, life's contingencies are seen rather differently. Prison becomes an occupational hazard which they wish to avoid rather than a haven which protects them from a hostile world.

The relationship between the 'straight' world and the 'criminal' worlds becomes more complex. Where's the borderline between 'thieving' and 'shrewd business'? Why do we condemn some forms of violence and not others?

These are articulate men who do not apologise – 'I'm a professional criminal, and I take pride in my trade'. They are not interested in gratuitous violence – 'I wouldn't kill anyone unless it was strictly necessary to get what I wanted or it was my life or theirs'. But violence still plays a big part in their lives. Archie says 'Yes, I'd hit a woman, I have', while Hank says 'I don't touch females, get somebody else'. Principles and expediency provide a colourful combination.

I'VE ALWAYS BEEN A
CRIMINAL[1]
Robert Allerton

*If you were to describe yourself in one word, would the description invariably
be 'a criminal'?*

Yes, definitely. That's what I am, I never think of myself in any
other way.

Have you any intention of changing, of going straight or reforming?

None whatsoever. There's one thing, though, I'd like to make clear
right at the start – and that is, I don't want to try and pass myself off
as a 'master criminal' or anything like that. I'm not. I've had successes
and failures in life like everyone else, and I'm nothing out of the
ordinary as far as criminals go. I don't consider myself cleverer than
most, or even cleverer than the police, for example: sometimes I have
been, and quite obviously sometimes not. On the whole I'd say I was
just the ordinary run of professional criminal.

*Is there any particular form of crime, or criminal activity, which you
wouldn't commit?*

A year or two ago I used to think I'd never go in for drug-
trafficking, but now I'm not so sure about that. I've never actually
done it yet, but as I get older I seem to be losing my inhibitions, I
don't feel as strongly about it as I used to. There's only one thing I
still feel I could never do, and that's poncing. To me it's the worst
thing of the lot, I'd never stoop to it – or at least I hope I wouldn't.
Maybe I'm old-fashioned, or sentimental about women or something
– but I just can't stomach the idea of poncing at all. I've nothing but
contempt, real, deep contempt, for ponces.

If it was ever necessary to kill somebody, well, I'd go up to and
including that. I'd kill somebody in a fit of temper, I'm quite capable
of that – or if they were trying to stop me getting something I'd

1 *The Courage of His Convictions* (1962) London: Hutchinson, pp. 85–111 (edited).

really made up my mind to have. Or if they were holding me down, and there was so much at stake that I'd just got to get away. But I think most people have it in them to do murder at some time in their lives, under certain circumstances.

The thing which I find most difficult to understand about you is that you're apparently quite undeterred by your repeated prison sentences. You've now reached the stage that when you're caught next time it's more than likely you'll get a very long sentence. I don't understand how you can be prepared to face that.

I'm not prepared. This is the thing which people like you can never grasp. I'm no more 'prepared' than you're prepared to knock somebody down in your car tomorrow. I don't think too much about the one more than you do about the other. It's an ever-present risk but one doesn't dwell on it — do you see what I mean?

I've always got this thing in my mind, and so have most other criminals like me — 'it won't be this time that I'll get caught'. Prison only becomes the dominant thought when you're actually back in the prison cell — or no, to be realistic, perhaps a bit before that, when you're actually in the arms of a police officer, although even then you've still got some hope you might not end up in the nick.

Occasionally I get the vague idea that if men who'd been in prison were to go back and contemplate the prison wall from outside, just before they set out on a job, they mightn't do it. But it wouldn't work. You see, three days after you've come out of prison, however long the sentence, you've forgotten all about it. You've forgotten the caged-up feeling, the monotonous food, the smell of latrines, the piggishness of the screws, the soul-destroying torture of visiting-boxes with your friends having to shout a conversation with you through plate-glass — it's all gone, soon after you come out, and you do everything you can to make it go, too.

Then one day one of your mates comes along and says: 'I've heard of a peter wants blowing, it's got two hundred grand in it, you want to come in on it and make one?' So you knock down the amount by 50% because people exaggerate, and you think: 'Well, at least I'll have a look at it, there's no harm in that.'

So he takes you along to look at the set-up, you weigh it up and work it out, and you think: 'Well, this is an absolute doddle, it can't miss; yes, of course I'll do it.' So you say to your mate: 'OK, sure I'll come in, when do we start?' It doesn't even occur to you that there's even a chance you might get nicked, it all looks so easy. And where's your 'prepared' gone then?

I don't want to do a long sentence — no — but if I have to I have to, and that's all there is to it. If you're a criminal, what's the alternative to the risk of going to prison? Coal miners don't spend their time worrying about the risk they might get killed by a fall at the coal-face either. Prison's an occupational risk, that's all – and one I'm quite prepared to take. I'll willingly gamble away a third of my life in prison, so long as I can live the way I want for the other two-thirds. After all, it's my life, and that's how I feel about it. The alternative – the prospect of vegetating the rest of my life away in a steady job, catching the 8.13 to work in the morning, and the 5.50 back again at night – now that really does terrify me, far more than the thought of a few years in the nick.

You don't think, then, that there's anything wrong in not working for your living?

I do work for my living. Most crime – unless it's the senseless, petty-thieving sort – is quite hard work, you know. Planning a job, working out all the details of the best way to do it – and then carrying it out, under a lot of nervous strain and tension – and having to run round afterwards, if it's goods, fencing the stuff, getting a good price for it, delivering it to the fence, and so on – all this needs a lot of thinking and effort and concentration. It certainly is 'work', don't kid yourself about that.

But anyway this whole point's not all that simple. A lot of other people don't 'work' for their living, in the way you mean – but nobody goes on at them like they do at criminals. Quite a large proportion of the 'upper classes', for instance. You can see them any day round Piccadilly, Vigo Street, Savile Row – nattily dressed half-wits who've never done a stroke of work in their lives, popping in and out of Fortnum's or Scott's, spending all their time trying to get rid of the money their fathers and grandfathers and great-grandfathers left them. And usually it's that sort who get fiercest about people like me, saying we ought to be whipped and flogged because we never do an honest day's work.

I can steal from people like that without the faintest compunction at all, in fact I'm delighted to do it. I remember once screwing the town house of the Duke of…well, I'd better not say who, because I didn't get caught for it. The inside of the house was the most beautiful place I've ever been in in my life – gorgeous curtains and furnishings, antique furniture, silver bowls and vases all over the place, exquisite miniatures on the walls – it was a fabulous place. My only regret was I hadn't got a furniture van so I could strip it from top to bottom. His Lordship I suppose was up in Scotland shooting wild birds, or some other civilized hobby, and his house was just standing unused until he chose to come back and live in it again.

I remember after I'd come out I passed an old man in rags, standing on the street-corner scraping at a violin to try and earn himself a few coppers, and I thought: 'You mug, why don't you go in there and at least get yourself a good sleep in one of his Lordship's unused beds for a night.'

All the things that were in that house, all those beautiful possessions, the Duke had got for himself without the faintest effort of any kind. Most of them had been handed down to him, and all he'd ever had to do to get the others was write out a cheque – and he probably didn't even do that for himself but had a flunkey to do it. Never in his whole life had he known what it was like to be short of anything. Well, I had, and I don't think it was wrong to steal enough from him to subsidize me for a bit.

And those people, when they have something nicked, they've got it all insured anyway, so they don't suffer. Sometimes they advertise for its return – you know, 'sentimental value' and all that. I'm sure I'd feel sentimental, too, about losing something worth a few hundred quid, only I'd be a bit more honest about it.

And the stuff I pinched from that particular house I appreciated, I did really. In fact, if it hadn't been too dangerous, I'd gladly have kept a lot of it to have around my own place, because it was so beautiful. But I never felt bad about taking it – why should I? I felt terrific. He'd got no cause for complaint, because it was taken, after all, by someone who could really appreciate its artistic merit, not one of those insensitive thugs who couldn't differentiate between Royal Worcester and a Woolworth's chamber-pot.

Oh yes, and one more thing. A couple of years later I read in the papers how this particular Duke was involved in a real sordid court case. The details that came out about his private life then made me wonder if he ever did really appreciate those lovely possessions he had. From what they dragged out he sounded a right stinking bastard. But if I'd been caught that time I screwed his place he'd have been all up in arms about me – and the Law would have taken his side too. He was respectable and I wasn't, that's the way it would have been put.

But how do you justify wage-snatches for instance?

Could we get one thing clear first? I'm not trying to 'justify' anything. There's always two points of view on any subject, a wrong one and an even more wrong one. There's so much injustice in the world that we could start swopping one for another all the way along, like me turning round on you and saying: 'You justify some of your respectable society to me – like a managing director of a company taking five hundred thousand a year for himself, from the efforts of people working for him whom he pays five thousand a year' – and so on.

So I'm not justifying anything; I'm just telling you what my point of view on a thing is when you ask me, and my point of view's probably as illogical and wrong as anyone else's is likely to be. I'm not saying: 'This is a hundred per cent right and everything else is wrong.' I'll put my point of view, but you're entitled to disagree with it and so is anyone else – in fact I wouldn't expect you to do anything other than disagree, because you belong in so-called 'straight' society.

If I can see a chance of earning myself – or making myself, if you prefer it – a few thousand quid all at one go, naturally I'll do it. It's only what people, millions of them, are trying to do on the football pools every week. You could say: 'Yes, but they're trying to do it honestly' – to which I'd reply: 'It depends on your definition of honest, because while they're trying to get themselves several thousand of someone else's money for the outlay of a few shillings and no work, I'm trying to get it by some careful thinking and plotting, some bloody hard effort, and the risk of my own liberty into the bargain.'

So who's doing more to earn the money – me or the pools 'investors', as they're called? (By the promoters, of course. It's the old con-man's trick of persuading a mug you're going to give him something for nothing, playing on people's natural avarice and greed.) The 'investors' trust to luck to bring them a lot of money – well, I back on my own efforts.

Who loses on a wages-snatch – the workers? Of course not. It's the company – and they can usually stand it. It's the same with banks – if I have a few thousand from a bank, theoretically, it's their customers' money I've taken. But you never hear of a bank apportioning the losses round their customers, do you? 'We're so sorry, Major Bloodworthy, somebody blew our safe last night and took ten thousand quid – and it was your ten thousand that was in there!' Mind you, I'm not saying they shouldn't; to me it's quite an attractive idea.

No, let's face it, most of these people are insured against robberies, so it's only the insurance companies who pay up.

But this doesn't in any way defend the use of violence to get it, does it, by coshing the man carrying the wages-bag for instance?

There you go again, using words like 'defend' and 'justify'. I'm trying to tell you I'm not defending it, because fundamentally I don't believe you can defend the use of violence at all, in any circumstances. It's wrong whoever uses it and whatever they use it for. It's wrong when I use it, it's wrong when American maniacs drop an atom-bomb on Hiroshima or Nagasaki, when a man commits murder, when 'respectable' society takes him and hangs him as punishment.

You get this in Parliament a lot, these politicians, usually the Tories, who start steaming off about the increase in crimes of violence, and how 'these thugs have got to be stopped' – Who are they to tell me that I'm beyond the pale for using violence?

So violence is wrong, on a fundamental level, I admit that. But on a day-to-day level it just happens that it's a tool of my trade and I use it – like an engineer uses a slide-rule, or a bus-driver the handbrake, or a dentist the drill. Only when necessary, and only when it can't be avoided. If I've got to whack a bloke with an iron bar to make him let go of a wages-bag he's carrying, OK, so I'll whack him. If he lets go without any trouble, I don't. That's all.

I don't indulge in it, you know, for the sheer pleasure of the thing. I'm no sadist. This has always been my theory, that I'll take whatever job comes along. If there's a vanload of stuff to be pulled, I'll pull it; a screwing job, I'll screw it; a safeblowing, I'll blow it – and so on. And if it's a coshing job, well then, I'll use a cosh.

There's another thing too that I think we ought to get straight. Violence is in a way like bad language – something that a person like me's been brought up with, something I got used to very early on as part of the daily scene of childhood, you might say. I don't at all recoil from the idea, I don't have a sort of inborn dislike of the thing, like you do. As long as I can remember I've seen violence in use all around me – my mother hitting the children; my brothers and sister all whacking one another, or other children; the man downstairs bashing his wife, and so on. You get used to it, it doesn't mean anything in these circumstances.

I've even seen, more than once, two men striping each other with razors – and then, a few nights later, those same two men, with their faces covered with sticking-plaster, drinking together in a pub.

So you see, to me there's nothing all that terrible, or special in any way, about violence. It's just like any other form of activity: eating, sleeping, drinking, screwing, whatever you like.

Perhaps this might sound a bit odd, but it's true – as I've grown older, violence has got divided into two categories for me: the sort that's used for what you might call 'personal' reasons, and the sort to be used on a job.

The first sort, the 'personal' kind, I'm always struggling to get away from. Perhaps it's because I'm getting older or more mature: but I'm reaching the point now sometimes when I'm having an argument with somebody, and feel myself starting to lose my temper, I try and take a grip on myself, say to myself: 'No, I'm not going to whack him, it's wrong, it's sheer bullying, that's all. I've got to use my brains and argue myself out of this.' If I feel I'm not going to be able to do it, I try and make myself walk away from him altogether.

I never carry a knife or anything, no razor, nothing like that now. I used to, and I've used one in my time, striping people I'd got a big personal grievance against: but never light-heartedly, only after thinking about it a lot, and not more than six or eight times at the most. But God forbid, I've given up carrying a chiv now; it's not quite nice, one can so easily become a hooligan.

A few years ago it was different, I'd have whacked anyone soon as look at them, but it's childish, uncivilized, undignified, to be like that. Now, as I say, if I get in an argument, I try to get out of it by walking away. Yet if the selfsame bloke I'm arguing with was walking along the street one day, carrying a wages-bag that I was going to have, of course I'd whack him then. It wouldn't be personal bad temper, you see, only part of the job.

I've almost gone through a complete change-round. When I was a kid I was always looking for a fight. If someone offended me, whoever he was and however big he was, I'd be up to him waving my fists and offering to fight. But it worried me to have to hit someone on a job.

I can remember the first time quite clearly. I was only a kid, sixteen or seventeen, and thought myself a real tearaway of course. There was an old woman, a pawnbroker I think she was, lived in a little house just off Cable Street somewhere. Me and a couple of my mates heard that on Saturday nights she always had a bomb in there. Money was short and we decided to have it.

We went along about nine o'clock one Saturday night with shooters, banging on the door and shouting out: 'Mrs Rosenbloom, Mrs Rosenbloom!' or whatever her name was. 'Let us in, it's urgent, we've got to talk to you.' She opened the door, and seeing we were only kids she let us in. When we were inside we shoved her back into her kitchen and knocked her into a chair, telling her to keep quiet while we turned the place inside out looking for the money.

So of course she starts screaming and raving like a mad woman. Before we went in it'd been decided it was going to be my job to keep her quiet. I rammed my shooter up against her ear and said: 'Belt up, you old faggot, or I'll pull the trigger.'

It made not a blind bit of difference, she just yelled all the louder for help. The other two were tearing everything to bits trying to find where she'd hidden her money, and this racket she was making was really getting on their nerves, so one of them said: 'Oh, for Christ's sake hit the old bag, can't you? If you don't lay her out she'll have the whole neighbourhood on us.'

And I just couldn't do it. All I could do was stand there bleating: 'Shut up, will you! I'm warning you, I'll pull the trigger.' Naturally it didn't stop her. Finally one of the other two walked over, took the gun out of my hand, and belted her unconscious. He put the gun back in my hand, really angry, and he said: 'It's her or us, you silly bastard, can't you see that?'

It taught me the lesson, and after that I was all right. But I've never been keen on the idea of hitting old women, or old men for that matter. Just a personal weakness, but I don't like it, I don't think it's right. Nowadays I don't go in for it at all: if there's a job involving old people, I back out.

Gradually, you see, as you go on, most of the squeamishness about things gets knocked out of you. Not long after the old woman, I was on a job when we had to push around a wages clerk from a super-market.

He used to be sent every week on his own to the bank to get the money for wages, and then walk back carrying several hundred pounds in a bag. We followed him around for a few trips first, and worked out the best place to stop him – at a corner junction, where he usually had to wait to cross the road. We came up by the side of him in a car, and hauled him in the back. It's better than starting a fight in the street, because sometimes if you do that passers-by try and join in and the thing develops into a rough-house.

I was in the back of the car, holding his face down on the floor so he wouldn't get a good look at us, and knocking him about a bit to make sure he handed over the bag. He did that without much trouble, and I told the bloke who was driving to pull up so I could sling him out.

But the driver wouldn't. He said it was too dangerous to stop, and I should push him out while we were going. It was the attitude of 'him or us' again. So eventually I shoved him out when we were going fairly slowly to get round a corner. Still a bit squeamish, you see, even then.

But not long after that there was another job, in a warehouse in Islington: and this one got rid of the last of my scruples about violence. While we were in the place the night watchman heard us moving about and he came up the stairs to the floor we were on, to see what was going on. On the landing were a couple of five-gallon oil drums. When I saw him coming up towards us, I lifted one of them up over my head and let him have it. It knocked him back all the way downstairs, but he lay at the bottom yelling blue murder, so I took a fire extinguisher off the wall and went down and laid him out with it. I didn't try to batter him to death or anything, just put him out and stop his noise. I didn't feel angry, savage, anything like that – I don't think I felt anything, just dispassionate about it, knowing it'd got to be done, because he was threatening us and our safety with his noise.

You felt no compunction at all about hitting him like that?

No, none. I feel if someone takes a job as night watchman he's got to be prepared to be hit if he tries to make a hero of himself. I wouldn't have touched him if he'd left us alone, but since he tried to stop us he got what he'd earned. Personally I think he was stupid, he should have kept quiet and kept his nose out of it. What was he trying to do, win himself a medal? And what was he hoping to get from it, anyway – a pat on the shoulder from the guv'nor, 'Good feller, Jim', a gold watch when he retired? Anyone who takes a job like that wants his brains testing, to me he does. Perhaps I'm missing something, but I can't see anything admirable in it at all, these heroes trying to win themselves medals.

You read it in the papers sometimes – 'Last night Mr Jim Smith tried to tackle some bandits and he's now in hospital recovering from concussion.' It always gives me a laugh, if it was a job I was on that it's referring to. OK, so the bloke's a hero and got his name in the paper. So what's he got for it? Concussion. And what have I got? What I went for, which is what I would have got anyway, and he needn't have got his concussion trying to stop me.

Lots of people take money off others, but they use other ways of doing it. Some of them are considered respectable. Personally I don't think they are – but it's a matter of opinion, that's all.

A landlord gets money out of people when he puts their rents up, by extortion, by playing on the fact they've got nowhere else to live. And the Law upholds him in doing it. Yet really all he's doing is stealing money from people. But if I go along and steal that money from him he screams to the Law, and they come after me to try and get his money back for him. If his tenant screams to the police that his landlord's robbing him, they do nothing of course. No: he perpetrates his crime upheld by all the respectability of society, without any risk on his part of going to prison. Well, personally, I think my method's a lot more straightforward and honest than his is. And I don't pretend to be doing anything other than what I am – stealing. But the landlord does. And, what's more, I don't go in for robbing poor people either, like he does. Thieving off your own kind, that's terrible.

Or take the case of a jeweller. He's a business man, and he's in the game to make money. OK, so I'm a business man too, and I'm also out to make money. We just use different methods. The jeweller makes a profit – and often a very big profit – out of what he sells. On top of that he fiddles the income tax and the VAT, and even the customs duty as well if he can get away with it. That's considered all right by him and others like him, and if he makes enough to buy himself a big house and a posh car everyone looks up to him as a clever feller, a shrewd business man. But how's he got his money? By rooking people, taking advantage of soft young couples getting engaged to sell them a more expensive ring than they can afford, and fiddling the authorities whenever he can. But at least he didn't steal it. Well, what's in a name? Tell me exactly where the line is between thieving and 'shrewd business' and I might believe it. What's more, the jeweller can insure himself against people like me going and pinching his stock. But I can't insure against the police nicking me, can I? The Law's on one side only, the side of the pretenders, that's all.

It's funny, there's a few criminals, you do meet them from time to time, who won't do any violence. A firm I was with once, there was three of them besides me, we were discussing some job we had in view – a wages-snatch I think it was – where it was obvious we'd have to whack someone to get what we wanted. One of the three was one of these humanitarian types, you know, had what you might call a conscientious objection to using violence altogether. He went on about it so long the other two started to dither as well. We had a long argument about it, and my line was the one I've already explained: if violence needs doing, then you've got to do it. Some people won't hand over to you what you want just like that, so you've got to whack them. Well, this whole job fell through because they didn't look at it my way at all, they were scared about the thing. Once you start drawing lines here, there, and everywhere about what you will do, and what you won't, you might as well give up villainy altogether. It's amateurism – and the amateur's the curse of thieving like he is of any other game. The only approach I can go along with is to be a professional, and get on with whatever comes.

What about the suggestion, made by certain people, offences such as robbery should be punished with violence?

Well, it's the old business of deterrence again, isn't it, and it only increases viciousness and bitterness, so far as I can judge.

What form of punishment does have any effect on you – any at all?

No, that's obvious, surely, isn't it? I can take punishment – in a way I can almost accept it as justified. The only thing that ever worries me is kindness; that gets under my skin a bit sometimes, it perturbs me. I haven't had a lot of it, so perhaps it's because I'm not used to it, but it does worry me all the same. Can I say this again here, though – that I'm not making a plea for more kindness in dealing with criminals. It's quite immaterial to me what method you try – but I think it's probably better for you, it does you less harm, to be kind.

You've explained how you feel about your own use of violence on other people, how you use it as a tool for the job. How do you feel when violence is used against you by others?

That depends on who's using it and what for, and under what circumstances. If I go after a bloke to give him a stripe for something, it's more than likely that if I do stripe him not long afterwards he'll come looking for me, trying to do the same thing back again. I don't object to this, in fact I expect him to do it: I know I'd do the same myself if it was the other way round.

But I think when the police use it for instance – which they quite often do – when they're trying to pin something on you and haven't got enough evidence unless they can get you to confess – well, this I think is wrong. They're supposed to be upholding the Law, not taking it into their own hands. Mind you, an odd beating from the police is just another occupational hazard, so one's got to put up with it, but all the same it doesn't make me respect them any more. They think I'm just a beetle-browed mental defective, but I've got my standards – and I don't go in for beating up people with a gang of my mates, all of us on to him in one room, like they do. I'll fight anyone any fashion he likes, fair fight or foul fight, and, like I said, if he comes off worst I'm not surprised if he comes after me again later, trying to even the score. But when the police give you a beating you can't go and do them up afterwards: you've just got to take it, and from the very people who are supposed to be getting you to lay off violence as a method. I know they've got their problems, the police, like everyone else: but if they're not clever enough to catch you out with all the resources they've got – cars, radio, tip-offs, grasses, forensic scientists, faked-up evidence, the lot – well, it's one-sided enough already without relying on beatings as well.

Mention of grasses reminds me – you can put them on a level with poncing I mentioned earlier as another thing I couldn't ever do.

Grasses and ponces are the two lowest forms of animal life. If a straight man is robbed or chivved, something like that, naturally you expect him to scream to the Law, and when the case comes up to go into court and give evidence against you. There's nothing wrong with that: he lives by his standards, you've offended those standards, and he'll do his best to see you get put away for it. That's OK. You might not like the bloke very much while he's swearing your liberty away in the witness-box, but that's his standard and it's what you've got to expect.

But when one of your own does it...I can't find words for this, only obscene ones – I live outside the Law, and I don't turn to it for help when I'm in trouble. If somebody screwed my house I wouldn't scream to the Law about it, because I don't have anything to do with them ever, I look after myself. Sometimes you get a crooked bloke who's been cut in a fight complaining to the Law, and I think it's disgusting. When he gives evidence against you, and you know damn' well if the fight had gone the other way he'd have slashed you to ribbons...well, you can put down grassing as even lower than poncing, that's where it belongs.

You get grasses in prison too, characters who try to get themselves favours by giving information to the authorities. They're the most universally hated and despised men in the nick. Whenever you read in the papers about a prisoner being attacked by others in a prison, it's usually a safe bet he was a grass. The men who attack him are not the ones who've been grassed either, they're other prisoners trying to uphold the law – their law – the prison law: Thou Shalt Not Grass. I'd do it myself, anytime I was in the nick – I have done it, in fact – given a grass a battering. I don't have to know him, have anything against him personally for something he's done to me. It's one of the things that's got to be done, the grass has got to be taught his lesson. I've done it, and been swagged off to chokey, and lost remission; fair enough. And next time a grass wants doing, I'll be ready to do it again.

This ties in a bit with one other thing I'd like to say on the subject of violence, which is that most violent men I know – people like myself who indulge in it when necessary – are all terribly high-principled and sentimental in a curious, twisted way. I don't know why this should be true, but it invariably is. You'll usually find that the more vicious a man is the more likely he is to be soft-hearted about women and children – particularly children. I've heard many violent criminals say this, and they mean it very deeply when they're saying it, that they don't want their own kids to grow up like they are, they want to make enough to take them out of the jungle and let them live like decent, upright people. Of course it's not true, they're only kidding themselves, I suppose, but they say it all the same. It's rationalization, that's all – but I don't know why that particular one should be so common in that particular type of criminal.

Was there ever a point in your life when you made a conscious decision to be a criminal?

No, I can't think of one. I remember when I was doing my first lot of bird, I was quite determined I wasn't even going to try and go straight when I got out. I made up my mind that as soon as I was out I was going to get on with the business of having more money for myself, whatever way I had to use to get it. And going out to work for a few quid a week wasn't one of the methods I even thought about. But there wasn't any one particular day when I got up in the morning and said: 'I'm going to be a criminal', like the kid who says: 'I know what I'll do, I'll be a fireman' – nothing like that. I more or less got accustomed to the idea gradually as I grew up.

What really made you a criminal? Do you know?

This is the point, isn't it, where I should lay back in my chair, put my feet up on the mantelpiece, and say: 'I never had a chance!' But it just wouldn't be true. I don't say I've never had a chance, because I have, I've had plenty of chances if I'd wanted to take them. But I never did

What made me a criminal?…I could reel off a whole lot of reasons, but they'd all only be part of the real answer. I'm always afraid of saying circumstances made me what I am, because I don't think they did entirely at all. Seeing my father, a straight man, getting only poverty all through his life for being straight…living in an environment where nearly everyone I knew was dishonest, where stealing was a necessity at some times, an adventure at others, but was always acceptable whatever the reason…wanting to impress other kids, getting a reputation for being a tearaway…seeing the terrifying dreariness of the lives of other people who were 'straight'…not being able to face working for a living because I hated the idea of work…

Those were the circumstances, but they were only part of the answer. I still think I'd have been a criminal, whatever they'd been. For one thing, there's this tremendous hatred of authority which I've got, this compulsion, almost, to defy it. I was born with that, I'm sure. Or I could say it was because I'd always had a desire for adventure, for living dangerously. That was true when I was young, but it isn't true now, and I still go on. Now crime's just business, that's all.

There's so many facets, you see, aren't there, to what makes anyone what they are? I don't think there's one reason for me being a criminal, there's many, many of them. Some I know about, some I don't – but they all contribute to a greater or lesser degree. I might say: 'If only I'd had this, that, or the other', or: 'If this had happened, or that hadn't…' My mother dying, for instance, when I was young: that's one example…If I'd been thrashed less, or thrashed more…I just don't know. I've never found one answer that convinced me, myself, in my own mind – you know, nothing I could think of and suddenly say: 'Yes, that's why I became a criminal.' I've thought about it a lot for many years and if I did know the answer, the answer you want, and could present it to you like that on a plate – well, I'd be a remarkable man. It seems to me that I've always been a criminal and always will be.

I'm no more acceptable to your class than you are to mine. This feeling of mistrust would be equally pronounced if I took you round to some of my friends. How could they feel anything else? You couldn't be trusted to keep your mouth shut about things you might hear. This doesn't mean we'd think you'd go rushing off to the police, nothing like that – but you might happen to mention to another straight person something you'd heard, and he might mention it to someone else, and that person would tell the police. That's the reason for the mistrust, and it's not unreasonable. But a thief knows of one of his own kind that he wouldn't ever take a risk by talking in the wrong places.

And your class of person has got a long way to go, too, before they ever accept a criminal as anything else but an insensitive second-class citizen. I remember a man coming to see me once, a straight man he was, and he looked along that row of books over there on the shelves, and he said: 'You know, it's really amazing you should read books like this, I'm staggered I am. I should've thought you'd read paper-backed thrillers, things with lurid covers, books like that.'

And I always feel this with straight people – that whenever they're being nice to me, pleasant to me, all the time really, underneath they're only assessing me as a criminal and nothing else. It's too late for me to be any different now to what I am, but I still feel this keenly, that that's their only approach, and they're quite incapable of accepting me as anything else.

A HARD NUT[1]
Archie

Most of the conversations between us took place either in his cell when he was officially supposed to be somewhere else working, or in my room late in the evening when all the staff in that part of the prison had locked-up their offices and gone home. He was softly-spoken, widely-read and highly intelligent, and serving a long sentence for an offence involving violence but which was not murder. Compared with the majority of the other prisoners, he was young: as he said on one occasion with a thin smile and a sardonic curl of his upper lip, 'The Judge said it was only my age which saved me from getting a very heavy sentence.'

★

—To me when I'm out crime is a way of life, a profession. At times it can be exciting, at times it can be something you're quite proud of. Not you personally of course, you couldn't, because you're not a criminal, at least not in society's eyes. You work for your living, and what you do is socially acceptable; and for all I know, where you live, in your own community, you might have a certain amount of prestige.

It's difficult for people like you to understand that I too, in my own community or what's the word, *milieu* is it – in that setting, I too have a certain amount of prestige. What's more, I don't want to lose it, anymore than you would yours. If you were caught embezzling the local cricket club funds or whatever it was you were connected with, you'd take a sudden drop; people would look sideways at you when you went in the local for a drink, your friends wouldn't send you Christmas cards, even your wife would get the cold-shoulder. Because suddenly you'd no longer be considered reliable. Exactly the

---

1 *The Frying Pan* (1970) London: Hutchinson, pp. 33, 36–8.

same thing would happen to me, in my world, if – well, let's be quite frank about it, even if it was generally known for instance that I was prepared to sit here and talk to you. It wouldn't matter how much or how little I was actually telling you: the mere fact that we were acquaintances would start doubt in people's minds. The code is that you don't mix with straight people. It's a very necessary law too, for self-preservation, my own and everyone else's. No matter what happens, what goes on, you don't know anything and you don't talk.

If it's a big robbery that six of us have pulled off, say, and there's been just one small error somewhere which brings the Law round to see me, the other five know – they have to know – that not only am I not going to let out a word about having anything to do with it, but even if by some incredible misfortune I'm so stuck with it that I'm obviously going to get ten years, I'll never so much as hint with a pause who the others were who were in it too. 'Joe Smith?' 'No, I don't know him.' 'Sam Brown?' 'I've never heard of him.' 'Jack Jones – you can't say you don't know him, he's married to your sister.' 'Is he really? That's funny, I've not heard from her for five years.'

You see, this is the only thing the criminal fraternity have got. It is a fraternity, though of course it doesn't operate down among the petty larcenists and what you might call the thoughtless one-man crooks who never plan anything. But amongst the firm, amongst the teams who work on a large scale and plan everything down to the last detail, which is what you have to do if you're after the big money, it does. Because all the other advantages are on the side of the Law. The radio-controlled cars, the forensic scientists, the squads of fifty or a hundred men on call at any one time, the legal experts, the barristers, even the judicial system – they're on the side of straight society. So the only thing we've got when it comes to the showdown is this absolute certainty, one with another, of a hundred per cent reliability. While you're planning a job, you won't talk one word about it to anyone, not even your own mother. And if one of you gets caught, the other five don't need to lose even a minute's sleep at night wondering about whether you might grass.

And if you haven't got that reputation, you're finished: you won't be asked to join in, you won't get a proposition, you won't even know a job's under consideration. The first you'll hear about it is when you read about it in the papers after it's over, like everyone else.

That's the number one thing: reliability. It's expected of you while you're outside prison – and just as much while you're in. Things get around fast: there's a man up in Durham prison now, I've never met him, and I don't know him except by name. But he was one of the boys – until about three months ago. He wanted to get his parole, so he passed on a bit of information to the prison authorities: something quite trivial, a prisoner had got something in his cell he wasn't supposed to have. That man now, he's finished for the rest of his life: there's not one respectable criminal, inside or out, who'll ever trust him, take him in on a job with them, recommend him to someone else, or would even point out a sixpence to him if they saw it lying in the gutter.

The second thing is violence. By this I don't mean you spend your time looking for fights, in fact anyone of that sort would be considered a menace likely to cause trouble for everyone concerned. But it's necessary to have the reputation of being prepared to use it. A certain amount of brains and intelligence is needed, ability to think things out, to plan and avoid stupidity; but on top of that you need to be known as someone who can, and will, use physical force without hesitation if the job calls for it, who isn't going to have attacks of conscience all of a sudden if, well for example, if a woman's involved.

Yes, I'd hit a woman, I have. A young one or an old one, if it's got to be done, either to get what we want or to pull out of a difficulty. You'll occasionally come across one who doesn't think you mean what you say – 'If you keep quiet I won't hurt you.' Instead she starts yelling her head off. Well, you did warn her: she's only herself to blame if you belt her to shut her up. I don't reckon myself a sadist, I don't get pleasure out of hurting people. But I can't say I lose any sleep about what I've done either.

PEOPLE LIKE ME[1]

Hank Sullivan

The security checks at the entrance to the inner cellblock were comprehensive, stringent and intense. Letters of authority and permissions to go in were examined line by line and compared with copies already held on file. Passport and driving licence were closely scrutinised, numbers authenticated, photographed and then retained. Signatures were matched, distinguishing physical characteristics such as eye colour and complexion were studied and noted. All jacket and trouser pockets were emptied and left hanging with their insides pulled out; shoes and socks were removed, felt carefully and minutely, and prodded, looked in and searched. Handkerchiefs and tie were unfolded and vigorously waved. Into a locker for items not allowed went wallet and billfold and all small change; as did tissues and aspirin, comb, keyring and keys.

Briefcase with tape-recorders, cassettes, batteries, notepad and notebooks, diary and calendar, two pencils and three pens: all were listed on a manifest and precisely described, then signed for and countersigned. Zips and Velcro-fastened compartments were opened and left exposed. Coded ultraviolet identification marks were stamped on the back of each hand. Time-in was noted at 13.29, projected length of stay assessed at three hours. Body search with a metal detector was protracted and precise; stepping through an X-ray arch had to be repeated before two different watchers in turn.

The procedure took an hour.

—'OK, everything's in order,' the Security Supervisor said. 'Have a nice day.'

Hank Sullivan was a prepossessing man: six foot two inches in height,

1 *The Violence Of Our Lives* (1996) London: HarperCollins, pp. 207–17.

he weighed two hundred pounds. His ginger beard was bristly, and short and carefully trimmed; he had lively steel-grey eyes. He wore a clean barrel-striped white sweatshirt with the sleeves rolled tightly up to the tops of his arms, and sat with them folded as he sprawled against the wall in an old wooden chair. His voice was deep and resonant and his basso profundo laughter came out frequently and loud. His talk was friendly and animated and his presence filled the white and box-like room.

—Glad to meet you Tony, finally we managed it hey after all of this time? Say just tell me one thing though will you right at the start? Don't mind my curiosity but how much in a year would you reckon that you earned?

Oh fuck come on, no kidding, only that much really, is that God's truth, that's all? Sweet fucking Jesus when I'm out I make more than that a week. I'd give up if I didn't, so help me God I would, it'd be far too much like work. But then so why'd you go on doing it, why not try something else: I mean do you like it, is it interesting, exciting or what? Pardon me for saying it but you've got to be a nut: I could never have imagined there'd be such crazy folk around. Let me tell you this though, I'm going to drop the idea of trying it myself.

Yeah sure I'll talk with you, like I wrote and said I would. I just hope it's interesting enough for you to feel you want to hear. My story's very simple you see, it's not at all complex: or least not the way I look at it it's not. I'm your ordinary professional criminal and there's plenty around: some of us successful, some of us aren't, you know how it goes? What's a professional criminal, what does it mean? Well all it is is someone who makes his living out of crime. Like you do with writing, it's more or less like that: you do your writing, I do my crime. Successful or unsuccessful, which one am I? Well successful of course, I must be, I'm here and still alive. I've never thought of giving up, I'm the same way as you: I just can't imagine doing anything else.

My basic facts are few, shall we start with those? You're talking to a man called Hank and his age is fifty-two: he's doing eight terms of imprisonment for life, plus six sentences consecutive totalling three hundred years. The life terms are for shootings in which people got killed, and the fixed sentences are for different offences like attempted murder, wounding, armed robbery, possession of explosives, robbery with violence, escape, resisting arrest and that kind of stuff. All of it straight though, nothing kinky or weird. Parole is something I'll never ever be given, no matter what: which I guess some guys'd take it to mean they'd never get out. Not me though, not me my friend, myself I don't look at it that way. Because for sure if I did, well then I'd be dead.

How do I mean? Well 'let out' and 'get out', they're two different things. They won't let me out ever, not from the front door, sure I know that. So what I have is the only alternative, you know what I mean? If it can't be the front then that only leaves the back: so escape's my ambition and the planning of it is all that keeps me alive. In twenty years I've made it twice so it's not an impossible dream. I'm not that sort of a man: I mean if I was I'd be frustrated wouldn't I, all disappointed and sour and eaten-up inside? But I'm not: I'll get out again one day, there's no doubt about that. Believe me, OK?

Go back to the beginning for you, my background and childhood, you want to hear about those? Sure I'll tell you then, it won't take too much time. You see there's nothing to tell. I'm from a white middle-class Catholic family, perfectly ordinary, straight down the line. As a kid I was happy and we weren't rich, but neither were we poor. We lived in a nice home, we were well raised and wanted for nothing or nothing I recall. My father was a production manager at a factory and my mother was a teacher: both of them are dead now, but they were nice people and good. They were very happy with each other, you know how some people are? They believed in family ties and values, and all that kind of thing. I've a brother and two sisters, all older than me: I've not been in contact with any of them since I was young, but as far as I know they've led conventional lives. Both my sisters are married and I couldn't tell you what their names are. That's about all I can think of that there's to say where my family's concerned. They don't really exist for me for practical purposes in any meaningful kind of way now, because that's how it goes.

Schooling, I guess that'd be interesting if I could remember anything of it that left any mark but I'm sorry no, I can't. I went to a Catholic high school for boys and the teachers were priests. I wasn't ever beaten or sexually interfered with: there were none of those things went on you sometimes read about, so there's no interest there, just nothing at all. I think I usually got good grades. My life was not unusual and nothing occurred in it for the first ten years I'd say: no one specially influenced me either for good or for bad, you know what I mean?

The fact I was secretive and had an inner life was all that made me any different I suppose. If you'd met me then you'd never have imagined more than anyone else what was happening inside. Exteriors conceal, right? In my case I was amusing myself from the age of ten on with stick-ups and fires. They were like kind of my hobbies, but they were much more than that: for me they were my all-consuming interests would be more correct to say. I guess to some folk that'd be unusual in a way: but if it is it didn't seem so to me. It wasn't my life was dull you know and I wanted to escape from it, and fizz it up a bit: I just found it interesting to do those things and watch how people would react. Guns were easy to get like they always are; and the first one I had was like a train set for me, I'd clean it and polish it and look after it like it was a treasure or my best friend. My very first gun, a Colt 45 automatic: gee I'll never forget it that one, I loved it I did. Like the way you remember your first woman, you know how I mean?

The other part intrigued me was the psychology thing: people are always more frightened of a kid with a gun than they are of an adult armed robber, have you ever noticed that? Because they think he's not going to be so reasonable and responsible in the way he handles it like a grown-up would I suppose. Might fire a shot at them for just a trivial thing like moving too quick or something of that sort. There was a cab driver once I stuck up when I was twelve: he'd pulled in an alley where I'd told him to go, and when I let him see the gun and told him to give me all he'd got, he got almost hysterical with fear. 'Don't shoot me, don't shoot me' he went on and on: I'd got to really make a big effort to try and talk him down. I said 'Look buddy I'm not going to shoot you' I said, 'just so long as you give me all there is.' You know this guy was shitting himself he was so terrified, I mean can you imagine that?

As for those fires, the arson bit I mean, when I first started coming into juvenile institutions and places of that kind, it used to cause so much fucking interest among psychologists and shrinks you wouldn't believe. Very unusual and significant, least that's what they always said. Going to bed with your sister or wanting to fuck your mother, that was ordinary stuff: but a fourteen-year-old who was a serial arsonist, well he really was, he was some special kind of a guy. All I did actually was set fire to warehouses and stores and offices and schools and that sort of place. Just for fun you know. But they'd never accept it was that, it always had to be symbolic of something: I found that kind of weird, I really did. One centre I was in a psychologist had me write down every single place I'd done. Sixteen as I recall and they divided them in groups: 'masculine' and 'feminine', 'aggressive' and 'passive' and some other categories I forget. It was a young woman who done this stuff, and I remember her better than I remember all the shit. She had a real short white overall and a pretty tight little ass, and she'd all the time lean over the table I was sitting at to mark up the blocks. So what I did naturally was I stretched it all out; then while she was arranging all the papers and covering them with marks I'd stand round in back of her and peek up her skirt or look down her front to try and see her tits. A strange kind of occupation for a young girl to have, studying someone like me. But I let her have her fun though, I didn't mind: but one of us was normal, right, and the other one was not?

My brain starts to ramble, it's a sign of getting old. I don't think I've any more to tell you about those fires, except how I worked. I read all I could about inflammable substances in the library and experimented making compounds of my own. Oh yeah something else there was which brings us back to psychology again. How it is with fire-raisers, do you know about that? They're always supposed to go and watch what they've done, the conflagrations they've caused and that's how the most of them get caught, they can't keep away. Well I was well aware of that so I avoided it, every single time. I'd set timing devices made from cheap stolen clocks, and when a fire of mine started I'd be gone far away. I usually went back to the roof of our house...from there you could see, and hear the fire-tenders' sirens. That was the best part for me because it meant a success. But if it didn't happen I wouldn't go back to see what was wrong: I'd just write that one off and try another time some place else.

You know I guess the best part of all though was hearing people talk. They sure caused some chattering, those fires of mine did. 'They've caught the arsonist', that I often heard; or words to the effect the owner of the premises was responsible himself, he'd done it for insurance because business was bad, you know what people say. How many I did in total I can't properly recall because I never did something stupid like keeping a list. Sixteen I told the psychologist about, but that sure was not them all: twenty-five or thirty say would be nearer the mark in around about a year. And then it all finished and came to an end: how I was caught was real stupid, no doubt at all. How it is when you're young, right, it's always the same? You want to impress some girl, and that's just what I did. I was boasting one night to her it was me who'd set the fires; and she said she didn't believe it, I was trying to pull her leg. So what did I do? I gave her a forecast: I told her wait and see, on the Saturday night I'd set alight a certain store. So when it went up like I said it would, what happened, well anyone could guess: she told her parents what I'd said. The cops were round my place in five minutes flat, and in my room they found things I'd not had time to hide. My parents were pretty shaken by it, especially my dad: he sat me down I remember and he said he knew I hadn't done such things and I must be protecting someone else, like parents always do. Finally he said he'd help me in every way he could, but only if I'd swear on the Bible to him to tell the honest truth. I said OK I'd do that, and that's what I did: I swore on the word of God that I'd acted entirely on my own, and I guess that made him feel pretty bad. He was a good man by his lights and he just couldn't understand. It taught me a lesson though, the experience I mean and I've tried to remember it since, all through my life but with varying success. What it is you'll know it, like every other man: never trust a dame.

What happened in the end was I was sent to reform school for an indefinite period, which was precisely four years. I'd say they were some of the best of my life: I mixed with guys like myself whose only aim was crime. There was a thousand juvenile offenders there of every kind you could imagine, and a lot I'm sure you couldn't, you know what I mean? That's an experience you know I'd not otherwise have had: it was good, it taught me possibilities and it opened up my eyes. Also it made me tough. You know I've often thought this since, the guys who do their time better are the ones who started early: that I honestly believe, now I've thought it out.

I don't know what was with my parents after that, somehow we seemed to grow apart. They visited a time or two, but I never went back home: it didn't seem to have no point, we sort of lived in different worlds. I'd say from eighteen up I only associated with my own kind. Funny, things like that, it's the way it often works: I mean some folks you fit with but others, you can only say if they hadn't been your relatives you'd never have known them even for a start. Then someone else you meet and it's like you've known them all your life. That was how it was with me and my first serious girl: she was the sister of a guy I was buddy-buddy with in there. We never talked it over or arranged it any way: but as soon as I got out I went to the apartment she had, and I think all we said was 'Hi there' before we then went straight to bed. That's the way it should be, so I've always found: then you know where you are and you won't get surprised by discovering you're with a vegetarian or someone like that.

She was a good kid that girl was, I owe a lot to her: she was the person gave me my first proper chance. Sheila her name was or Sheena, something of the kind: she had some Irish in her you know like I do as well. And we were both brought up Catholic, which was another thing: we were ideally suited to each other in most every way there was. She wasn't much of a looker but I don't think you should let that count: what mattered was she had brains, was good with figures and intelligent. She had a job in the central cashier's office of a chain of carpet and furnishing stores, and she knew the days of the month where their different cash drops were made. That was very useful for me because she could point me to all the places where I needed to be, tell me what time the armoured truck with the wages in it would arrive and all stuff like that.

Honestly I did, I learned a lot from that girl: not just where and when to make the strikes but how to plan them out so's they looked like they were at random and no one could trace a pattern in them, point a finger, you know? That stuff was very useful for a young guy like me beginning on a criminal career. I think she was hoping one day I'd make a big enough pile for us to retire and settle down. It was sad for her it didn't happen like that. My trouble was you see I had a wandering eye: something I've never come to terms with in my life. I don't attach myself to people, there's too many risks: lays you open to their moods instead of keeping them to yours. Me and her, Sheena or whatever her name was, things were going along very smoothly for a couple of years till she started talking about wanting to settle down. There was nothing else for it: one night I upped and I didn't come back because you don't want discussions, you just make the break like that. Besides women can peach on you, threaten to tell, and that can lead to awkwardness: I've had it happen and it's not very nice. As soon as they say they might, the best thing to do is make for the door.

I'd say on the whole though I've been lucky with my women, they've mostly given me good times. There was one I remember, now she was one of the best, a feisty little girl: only sixteen, fast-legged and sprinty like a quarterhorse. Got me to train her how to use a thirty-eight; and she was the sort to go out and pull jobs I myself'd think twice about first. She was some kid she was, red hair and not all that tall, only came up to here. You know what she'd do? What she was good at especially, it was usually hotels: she'd sit in the bar of one and when some guy propositioned her they'd go up to his room. Ten minutes flat and she'd get him stripped naked, down to his drawers. Then she'd take off all her own clothes and get him so dazzled he'd fall on the bed: and when he did that then she'd reach for her purse, pull out her gun and make him give her his last cent. Takes courage to do that you know, for a girl on her own. I used to tell her if she was my daughter I would, I'd feel real proud.

Say you know what Tony, let me tell you something…I'm really enjoying talking to you, it's great to reminisce. Put a new tape in? Sure, go ahead.

—Women eh, there was other ones too, plenty in my time. I met a broad once, believe me she was sixty-five…she was a little old granny and she drove a big truck and suggested we go into partnership. Only let me tell you, that's something I've never ever done: take on one other guy and the risk grows three ways. One is he could let you down and not play his part, two he could get injured and captured to follow, three if he is he could try to save his neck by telling what he knows. I'd say to any young guy to always bear that in mind: wherever it's practicable, stay on your own.

Let me tell you an example: the first time I ever came to prison, it wasn't my fault. Me and another guy, we'd held up a security truck that was taking wages to a factory: I'd done all the planning about where exactly we'd stop it which was on a bridge over a canal. Then at the last minute I heard it had four armoured guards, not two like I'd been told. I always reckoned I could deal with two when I worked on my own; but four was rather different, you'd need eyes in the back of your head. So what did I do but I took on an assistant; and when the shooting started he took a bullet in his hip. He wasn't wearing body armour like I'd told him he should so of course he was caught. They beat it out of him where I was making for and they had twenty police vehicles and dogs and a helicopter too. They got me in a wood and threw a cordon round it: and all because this guy gave them knowledge so they could work out my route. I had no way out except firepower: in the confrontation I shot more accurately than they did but one against twenty's not fair odds and I surrendered in the end. I gave a good account of myself first, I think I took out a total of four: but I finished up with two life sentences plus two hundred years.

Considering for ten years I'd been working nice and steady and never once been caught, as you can imagine I felt very bitter about that result: I still think if I hadn't had that amateur along, I'd most likely have shaken off pursuit. I've learned my lesson about that, or mostly I have: I don't want to be boastful, but if someone wants to hire my services for something big when I'm out I always lay down strict conditions that they leave me alone to work the way I want to, which means on my own. I won't do nothing for anyone if I have to follow their instructions, they must follow mine.

Another thing is this: I won't do just anything, I always make it plain that there's lines. An obvious one from which I'll never deviate is I'll never hurt a woman, not for any sum at all. I don't know if it means I'm soft-hearted or what: I've been offered contracts and some of them were big ones, but if it's a woman, then the answer's no. I don't touch females, get somebody else. On the whole though taking individuals out, that's really not my line. I've only done two contract hits in the whole of my life; or three at the most. They're sneaky, know what I mean? I wouldn't ever touch them unless business was real bad, I'd sooner stand up and fight: I don't like killing people when they're not armed.

The excitement, you know, that's the part I like: I'm not the sort goes round shooting at random anyone I see. All of my killings they've all had a purpose, I'm a professional criminal, not a fucking psychopath. Those first two I told you about, I was trying to get away; then the next three again, they were all of men with guns who were moving me to a different state or other to face some more charges. The chances of breaching a maximum-security establishment are low because you're outnumbered by the guards, so the best times are when they're moving you. Then the same thing again two years ago, there were just two prison guards. That's only seven? One two thr...oh yeah you're right, so who the hell was...yeah wait a minute, I've got it now: the second escape it wasn't three it was four, a State Trooper turned up and thought he'd join in. Though I'll be honest with you, there's been a couple of others too that haven't come out and I think they never will. How many in total? Jeez I've no idea, more than ten it must be I guess.

Let me try and tell you how it is. Firstly I don't have to justify myself, there's no need. I guess the way I'd put it would be to say it's like we are at war, me and society I mean. I see myself as a law enforcement officer: only my laws, not yours. Or another way to say it would be there's one set of guys whose uniforms are blue: they try and hang on to things like money and possessions and power. And then there'd be other ones whose uniforms are green: they want to get a slice of things themselves too. The one way they'll not do it is work from nine through five so they have to think of other ways. I've chosen one which I thoroughly enjoy: it's plotting and scheming and working out a strategy, then putting it into action and seeing if it works. And again I'm not boasting in saying this to you because it's true: I've been successful a hundred times more often than I've ever been caught for, that's certainly a fact. We're cleverer than we're given credit for, people like me, we certainly are.

I'm a professional criminal, and I take pride in my trade. An amateur, you see, he's not like that at all. How I'd define him would be a guy who makes a quick hit and relies on his luck for the amount of cash he gets: could be a few hundred dollars, might be nothing at all. But for me I need to know first what the amount is involved, and the amount of risk I'll take's got to be commensurate with the financial reward. If it looks like it's going to be a combat situation I wouldn't go in under-armed: always at least I've got to have an automatic rifle, two pistols and at least some hand grenades. 'Armed to the teeth' would be the phrase, right?

Obviously if it's something big other guys are going to try and stop me, right? They'll go as far as they think's necessary to do that, including killing me of course. Then I'm saying in return that to stop me that's what they'll have to do: and if they try, then I'm going to try and kill them first. That's common sense, OK? But don't get me wrong like I said before: I wouldn't kill anyone unless it was strictly necessary to get what I wanted or it was my life or theirs.

Would I ever kill you, you want an honest answer to that? Well the answer is no, probably not. I can't envisage the situation arising can you, where it would be necessary? I mean if you were a guard here and I had a gun, if I wanted your key I'd ask you for it, I'd say 'Give me your key.' And if you were sensible about it as I think you would be and did what I asked and stood to one side, then of course I wouldn't kill you, because there wouldn't be a need. On the other hand though if you crazily decided you wouldn't give me the key and went for your gun, then of course I'd blow your fucking head off. I'd have to wouldn't I, otherwise you might do me harm. That answer your question, do you understand? Good: no hard feelings I hope?

—Oh boy Tony I've enjoyed this you know, I truly have. It's been like the kind of conversation you usually have with yourself, know what I mean? Good luck with the book.

THIS IS THE QUESTION[1]

—'I'm going to ask you something which I don't want you to try and answer straight away; instead perhaps you'd think about it over the weekend on your own, preferably without discussing it with anyone else. Come back on Monday and tell me your answer. This is the question:

Imagine it's about a year after your present sentence, and you're in trouble again. You've been found guilty of yet another offence exactly similar in nature to those you've already committed in the past. Imagine also that I'm the Judge you're eventually brought in front of, and I then have the unavoidable duty of dealing with you. But when you appear in court I say 'I've no idea what to do with you at all: I can't see much point in sending you back to prison yet again, but on the other hand I can't think of any suitable alternative. So what I'm going to do is remand you in custody for forty-eight hours; in that time I'd like you to think about the situation, and tell me yourself what you suggest I ought to do.

In other words, if you offend again, what sentence do you think should be passed on you?

*

Archie

—A funny question I thought; I had quite a chuckle about it, it amused me. It made me try and picture myself as an honest man who genuinely wanted to go straight, which is what I thought was the first thing wrong with it from my point of view. Because I'm not,

---

1 *The Frying Pan* (1970) London: Hutchinson, pp. 200–10.

and therefore I can't answer it. If I had any intentions of being genuine about giving up crime for good, then all I could do would be to ask you to try and find some way of correcting my twisted thinking, which I suppose is the whole idea of this place here. But you're saying, aren't you, that I've gone out from here and yet I've still got nicked again? Which means it hasn't worked: as the Judge, you look back at my record and you see I've been in Grendon and even then I'm still thieving, so what can you do after that? Right?

I was reading a book a few weeks ago, I don't know if you've come across it, *The Seventh Step*? It's about an American geyser, an ex-con himself, he runs a system of what he calls 'bonding' men when they come out of nick. Some businessman puts up a few hundred dollars to help the man get on his feet and find himself somewhere to live and a job: then over a period the ex-prisoner has to pay it back. Until he does so, out of his earnings, the businessman can't put up money to help another prisoner. The con is told this, and the idea is that as he knows some other feller in the nick won't be given a chance till he's paid off his bond, out of loyalty to his pals he does his best so someone else can have a chance as well.

That's the theory of it, but I don't think it would work in my case; at least not the way it was intended to. If you were to bond me for instance, I'd pay you back alright, and in double-quick time so I wouldn't be obligated to you myself and so another feller could be given a chance. I'd pay back within a week after I'd got out: but the way I got the money for it, it wouldn't exactly be one that met with social approval.

So we're back at square one: what are you going to do with me? If you were a Judge naturally I'd tell you this was definitely my very last crime, and if you cared to give me one more chance I would give you my solemn oath that I'd never offend again. Equally naturally I wouldn't expect you to swallow it for a minute; if you did I'd think there was something wrong with you.

To my mind you see the problem really is that you yourself are presumably a law-abiding member of the community, and therefore you tend almost automatically to think I'd like to join you. In that, you'd be making a fundamental mistake. And if we were to sit here for hours and argue it out, I don't think you could give me any really convincing reason why I should want to be law-abiding. I don't like the pattern of crime, prison, crime, prison: but the way society is, and the way I am, what's the alternative?

Really all I could say to you would be 'Set me free.' Just like that; no threats or warnings on your part, and no promises of good behaviour on mine. Obviously with things as they are, you wouldn't do it; you couldn't, society wouldn't let you. So then I'd just have to say to you 'All right, get on with it. The social justice of your society demands that you impose a prison sentence, and I think you're being a bit of a coward in trying to put it on to me to decide what should be done with me.'

Because we were friends I'd ask you to make it the smallest amount you could, of course: I'd make varying calls on that friendship with each little twist and turn in the conversation, to see if I could get you to feel bad about it. The first sign you gave me, perhaps just by no more than a note in your voice, that you were having doubts, I'd play like hell on that aspect of the case in an effort to get your sympathy.

Prison's no good, especially for those who are weak-willed and incapable rather than deliberately ill-intentioned. Rightly or wrongly I don't include myself in that category: I know perfectly well I've got more than enough will-power necessary for going straight if I really want to. But this only brings me back to the point I made at the beginning, that I can't yet even picture myself as wanting it.

All the same, an interesting question put to me, I thought; I'm only sorry I couldn't be of much more help to you in answering it.

Ron

—I gave this a hell of a lot of thought. I felt I had to, that it was worth thinking about; if you like I felt it was the sort of thing I had to be made to think about. I'm afraid I haven't been able to come up with anything very bright in the way of suggestion, except that you should send me back here to Grendon again for a further period of two years.

I don't see what else I could ask you to do in view of my condition of mind and my antecedents. If you let me off, I'd be straight back in trouble within a week, so you'd only be postponing the problem of dealing with me. Probation would be no good whatsoever: hell, I've already had five probations, I can't see that a sixth would stand much chance of changing me.

The thing is that I am going to be me until the day I die; and you simply can't tolerate me. By 'you' I mean society in general, not just you the Judge or you the person. Somehow or other as far as you're concerned, I've got to be taught to conform; and until you can find a way of doing it I'm going to go on making a bloody nuisance of myself.

How you could teach me, I don't know. One of the things I read in that definition of psychopaths was that they couldn't profit from experience, they couldn't be taught: the only hope for them was that one day they grew out of it. It was quite right as far as I'm concerned in another way too: when it said they always destroyed personal relationships. I certainly do that, I always have done. I'd like to be able to say to you 'Please don't send me back to prison, put me in the care of someone who'll try and deal with me without taking me to court or punishing me or rejecting me.' But I couldn't honestly say if you did it would necessarily make any difference. It probably wouldn't, because I'm lacking in something, I'm lacking in a feeling for other people just as a one-armed man is lacking a limb.

Why I should ask for Grendon rather than any other prison isn't just because it's more comfortable, but because I definitely do think they're on the right lines here. I wouldn't say it was anything like ideal, or that it couldn't be made ten times better. But at least in my opinion it's a place where you do get opportunities to give a bit of time to thinking about yourself and your problems and discussing them, instead of the insane wasting of time which goes on in other prisons, where the following of petty rules and regulations is the sole occupation of everyone concerned.

So that would be my answer. 'Give me some more of the same thing.'

Yes, as soon as I say that I realise the implication of what I'm saying. I'm asking you to keep me a prisoner, aren't I? Well I wish I could answer that. I think I must have a very deep sense of not really belonging outside in the community at all. Imprisonment is a very dehumanising experience, it takes away your manhood and your sense of identity and everything; the more you have of it, the more dehumanised you become. I suppose that's why I'm now incapable of thinking properly about myself as a person, as an individual any more. Not that I'm saying I was much of one ever, so far as I can remember; I think there's always been something lacking, something that makes me think of other people in the same way as I think of myself: impersonally, not as individuals.

All this isn't much help to you, I'm afraid. But if you can ask me that question, as you can and did, perhaps I can ask you one too. In the same way I'll ask you to take it away and think about it after you've gone. You've asked me what you should do with me: my answer boils down to 'I don't know, I think all you can do is give me the same treatment again until something changes.' But that something might not be in me after all: it might be I can't change ever. In that case I think I've a right to put the same question: are *you* going to change either, in your methods of trying to deal with me? Or are we both – me as an individual and you as society – approaching the whole thing in completely the wrong way?

Donald

—I think myself that for someone like me the answer'd be very simple: there ought to be some kind of homes we could be sent to, where people would look after us and see we didn't get into trouble. Not prisons because they're no good at all: they kill all the feeling in you, I think you come out worse than you were when you went in.

These homes'd have to be proper places with comfortable furniture and nice carpets on the floor, not institutions with bare boards and all things like that, but somewhere better. The sort of place you could live in without feeling ashamed about it, where you could take people back to for an evening if you met them. Like a big house with lots of lights and nice things in it; you could take a person there and say to them 'This is my home, this is where I live; and these other people here, they're all my friends.' If you could send me to somewhere like that, I'd feel I might have a chance of making something out of my life.

One of the troubles, you see, is that I always get so depressed when I'm out, I don't seem to fit in; and if there was something of that kind I could be forced to stop at, I think for me that would be the best possible arrangement there could be. Only I know there aren't many places of that kind; it would be very difficult for you to find somewhere that would have me, wouldn't it? But perhaps there might be a lady somewhere, a motherly sort of woman it would have to be, who'd take me in to live with her as part of her family. It'd be asking an awful lot of her, I get these terrible moods and depressions and she'd have to put up with me; and then I suppose in the end she'd get fed up, wouldn't she, and ask me to leave?

This is a very hard question for me, and I've laid awake nearly the whole of Saturday night thinking about it. Because you see one of the things you said when you asked me it, was what should you do if I came in front of you and I'd committed another offence? And when I thought of that it made me worry because I suppose really if I go on committing offences sooner or later I'll have to be put away for a very long time indeed, there'll be no alternative.

If you were a nice Judge perhaps you'd give me a chance to say to you I wasn't really a bad person at heart, just an inadequate one; almost like a child in some ways, no more fit to run his own life and manage his own affairs than a kid. This is a terrible thing for a grown man to have to say; but at least I think it would be honest if I was to say something like that about myself. I'd tell you you'd have to be very firm with me, you'd have to be standing over me and directing me in what to do and how to do it.

Otherwise I don't think I could exist for very long, if I didn't have somebody watching over me all the time. It's not my wish I should be like this, I didn't ask to be born a thoroughly weak person; in fact I wasn't given any choice about it, I didn't ask to be born at all. But I'd have to admit that was what I'm like, someone who isn't capable of managing to go through life somehow, without a lot of help from other people.

They tell you it's your own responsibility, that a man ought to be able to look after himself, he shouldn't go through life all the time looking to other people to solve his difficulties for him. I've had that said to me often enough, I could repeat it off by heart for you: but no one has ever told me yet exactly how I ought to do it. They think I'm like they are, that I must have *something* in me: but sometimes when I come to think of myself, I feel like one of those rag-dolls you see in shop windows that flop down all on one side, kind of sagging because they haven't got enough stuffing in them, do you know what I mean?

All I could do was try and find a way somehow of appealing to you, trying to tell you exactly how I felt. I'd say 'Yes, I'm a guilty person, yes I did whatever it was and I'm very sorry about it; in fact I think I'm more sorry about it than you are, because it's me that's got to pay the penalty for it now. Only please, if you could, would you have just one more try with me?' That's not a very good answer for you, I know, but it's the best I can do.

Clive

—I was, I really was, there's only one word for it, I was absolutely shattered. I thought 'My God, what a question!' It really knocked me sideways, I've never had to think so hard about anything in all my life. Because in all my thinking up to now, I haven't even allowed the prospect of being in trouble again to enter my mind. I'm quite determined when I go out to lead an honest life; and this is something totally different from saying that when I go out I'm going to make sure I'm not caught again. I really mean it; I can't even contemplate letting down those two friends who've stood by me, Martin and Helen, it would be out of the question, it doesn't bear thinking of…does it?

Oh Christ yes, I suppose it must be contemplated; that's the whole point, isn't it, of what you meant by the question? Really you know, my God, it's a shattering thing to face.

All right, let's say it then: 'Here you are, young Clive, after all that's been done for you, and after the limitless friendship that's been extended to you by Martin and Helen, here you are again and you're in trouble.' I think if that did happen, then there'd be no escaping it, no dodging the issue, no trying to evade it: the point would be, quite simply, that I'd have to face the fact I was insane – or at least so totally mentally unstable I wasn't fit to live out in the community, I'd have to be committed for a very long period to some kind of mental institution.

I certainly wouldn't ask you to send me to prison again, I think that would only be making things still worse. I'd tell you I wanted just one more chance to find myself, to prove to other people and to myself that I wasn't utterly and irretrievably bad, that I didn't want to let down these good people who've put so much effort into proving to me that whatever happened, they were never going to reject me.

But oh my God, I can hear myself saying it you know; I've said it in so many words so many times before, haven't I? Yes, yes, I have, it's only too true, the same old flannel. You'd look at me and you'd say 'But this is nothing different, we've been through all this' – and you'd be only too damn right, you would. You'd have got yourself a problem with me, and there's no escaping that, my God there isn't.

If it was me you know, and I was the Judge, I'd look at me so hard and so cold and I'd say 'You sod, Clive, you absolute bloody sod. There's only one conclusion I can come to, and that is that you're now so utterly institutionalised there's no hope for you at all. You're an out and out bastard, mate, and I'm going to send you to prison for ever.' I'd phrase it in more legal terminology of course, but that's what I'd mean. What a bastard, what a shit: that's what I'd be thinking about myself.

De-institutionalise me, how to do that: that's what I'd have to be thinking about, isn't it? VSO, Voluntary Service Overseas, send me to work with something like that: would that be any good? I wonder: it just might. Perhaps it'd give me a feeling that even if I was no good myself, at least I was being of some use somewhere to other people. But then you as the Judge couldn't do that, could you? It's not realistic: the whole point is that I've done more people out of more money, and I've got to pay the penalty for it. Restitution's no good; even if I worked and paid it back, it wouldn't alter the fact that what I'd done was committed a crime, I was still culpable and blameworthy and all the rest of it. We can't have VSO just for the people who want to work off their own sense of guilt, can we? No we can't. I tell you, it's awful, I'm still shattered, I really am.

You see, I said to you before I think that Grendon does work if you'll let it. But you know, deep down this is a prayer: that it will work, that it must work, that it's got to. I'm holding on to that, like hell I'm holding on to it. When you asked me that question and told me to go away and think about it, when I really did begin to think I was absolutely terrified; because if it was to turn out that Grendon hadn't worked, then I'd be brought slap-up against the fact that all the time I've been here I've still been nothing but a con-man – and the person I've conned most of all has been myself. And that's about all I can say now: I'm going to make it work, I really believe it is affecting me. Because any alternative, as far as I'm concerned, is just too absolutely awful to contemplate.

Bernie

—A poser, you know, that question of yours. It's been in my mind all weekend, I thought I'd be able to shrug off but I haven't. I came up with all sorts of clever answers for you, I thought 'Right, that's it, that's the solution, now I'll get back to the book I'm reading and forget about it.' But it irritated me, really it did, because it kept creeping back. At one stage I'll tell you frankly I considered doing exactly what you'd asked me not to; asking somebody else's opinion. I thought I'd stop the next man I saw, put it to him, and then come back to you with what he said as my own opinion. Anyway, in the end I didn't: I kept it to myself. I'd like to express my total lack of gratitude to you for giving me an extremely awkward and uncomfortable weekend.

I think the first thing I'd better say to you is that you'd better bear in mind all the time the case had been coming up for hearing, I'd have been working like blazes to find every scrap of assistance that I could. I'd have got a good solicitor, a good barrister, character-witnesses to come and speak on my behalf, offers of a job ready and waiting for me, promises of accommodation and supervision from people of unimpeachable integrity, and anything else I could think of. If I thought there was any chance of getting away with it, I'd even offer you a bribe; but of course in England you're liable to find yourself in trouble for that on top of everything else if you come unstuck.

All right; let's say I've done all the wriggling and twisting and chicanery that I can think of, and we arrive at the final point which I presume you've had in mind all the time, that everything's failed.

Here we are in court: all the excuses have been given, all the appeals have been made, everything that could possibly be said has been said, and now inevitably you've got to do something. Well, you've done something: you've told me to go away and think about it, and come back with an answer: and now here I am.

I would say to you that there is only one possible thing you can do. Which is to put a revolver right up against my head and to tell me quite simply and frankly that the next time without any hesitation at all you're going to pull the trigger. The revolver you put there should be, I suggest, a suspended sentence of ten years' imprisonment; with the clear proviso that if I offend once more in any way at all, there'll be no trial, no hearing, no defence, nothing: just 'bang', ten years.

I really do think that would terrify me, so long as you made it absolutely plain to me you really meant it, and on any future occasion there'd be no ifs and buts and whyfors and wherefors: there'd be nothing only that simple fact of ten years' imprisonment. Oh and you might add to, to reinforce it, that it wouldn't be subject to remission: it'd be the full ten and not a single day less.

Yes I do think I would be deterred. I know with a lot of people deterrence doesn't work, but I think in my case it would. Because I'm not a young man; I couldn't console myself with the thought that when I came out I'd still have a good few years left to enjoy myself in. I know I wouldn't: I'd know that ten years inside to me now, at my age, would mean when I was released I'd be nothing but a zombie and it would be the absolute end of my life. I hate prison, I loathe it: and that's the only realistic thing in the world you as a Judge would have to work on: my fear of it, my loathing for it.

True, it's never deterred me before, that's perfectly correct. But most times I've always had some faint idea in the back of my mind I was going to get away with it somehow; and when I haven't, my main feeling has been irritation with myself for not succeeding. But this time, in this hypothetical case we're discussing, I'd know there was going to be no getting away with it. You'd already in fact passed the sentence on me, of ten years: I couldn't even hope you were going to be moderate or tolerant or humane or anything. There it was, staring me in the face, unavoidable: one more slip, no question about it, I was actually going to do the sentence.

In that situation, I would, I'd think a thousand times before I took one false step. Up to now, I've only in the past thought six times; and then I've gone on. But with ten years pressed up against my head, and no chance whatsoever of avoiding it I really do believe something like that couldn't fail to hold me back for ever after.

Geoff

—I'm dangerous, I think you'd have to face that; you couldn't go on letting me wander around, give me probation or anything of that sort. The offence I'd probably be up in front of you for would be the same as usual, possessing drugs and maybe carrying firearms; but after what I've told you about myself while you've been here, you'd know the actual charges didn't really matter: what was much more important was what was inside me. You'd have an unfair advantage, because you'd know much more about me than the ordinary Judge would; or at least if not an unfair one, you'd have some kind of advantage.

What you should do with me; I wouldn't envy you having to decide. Worthless, a wastrel, and a potentially dangerous one too. I don't suppose you'd have much alternative but to put me away for the protection of society, and for as long as you possibly could.

I have a feeling though that there was more to the question than that: you were trying to get me to think about what I would do, you were putting the onus on to me to come up with a constructive suggestion, you weren't going to let me shirk my own responsibility. Was that right? Yes, OK. Well then here we go.

I think the only thing would be an indeterminate sentence. Not six months or a year or five years, nothing like that: simply a sentence of imprisonment which would last indefinitely. Or rather one which *could* last indefinitely, depending on me. 'Her Majesty's Pleasure' I think they used to call it, didn't they – 'to be detained during Her Majesty's Pleasure.' For that to work properly, you'd need all sorts of things which at the moment we haven't got: regular facilities for psychiatric examination, constant reviewing of the situation every few months, regular paroles for me now and again to see how I got on. Backed by very strict control; at the first sign of trouble, bring me back inside for a further period, a few months maybe; then let me out again. You'd have to contemplate the possibility – so would I – of the situation going on for months and years, trying this, trying that, failing, starting again, failing.

I realise what I'd be asking is impossible, because it'd mean one person, one social worker with authority, giving up more or less the whole of his time to me. And I reckon I'd be a full-time job for anyone. Meantime there's thousands of others in trouble and needing help, so why should I expect anyone to bother simply and solely with me?

I don't think it would be any good putting me with a family, I'd just wander off. No one would know where I'd gone or what I was up to: in a few months sooner or later it'd be absolutely certain I'd be back in trouble again. There's only one way of making absolutely sure people don't do any more wrong, and that's by keeping them in prison. But this only holds the problem in suspense: the day a man's let out, it starts all over again. Pointless, prison, I think: keeping people in a kind of vacuum, but not altering them much at all, and eventually turning them out as bad as they were to start with, or perhaps even a little bit worse.

But me it was you were asking about, wasn't it: not other people, but me myself, me. Yes. And I'm the one supposed to solve it. Hard, you know, very hard: I'm all mixed up about me. As mixed up as you are, or the judges, or society in general. You can't think of what to do with me or how to deal with me any more than I can.

A funny thing: when I was thinking about it, it suddenly struck me that really what it came down to in the end was all purely and simply a matter of coincidence. Coincidence like walking round a corner, meeting someone you've never set eyes on in your life before, a girl or a woman maybe, and getting involved with them to such an extent that you start thinking about their problems rather than your own. As soon as another person starts getting important to you, it changes you.

Here in prison no one else is important; you think about your own problems to the exclusion of everything else. That's what Grendon does for you, and I'm not so sure it's a good thing. Life's like a fire, I think: and when you come here, slowly you begin to realise that what's happened to you is that you've jumped straight out of the fire into the frying-pan.

Norman Edwards[2]

—The exterior is not just an exterior for the sake of deceit. I've never really used it to its full advantage, to take me up to a position where I could really do someone out of a fortune. It's also an exterior which I like, which I want people to accept – or part of me wants them to accept it, while another part takes a rather mischievous pleasure in knowing that I'm deceiving them – not just financially but in their whole estimate of me, and the thing I enjoy as much as anything is this. It becomes a little game that I play with the world, and I can't help playing it wherever I am – outside, in a job, in the dock, in

2 *A Man Of Good Abilities* (1967) London: Hutchinson, pp. 147–53.

prison. Doubtless it's very deplorable and improper – but there it is, it's not only in me but it is me. And well, there it is.

When you say 'There it is', like that, it suggests you've accepted that there's little prospect of your life being any different now.

It'd be unrealistic, wouldn't it, to take any other view? The probation officer I'm now on licence to for the unexpired portion of my sentence – the next two years or so – is bound when he looks down my record to say to himself, 'Well, this chap can't be a very good risk', isn't he?

What would you say the odds were?

Well, at the very best, with all those previous convictions and at my age, it couldn't be better than evens and it'd probably be about six to four against, I should say.

If you were that probation officer, how would you handle a case like this, like yourself, if it was presented to you?

Well, I think having looked at his record and seen that there was that long period of ten years or so when he didn't get into trouble, I'd want to see if he couldn't sort out some kind of job where we could repeat the performance.

Two things you've mentioned earlier, I think you would have to take into account – one is that during that period you were in fact, as you said, avoiding detection rather than avoiding committing any crime; and the other that you have a tendency to make sure that you do get detected. As the probation officer you know these two things – so what sort of a job would you try to find?

A clerical one, some kind of book-keeping perhaps, but one that didn't entail handling actual cash.

Why wouldn't you trust him to handle cash?

I would think it would be putting temptation too much in his way, it would be rather asking for trouble and I'm not sure how he'd react, so it would be better to try and avoid the situation arising.

Like the firm you were working for did when they asked you not to use their banking facilities?

I'm not an entirely rational being; and although intellectually you gain a point, I know that you wouldn't really expect too great a degree of consistency from me.

No, quite true; well, what else besides finding the right job would you, as the probation officer, do?

I think I'd try and make a friend of him, or get someone else to try and do it, someone to whom he could unburden himself if he wanted to. It'd be important to try and get his co-operation.

Would he unburden himself ever, do you think?

To a degree, to a degree he would – though of course there are areas he wouldn't want people to pry into, certain aspects of his private life and so on.

And what would you do if he committed another offence while he was on probation? Would you have him sent back to prison?

Not if I could avoid it, no. I think he's got to learn somehow to live outside without committing offences, and he'll never do that in prison. I'd try and find out what went wrong and hope to avoid the same pitfall again in the future.

And if he offended again after that?

Well there are people of course who no matter what you try to do to help them, it's quite useless; and unless you're willing or able to make a full-time job of being a nursemaid to just one person, then you do reach a point – as this probation officer probably would eventually – of having to turn the problem over to someone else.

Such as who?

Well, what I mean is, he might just have to wash his hands of the whole business and let events take their course.

So that the problem would then be one for a Judge?

Yes.

All right, if you were the Judge now, what would you do with this offender?

Poor Judge, he'd be in a bit of a state I think, wouldn't he? Here's this man been locked away for ages and given chance after chance in between, and yet he still goes on and on doing exactly the same things. The Judge hasn't really got the tools to do anything very much, to get psychiatrists to work on the man and things like that.

Do you think psychiatrists might be able to help if they could work on him?

They might – though it's doubtful, with someone of my age. I think the Judge is more likely to shake his head sadly and send the man back to prison.

You're sending yourself back to prison, then – is that the answer?

No – or at least I hope it isn't. It seems so pointless, it seems so wasteful of everybody's time and energy including my own. With my advancing years I feel rather less inclined now than I used to, to look round for some activity outside the law, but one hesitates all the same to say that all danger is past and I suppose I must face up to the possibility that I'll go back inside again.

Are you actually doing anything at the moment, in the place you're working, that could get you put back inside?

No, not yet: in fact where I am, there's no opportunity to do anything, I only handle figures but no actual money.

The ideal job in fact that you said you'd try and find for yourself if you were your probation officer?

That's true.

So will you stay in it?

No, not for long, I shall be moving on to another job when I can find one. You see I'm only an ordinary clerk where I am at the moment, and in fact it's well below my capacity. I could earn myself a great deal more in a job with more responsibility.

When you say 'earn', do you mean legitimately?

Oh yes. I could look after a small office, control a staff, supervise accounts, that sort of thing; and I think I'm wasting my abilities to be doing anything less. This feeling sweeps over me, and it's quite irresistible, really, that I ought to be doing something much more responsible, I ought to be in a higher position, one with more prestige and status attached. Those things, those values – they may be unreal ones or false ones to other people, and perhaps they are to me also, in that I know they're not really the things that matter at all but they are the values I've lived by all my life and I can't really be expected to give them up now, to reassess my standards, to change all my concepts.

You say you know they're not really the things that matter: what are the things that do?

If I repeated them to you, they'd be words, that's all; and they'd be words used to conceal rather than to express. Happiness, contentment, peace of mind, self-respect, self-knowledge, integrity – those would be some of them, and I could say them and make regretful noises about not having them. But they wouldn't really be valid for me and to me – they're all values that I know other people have, but as concepts in a personal sense they're almost meaningless. Of course, I'd prefer not to go back to prison, I'd prefer not to have lived the utterly futile and useless sort of life that I have – but I may as well face the fact that I've lived that life, it's over, and I can only concern myself with myself as I am now, and what lies before me.

And I say, without any sense of making a grand declaration of faith or anything like that, that I accept the values of position, prestige, status. I accept those as things to be strived for and I accept that now, if I'm ever to get them, I shall have to continue to try, as I've always done, to find short cuts towards them. I can't look back on a lifetime of dogged devotion and service to a company which has eventually brought me the just reward of a high and responsible position. So I have to forge my references, otherwise I'm never going to get there, there isn't time. And if anyone finds out about me, discovers my long and nefarious past, I'm not going to remain in the post either – so therefore, all the time, I have to live with a pretence and live under the fear of someone finding out. But I'm not going to make myself miserable doing it; sufficient unto the day and all that. The man who said to me that he'd lived under the shadow of Wandsworth – well so he had, to him it was a shadow even though in his case it wasn't a very real one. To me it is a real one, but it's nothing like the shadow that hangs over him. If I get into trouble and get caught, well I get into trouble and get caught, that's all. When I get back in Wandsworth or wherever it is I'm going, if I go, I shall do my best to get myself as congenial a job as possible, and one that makes the best use, in the circumstances, of my abilities.

But while I'm outside, I shall go on until I find what is in every way a suitable job. I think I could best describe it like this – it must be a job, as I've said, with a certain amount of standing and prestige, which earns me about twenty-five pounds a week or thereabouts. And in addition it must provide me with the opportunity to exercise my brains and ingenuity so that I can consistently fiddle for myself another two or three pounds a week on top of my salary. I don't want to double it or anything like that, but I do want to be able to give expression to this little bent I have, this little quirk or twist that gives me the satisfaction of knowing that just in a minor and unimportant way I'm being cleverer than the accountants or the auditors. This is what gives spice to life as far as I'm concerned, gives it an extra little dimension, a secret room that no one else knows about and that's entirely private to myself alone.

Without that, nothing really will occupy my interest for any great length of time. It wouldn't do either if the boss were to give me a rise of an additional two or three pounds a week – I'd still have to have my little fiddle, on top of that, to satisfy the – well, I suppose it sounds absurd to describe it in these terms, but I was going to say to satisfy the artist in me. To you perhaps and others like you, it wouldn't be worth doing – especially not now, when the consequences of discovery are likely to be so heavy and so disastrous. But that only makes it now all the more appealing, somehow, the thought of the high stakes on such a trivial game. It's all, without a shadow of doubt, deplorable in the extreme, and I don't expect you to understand it. But it's essential to me now, it's so much a part of me that without it I honestly don't feel I'm properly living. And after all, I don't have much other excitement, do I?

Part IV

NONCES

Sex offending is currently on the political agenda. However, sex crime has always fascinated. Each decade seems to produce a particular focus of interest which dominates. Concern about organised prostitution emerged in the 1950s, the move towards a partial decriminalisation of homosexuality was the focus of the 1960s, the new wave of the women's movement took rape as a major issue in the 1970s, child sexual abuse was recognised as a serious social problem in the 1980s. Concern about sex crime has dramatically escalated in the 1990s. Media coverage has encouraged a moral panic. Various proposals, such as sex-offender registration schemes, are being put into place. However, the voice of the sex offender is rarely heard.

Tony Parker's conversations with sex offenders are among the most powerful of his work. They place the offending within the wider context of a life. Wilfred, Harry, Norman and Stanley provide some illuminating insights. It is always tempting to categorise, but Tony's own words provide a cautionary reminder: 'None of them is representative of a type, only of himself. These are personal statements made at unknown cost and with inestimable bravery and to try adequately to thank those who made them by allowing themselves to be subjected to persistent questioning is beyond my power; I can only state my respect and admiration for their courage and dignity.'[1]

1 'Introductory note', in *The Twisting Lane* (1969) London: Hutchinson, p. xi.

A MALADY COME UPON YOU[1]

Wilfred Johnson

A month after the season had finished the holiday resort was characterless, uninhabited and depersonalised with the colourful summer-thronging crowds gone from the streets and cafes and amusement arcades. Along the concrete promenade with its decorated lamp-posts and regularly spaced shelters and benches there was no one to be seen; the steep flights of steps and the sloping paths coming down from the cliffs were deserted, and between them the formal flower beds were now only empty and unplanted bare patches of soil. Over the lines of abandoned beach huts and shuttered refreshment stalls a ragged group of mute seagulls flapped and dipped hungrily and the distant pier unused and silent stretched out like an atrophied arm into the sea.

In the honeyed afternoon sunlight he stood by the balustrade of the sea-wall, staring intently at the glittering white-flecked waves of the grey North Sea heaving slowly one after another to break hissing and frothing on the beach below. A small frail man of sixty with dark green eyes in a thin and troubled face, and the collar of the military-looking macintosh the prison had lent him for the day turned up against the breeze from off the water which blew through his short-cropped and neatly parted greying hair. His hands resting on the wall, he stayed for a long time silent, looking at the pastel colours of the sand and sky, breathing the salt-fresh air and watching the ocean's endless sullen surge.

—The sand, he said after a while, it looks like brown sugar, doesn't it, don't you think it does? Barbados Muscavados, 'brown moist', that's what they used to call it if I remember, in the trade. Oh this is a lovely scene isn't it, all very peaceful, so beautiful, it really is.

1 *The Twisting Lane* (1969) London: Hutchinson, pp. 36–68.

Do you believe in God? No? I do. I'm sure there must be a god somewhere, you know. I don't see how else you can explain it otherwise – that you should say a prayer and then that it should come exactly true. I did, yes, I prayed last night before I went to sleep: that today would be nice and sunny, that it'd be a happy day and we'd get on well together, and we could be somewhere quiet and peaceful where we could have a good long talk. I never expected the seaside though you know, somehow I hadn't thought of that, that's made it even better still. So it's all turned out like I hoped, just like I prayed it would; absolutely perfect in every way. He answered my prayer, I'm quite convinced of that.

It was good of them to let me come out with you wasn't it? I've never heard of that being done before, somehow in prison you never expect they might let you out for a day. Three years is a long time to spend locked up in a place; and you completely forget what it's going to be like outside, you've put all thoughts of it out of your mind. I was a bit frightened at the idea, yes, I thought it'd be too over-whelming for me somehow, with all the bustle and the people and the noise. That was why it was such a good idea to come here. Look – not a solitary soul in sight is there, anywhere? We might almost be the only people left in the world, mightn't we, it'd be funny that, wouldn't it, if we were? When we went back into the town we found everyone had vanished and there was no one left but us. What should we do then? Sometimes the mind runs on like that, doesn't it? Mine does, does yours? I often think it's going to happen you know, everyone wiped out in a war perhaps, and I'd be the only one left alive.

It wouldn't be too difficult for me, having no one to talk to; I wouldn't miss other people, I don't think, very much. There's often no one at all that I talk to anyway. You can't, you see, in prison: it's not possible, it's too much of a risk. All the other prisoners talk: they boast, even, a lot of them. Because to their way of thinking they've got something to boast about I suppose; big robberies they've done, safe-breaking, smash-and-grab, wages-snatches, cleverly worked-out frauds. They can't be all that clever though can they, otherwise they wouldn't be in prison for it? But it's funny, that aspect of it never seems to cross their minds. They concentrate on the jobs they did without being caught for, or the big ones they're going to do when they eventually get out. 'Next time it'll be different, I'll be more careful, I definitely won't get caught again' – that's what they all say.

There's a man like that I walk round with on exercise; he's in for what they call 'kites', dud cheques you know, that sort of thing. Always describing the details of it, how he does it, the ones no one's ever found out about, the marvellous living he was making at it before a little bit of bad luck brought it to an end. 'And in the future I'll never be any different', he says, 'only much shrewder, they won't get a chance to catch up with me next time.' A nicely spoken man he is too you know; well I suppose you've got to be, haven't you, for that sort of thing? I quite like him, he's honest according to his own lights anyway about himself and what he is, he never pretends.

But the thing I like most about him is that he doesn't ask me any questions about myself. He never has done, not once in three years. Perhaps he's not interested, perhaps he doesn't care. Now and again though I suddenly get the feeling he's going to: I'll be lying in bed one night and it comes over me like that, out of nowhere, and I start thinking he's going to ask me about it the next day. I'm sure he is, I'm convinced of it. He's going to turn round to me and say 'Oh by the way' – that's how he'll put it – 'oh by the way, you've never told me before, but just exactly what are the details of your own particular case?'

I get so frightened you know, really terrified. I convince myself that he'll say it, that he's going to come out with it; I'm certain he is, and I feel myself starting to sweat all over. Then for the next few days, perhaps for a week even, I won't walk round with him, I make some excuse like I'm not feeling very well, I'm not up to walking round with him on exercise. I go off out of sight somewhere on my own then where he can't see me, keep right out of his way until the feeling's worn off again.

You just can't risk it you see, you never can. All your time in prison you're scared to death that someone's going to find out. You know from how you hear them talk when there's some sort of similar case reported in the papers, and they all start discussing it among themselves. 'Make a note of his name', they say, 'so that if he ever turns up in here we'll know who he is, we'll see he gets what he deserves.' The way they talk, the way they look; they mean it all right. In fact there's instances I've heard of where it's actually happened, someone like that's been set on by the others; and the screws won't lift a finger to help them either you know, they feel the same way about it themselves. As soon as something starts they don't interfere to try and break it up or go to the man's assistance, they just turn their backs and walk away.

You wouldn't get a chance to explain it to anyone, you couldn't tell them anyway how it was because they wouldn't listen, and even if they did it'd make no difference. In their eyes it's absolutely contemptible. And they're right you know. It is: it is contemptible, there's no other word you can use for it, really there isn't, not when you come to think about it.

*

Wilfred Johnson
Date of birth: 19 April 1908.
Address: 'Rosecot', Field Bank, Walthorpe, Sussex.

16 June 1945	Kent Magistrates' Court. 6 months' imprisonment. Indecent assault on boy aged 10.
29 August 1951	Sussex Quarter Sessions. 2 years' imprisonment. Indecent assault on boy aged 8. Two other charges concerning boy aged 9 and boy aged 11 taken into consideration.
22 July 1953	Sussex Quarter Sessions. 21 months' imprisonment. Indecent assault on boy aged 11 and boy aged 10.
11 March 1957	Sussex Quarter Sessions. 8 years' preventive detention. Indecent assault on boy aged 10, boy aged 8, two boys aged 9, one boy aged 11.
18 August 1965	Sussex Quarter Sessions. 5 years' imprisonment. Indecent behaviour with boy aged 12, boy aged 11, boy aged 9.

—The first thing I remember must have been in the war, I think, the Great War, when I was about seven I suppose, and there'd been a house bombed in Golders Green. At least I think it'd been bombed but I couldn't be sure; my sister who was two or three years older than me, she was always a great one for a lark and a joke you know, she might have been pulling my leg. It was a rare event of course in those days, a house being bombed, not like the Second War. 'Come on, Wilf!' she said, 'we'll go and see if we can find it', and the two of us went off, it was miles and miles from where we lived. There wasn't all that much to see now I think about it when we got there. I know it was very late when we got back, our mum didn't know where we'd been and she was getting really worried about it. But Sally she couldn't have cared less, anything with a bit of excitement or fun in it always appealed to her.

My father was often away at sea during the Great War so my mother was having a hard time of it nearly always. No, he wasn't a sailor, he was a kind of a clerk on board ship, looked after the book-keeping and stores and that sort of thing. I believe he was called a 'ship's writer', something like that. Of course at school with the other kids, I always told them my dad was a sailor. I remember I was very disappointed when he came home on leave and he didn't have the outfit, bell-bottomed trousers and all the rest of it that I thought a proper sailor should have.

There were three children actually all together; as well as my sister I had an older brother, his name was Harold. He was my father's favourite, my brother was. They used to spend a lot of time together when he was at home going out a lot and that sort of thing. There was something about Harold, I don't know what it was: he was quite studious I think, and my father was always saying he'd go a long way in life.

I remember the shortages too in the war, how our mum sent Sally and me out once round the shops to see if we could find a pound of sugar anywhere, I think it was threepence she gave us for it. She was really delighted when we found a shop that had some and brought it back. I was fairly clever at school, I know I got some sort of a scholarship when I was ten or eleven, to go to what would be the equivalent of a grammar school up in Edmonton somewhere. But I never stopped at one school long, we were always moving about; my mother was a very restless sort of a person, adventurous you might have called her almost. She'd say, 'Oh I'm fed up of living in this place, let's move somewhere else', and the next week we'd be gone. Flats, parts of other people's houses, a little detached house of our own I remember once: south London, north London, we must have had a dozen different addresses at some time or another. But she always seemed to make friends wherever she went, she was never short of company: of course she was a very gay and lively woman in those days, and very good looking. She had beautiful long brown hair which she wore sometimes up and sometimes down to her waist, whatever the fashion decreed at the time. Lovely grey eyes, a nice wide mouth, a slender figure, only about five foot two she was; what you'd call 'petite', that'd be the word. And she played the piano a lot, and had a nice singing voice, and a very good dancer too, very light on her feet. It wasn't surprising everyone liked her. Originally she was of Austrian descent, her great-grandfather on her mother's side, something like that. She came from a very well-educated family, sensitive well-bred sort of people they were with good educations, and talented at music and things like that. When she was younger I can remember she used to give what they called 'musical evenings' – a few friends in, and she'd play the piano and sing for them. Not jazz, you know, but good stuff, classical music. It was from her I got my own love of it. I can't stand this present-day 'pop' stuff, but really decent music – Ivor Novello, Irving Berlin – I'm very fond of all that.

We hadn't a lot of money ever and I've known her cut up one of her own skirts to make a little pair of trousers for me when things were hard. 'I don't need this old thing', she'd say, 'I can find a much better use for it for something for you.' And perhaps it'd been only the week before, you know, that she'd got it for herself. But she never complained, she always did it with a laugh and made light of it. A really lovely person in every way, the best sort of mother anyone could ever wish for, she was.

She wasn't happy though; she can't have been with my father, not for years. When he was home there was always terrible rows. My brother would come running into the room. 'A-B-U', he'd say, 'A-B-U!', and then he'd run out again. 'Another Bust Up', that was what it meant. And I'd go down to wherever they were – and if I saw my mother crying I wouldn't hesitate for one moment, I'd set on my father and pummel him like that with my fists; only eight or nine years old I'd be but I'd really go for him, I would. I could never bear to see her cry. Sometimes I think I could have killed him, I honestly would have tried to kill him you know, I was so wild about it. I hate people rowing: I did then, and I always have done, right through the rest of my life, it upsets me terribly.

Of course looking back on it now later in life, I can see he wasn't really all that bad a person as I used to think he was when I was a child. It was something in him, just an unfortunate habit he'd got that he couldn't keep his eye off the ladies. My mother used to get so jealous always, I think she used to be quite unreasonable about it sometimes. We'd all go out for a walk, or shopping or something like that, and when we got back she'd burst into tears and say she didn't like the way he'd been looking at one of the girl shop assistants perhaps; his eyes all over her she'd say, and asking us to back her up and say that we'd noticed it too.

With him being away a lot I suppose he might have got the taste for it when he was in the different ports and places. Other women, that's what started it all. When he came home he was always pacing up and down, he couldn't hardly bear to be in the house sometimes, he was so bad-tempered. Till eventually mother would say to him, 'Oh go down to the docks', she'd say, 'see if you can't find yourself another ship, I know you don't want to be here with us.' He always wanted to return to the water, so off he'd go: we wouldn't see him again for months and months until he came back then from his trip.

While the war was on I think, sometimes he was away for perhaps as much as a year at a time. I was never sorry really myself to see him go. He was a bit too heavy-handed for my liking, he'd hit you first and ask questions afterwards, you know how I mean? I got quite a few tannings from him, usually for very trivial things.

I know at the finish it got just too much for both mother and father, they couldn't get on at all together, and they had a legal separation. That was not long after the war was over, about 1921 perhaps or 1922, when I'd be about fourteen. In fact that's right, it was just when I was fourteen, because I know I had to leave school then and get a job to help out with the money. My brother he'd gone off somewhere working, I think it was up to Birmingham or some place like that, and we didn't see him any more. He got married and settled down and had a family of his own. He's done very well for himself ever since; at least he seems to have done, whenever I've seen him, which hasn't been a lot of course in the last twenty or thirty years. But I don't think my mother minded all that much as long as she'd got me. I was always her favourite, I know that. You can tell it from the way a person looks at you, I think, can't you? A child's always very sensitive to things like that.

And myself, I was glad to leave school, I preferred being at home. I had a terrible squint, all the other kids used to call me 'Boss-eye' and things of that sort, they can be very cruel, children, can't they sometimes? My mother was very good about it, she used to comfort me – and at the same time she never tried to make me go to hospital and have something done about it, which I was terrified of. She'd say, 'It's all right, Wilfred, you don't need to, it makes no difference to me.' In fact I was over thirty before I summoned up the courage to have it done, and in all that time she never tried to push me into it, not once she didn't.

The first job I had was in a grocer's shop, a kind of general assistant and delivery boy. Fifteen shillings a week I was earning, my mother was very glad of it. She got some kind of an allowance for me and my sister from my father, he always paid that regular, but even so there wasn't a lot to go round. But things were a lot better and more settled then, my mother certainly seemed to be happier and not so restless. We lived in one place for a long time then, a little house we had in Lewisham just big enough for the three of us and she made it into a very nice home. We were used to dad being away anyway, so we didn't mind much that he wasn't there – and he still used to come and see us, you know, from time to time. In fact him and mother got on much better after they were separated, they remained quite friendly really all the time right up to when he died, not long before the Second War.

I liked the grocer's, I've always thought that was an interesting sort of trade. Nice clean work, isn't it, with foodstuffs and packages and things? I've often wished since I'd stayed there. You never know, things might have turned out that little bit different for me if I had. They were good people to work for too. I had a bit of an accident while I was there, hurt my foot when I was knocked down by a bus. I was off for three months with it, and eventually I got compensation, from the insurance you know. I believe it was a hundred pounds – a huge sum in those days. And this firm kept my job open for me until I got back. I was with them quite a long time, seven or eight years. Then my sister got married and went away too, so that only left me and my mother, and I wanted to get a better job because she was ill; more or less a permanent invalid from then on she was. I always wanted to try and do the best I could for her and have her looked after properly. She was treated for years and years for pernicious anaemia, that's what they thought it was – and it was only right at the end they discovered it wasn't that at all, it was a cancer, and a very bad one; and of course it was too late to do anything about it by that time. But she was a brave woman, she never made a fuss of herself, she used to spend all her time taking care of me.

She never remarried, she never wanted to, she didn't believe in that sort of thing. She was like a wife to me really. In fact better than a wife because I'd known her all my life you see, and you can't get any closer can you to anyone than that? You're longer with your mother than anyone, aren't you, even your wife? Oh a lovely relationship we had together all those years, never a cross word between us, nothing; it was just perfect. Real pals we were, we neither of us wanted anyone else, you know, at all. I was a great home-bird myself, I didn't really have any other friends except her. She was my best friend and I was perfectly happy like that – great friends we were, real chums. She understood me and I understood her, our minds always seemed to be in keeping with each other. We could sit for hours in the evening, you know, in the same room, never talking: we never needed to talk about things, each one knew at once what the other was thinking; and that's a wonderful thing when it's like that.

I had a little Austin Seven in those days, we used to go out for a run every single week-end without fail – Brighton, Margate, Hastings, all sorts of places – once we even went as far as Portsmouth we did, and then the car broke down on the way back and we had to spend the night pulled up at the side of the road! She had a canary in a cage she was very fond of, she'd never be parted from it, so that had to come everywhere with us on the trips too. And still the same sort of venturesome person she was, always. 'Where should we go today, Wilfred?' she'd ask me, and I'd say, 'Well how about Birchington, do you think the car'll make it as far as that?' and she'd say, 'Well come on, let's give it a try shall we, eh?' So we did. A really great sport she was, ready for anything. She'd make up sandwiches for the day for us, we'd pack all our things in, the canary as well, and away we'd go. Oh some very happy times we had, really happy times.

I'm only sorry you can't meet her, you'd have loved her, really you would. Well there it is, she's gone now, and that's the way it is, isn't it? But you can imagine, I expect, being a married man yourself: what it would be like after years and years of happy marriage if your wife was to die. It's like the end of your own life somehow, a light going out, you can't ever really grasp it, what it means that a person's gone for good; not when you've been like we were you can't. Everything to each other, everything. Very wonderful it is, of course, too, when you look back on it, lots and lots of happy memories, places you've been together, things that you've seen. A dear soul she was in every possible way. An angel, in fact, that's what I think, that's the word I'd use for her, it's the only word there is. Life with her was marvellous, it really was, and I look back on it as something very beautiful. There's a lot of people would think there was something strange about a man feeling like that about his mother. But that's because they've never experienced anything like it themselves.

Perhaps you think me foolish, soft like, to go on like this about her. But I want you to know me as I am, you see, there's nothing I want to hide from you, nothing I wouldn't say. And it is true that my life virtually ended for me when she went; it left a great sort of gap in the world for me that could never be filled. My sister's said to me that I've got to get over it; but it's easier for her I suppose isn't it, with a husband and family of her own? And she never saw her like I did you know, she wasn't there herself at the end. But I was; I was with her when she died, I saw her in such pain she was trying to get out at the bottom of the bed, and I had to lift her up and put her back on her pillows again. And then soon after, she just put her hand gently over mine and gave a big like a sigh it was, and then she died. Silly, isn't it, a grown man in tears, I do beg your pardon, I'll just blow my nose. But it's nice to talk to someone about her, after all this time. It still feels almost like last week you know, just as recent as that. I can hardly believe it myself that so much time has gone past since she went: it's quite a long time now, nearly twelve years.

★

From far along the promenade the faint yelping of an approaching dog; louder and nearer, and then still yapping unceasingly as it came by with its head down and went on towards some vague aim a long way ahead, a portly cairn terrier scampered past and disappeared into the distance.

–Poor old chap, I wonder where he lives, he looks a long way from home doesn't he? Well I know where I live; and I suppose now you ought to be taking me back, shouldn't you? Not a minute later than five o'clock I had to be in, they said. Will you come again? Oh good, yes I'd like that very much. Perhaps next time we ought to get down to facts hadn't we, really try and talk about my cases and things of that sort? Yes, I think I'd like to try, I really would, yes.

★

—I remember every single little detail of that day we had together last month, you know – the sunshine, the sea, that lovely old church we stopped to have a look at on the way back. It was just the sort of day my mother would have liked if she'd been alive. Afterwards when I was in my cell thinking about it, it reminded me of her favourite piece of music, the one she used to like to play on the piano. It was called 'A Perfect Day'. I can see it clearly in my mind's eye now, an old-fashioned cover it had, a drawing of a country scene. She used to prop it up in front of her while she played, though I'm sure she didn't need it you know, she must have known every note of it off by heart.

Today's not so nice though is it, all this rain; I think the winter's here all right now, don't you? We were very lucky with that other day weren't we? An Indian summer wasn't it, that's what they call it, yes. Well never mind, it's nice in your car, we're all right up here on the cliffs, warm and dry and no one to disturb us. It was jolly cold though, down there on the shore, wasn't it? I couldn't have stood longer than ten minutes of that, could you. No. It's good of them at the prison to let me out a few times with you, they're not all bad people in those places. That assistant governor, Mr. Whitaker, he's a nice man, the sort of person you could talk to if you got the chance. But there's so many isn't there, so many prisoners I mean? It's all the staff can do most of the time just to remember people's names. He did talk to me once a year or so ago, Mr. Whitaker; and what he said to me was true all right. 'You know, Johnson', he said, 'the other side of that wall at the bottom of the yard there, there's rows of little wooden crosses in the ground, just with names on them that's all – and one of them one day's going to have your name on it, if you don't try and do something about yourself.' He meant well by it, he said it kindly; it wasn't his fault what happened after that.

I put my name down for the doctor from the Home Office and when he came I was called up to see him. You wonder where they get some of them from, don't you? To my mind he wasn't like a doctor at all. It was a hot day but somehow you don't expect a medical man to be sitting in his shirt-sleeves and braces do you, chain-smoking all the time? Even though it's only prison, that sort of thing doesn't seem the right kind of behaviour for a doctor. A great big man he was, more like a publican than anything else, very loud-voiced and rude. 'Well come on, what do you want?' he said. When I told him I wanted to try and have something done about my trouble, he looked at my record he'd got in front of him and he said, 'Oh yes', he said. 'Well, it's taken you long enough to come round to it, hasn't it? Twenty years or more, and then you suddenly turn up today and say you want to try and do something about it. Why haven't you thought about this before? Why haven't you tried to get treatment for yourself while you were out, instead of waiting till now? Anyhow,' he said, 'there's no treatment we can give you, so you're wasting my time.'

Even if it's true, I think he could have put it over in a different way. I don't think it's much help to someone, that sort of attitude, is it? In a sense he's right I suppose; I mean it is up to me really when I'm out, you can't argue with that. There's been times when I thought I would, I'd put my mind to it when I was released and see if there was anything could be done. But when you get out your mind doesn't work like that. First of all you're glad to be free and all you want is a few days to settle down, get back into the swing of things. It does take time to get accustomed to it. When I came out from my PD for instance, all the telephone boxes had been altered, you needed completely different coins for them. Trivialities of that sort, it's very unsettling until you get used to it. You're all the time wondering what the next surprise is going to be, how you're going to explain it to people when they give you a funny look because you don't know.

And there's so many things to get on with; you've got to fix up for milk to be delivered, get your clothes in order, have your shoes mended, think about finding a job – dozens of things to occupy you.

So you push everything else to the back of your mind. You think, 'Well, I'll just get myself organised, start earning some money again, that's the first thing.' And the weeks pass, time goes on, you still haven't got round to it, to thinking about yourself. In fact you don't even really want to think about it; you can't face going along to your doctor and telling him what it is or anything of that kind. Then you start a job and you think, 'Well, I'll be all right now I'm working.' That's how it goes on; six months'll pass, a year, sometimes even two years before you begin getting yourself into trouble again. And there you are, it's happened, and it's too late.

—Last time I think we were mainly on my childhood days, weren't we? I'd been telling you about my father leaving home, my brother and sister getting married and so on, yes. I'd be in my early twenties then. In every way just an ordinary sort of young man, except I wasn't much for the social life or other people, I'd sooner go about with my mother like I told you. There was nothing of importance in those days of my life at all. Just long happy years, me and my mother together on our own. The car I told you about didn't I, the little Austin Seven we had? Yes. I know what it was, the new job that I took – that was it wasn't it, where we left off?

Well I got the job like I told you, because there was more money in it than the grocery trade. It was with a retail wine merchants, they had a big chain of places all round south London. Selling in a shop, delivering orders in the van, that sort of thing mostly. Altogether I must have been with them eleven or twelve years. I think it was while I was there I first developed my taste for drink. Not a lot, I wasn't a heavy drinker or an alcoholic, nothing like that – but just at weekends I'd take home a bottle of wine or a half-bottle of whiskey at trade price. I was never one for going in pubs; instead my mother would cook a nice meal and we'd have a drink with it. She never touched it herself. I used to enjoy it but it wasn't a problem, though; I don't want to give you that impression. In the week when I was working I never drank at all, and as I say at weekends it was not a large quantity. I wouldn't be incapable, nothing of that sort. But I got used to it, that was the point; and later on in life that turned out to be not a very good thing.

I wish I could remember some occasion or incident from those times that was particularly memorable that I could tell you about; but I can't. An even, regular sort of life, a steady job, no excitements or troubles. Looking back on it I'd say it was perfect contentment; both of us happy, devoted to each other. I used to think it would go on for ever just like it was. The only thing that worried me was my mother's health; it was never good, often she'd have to stay in bed for days at a time and I'd have to look after her, do all the housework and shopping after work and so on. But I never minded; after all when she was well she gave up all her time to looking after me, didn't she?

When the 1939 war came I got a low medical grading because of the injury to my foot. We were both glad of that because it meant I wouldn't have to go away in the Army or anything. But then when they brought in the direction of labour later in the war I had to change my job and go and work for a ship-building firm, marine engineers they were, down in Sheerness. It was just about possible from where we lived in London for me to travel up and down each day. It meant a long journey, but it was better than having to leave home. I was very worried about mother in the bombing, but she bore up bravely you know, she was wonderful. Sometimes I'd say I wanted to get her away, out into the country somewhere, where I'd know she'd be safe. But she wouldn't hear of it. 'This is our home,' she'd say, 'and this is where I'm going to stay.' It was on the outskirts of south London so it was never too bad.

Round Sheerness was very nice in the summer, and I began to take an interest in all the little boats that there were lying about. Some of them were going very cheap indeed: towards the end of the war there was hardly any private sailing, people weren't so much interested in it as they are these days. I bought myself one of those very small sort of cabin boats, just about big enough for two people, and I spent most of my spare time on the engine getting it back into running order. I never went far out to sea in it, only round the coast or up some of the little inlets and creeks and places of that sort. It was a hobby for me at week-ends. I often used to try and persuade my mother to come down there with me for a bit of a sail, but she never would, she didn't fancy the idea.

And that was when my first trouble came on. There were always lots of kids about in the boat-yards, asking could they help you, would you take them out in your boat for a ride. One Saturday afternoon there was two of them, two little boys, I said all right they could come out with me because they'd helped me push my boat down into the water from the shed. A very hot day it was. They went over the side for a swim. They'd no costumes on. When they got back in the boat they were running about skylarking and laughing. And I did you know, I must admit I did go so far as to forget myself, I laid hands on them. Nothing serious, please don't think that, I didn't attack them or anything of that kind. Only playing about, touching them, that was as far as it went. They didn't object, they didn't complain, it was a harmless bit of fun you might say. It never crossed my mind they hadn't liked it, they seemed willing enough.

That was why it was such a surprise to me the next weekend. I was down there again tuning up the old engine, and these two plain-clothes policemen came into the shed. They asked me exactly what it was had happened the Saturday before, and I told them. I didn't hide anything, I told them just how it was; no more and no less. They weren't even boys that I knew, I hadn't made arrangements to see them again, nothing of that sort. But they'd told their parents I suppose about it. Anyway there it was, that was it. The police took me to court straight away for it, and I was given six months.

I couldn't believe it at first, I really couldn't. Six months, just like that; no other enquiries, nothing. The magistrate said, 'There's too much of this sort of thing going on, I'm going to put a stop to it.' Being near the end of the war as it was, I suppose they were short-handed, they wouldn't have time for probation reports and so on: in fact they didn't seem to be even thinking of probation at all for my sort of case.

Before I knew where I was I found myself in Canterbury prison, sewing mail-bags. Thirty-seven I think I was then, or thirty-eight. To end up suddenly one day like that in prison, you don't believe it could happen to you, especially when you've lived all your life in an ordinary respectable manner. There wasn't one person I knew or had ever heard of who'd been convicted before.

As for my mother, well, she simply couldn't grasp it at all. She came to see me when I was due for a visit, even though she was very ill – she'd gone to live at my sister's, they brought her and took her back all the way in the car. She cried, she looked terrible, she did. 'What is it, Wilfred?' she kept asking me. 'What's it all about, what's happened?' What could I say to her? As soon as I started trying to explain she said, 'I don't believe it.' She wouldn't listen, she just couldn't believe it at all. She wrote me some lovely letters you know, while I was inside, never blaming me or anything; just saying I must look after myself and not to worry about her, and when it was over we'd forget it for ever.

I looked at it the same way too – it was just something that had happened that there was no accounting for. I'd done wrong, it was no use pretending about that: but I was being punished for it, and it was up to me afterwards to see it didn't happen again. I think one of the things was that it had never occurred before, you know: it'd come on me suddenly, without any warning at all. A hot day, two little boys on the boat without any clothes on: I couldn't think what had possessed me.

When I came out there was no question of me going back to the same job, the people at work would know all about it, it would be too embarrassing, I couldn't face that. We didn't know what we should do really. Then one day my mother said she thought the best thing would be if I was to get away, make a completely fresh start, widen my horizons and that sort of thing, make a new life for myself altogether. My brother-in-law had a bit of influence with one of the shipping lines, so he put in a word for me and got me a job as a steward on a cargo vessel. It had a few passenger cabins, but chiefly it took engines and machine tools to different places round the Mediterranean, and then loaded up with fruit, oranges and lemons, for the journey back.

When I got used to it I quite liked the seafaring life. I think I probably took to it because it'd been in the family, hadn't it, with my father? We went to some nice places, Gibraltar, Valencia, Barcelona, Majorca, Malta, and on all round the Greek islands; some lovely places there are round there, you know. Each trip would take almost a month to the day, then I'd be home for a few days, and then off again once more. It was ideal for me really, took me right out of myself; there was no trouble of any kind. I could look back on the incident I'd been to prison for as something completely in the past. Once in Barcelona I met a girl, Spanish she was, very bright and jolly, working as a waitress in a cafe. I even thought sometimes if I got to know her better I might bring her back to England with me and marry her; we struck up quite a correspondence between us for a few months. But I was never on a ship that did that particular run again, so I didn't get the opportunity to see her any more, and it just fizzled out. A pity that was, I think, looking back on it; a nice woman of that kind might have made all the difference to me, you know.

Altogether I was at sea for just about two years, ending up with a very long trip over to Singapore and Hong Kong. That meant I was away for four months or more, it was a long time, my mother wasn't very keen on it at all, she missed me terribly. I missed her too, and after another long trip like that I decided to give up the life then, and come back. We bought a house, a cottage it was – well, more of a what you might call a prefabricated bungalow really; one of those summer-places, you know what I mean, two rooms, made of corrugated iron and asbestos mostly, a wooden roof and an Elsan out at the back, and a stand-pipe for water just over the road. It wasn't meant for living in all the year round. One of my uncles had it originally, and he sold it cheap to us for somewhere to live. 'Rosecot' it was called – it's a terrible name isn't it? I can't think why we've never changed it, we often used to have a laugh about it and say anyone would think that it must be very picturesque with a name like that. Actually it's in a field at the end of a road all on its own, near a little village on the coast. Not a proper holiday place, more like somewhere people go to out of London at weekends to be on their own. It has electric light, we had that put in; and over the years from time to time I've cleared a bit of ground round it and laid out a sort of garden.

Yes, it's still there, I've still got it. Really ramshackle it must be now, I don't like to think of it. When I went back after my PD there was great holes in the roof, all the fencing down, everywhere overgrown with grass and weeds; it was in a shocking state, it broke my heart to see it, it did. But in those days I'm telling you about now, when my mother and I first took it over, we got it really nice; painted it up, put up an archway of roses round the door to fit the frame – it was a real home it was, and we had many happy years there. It could be a bit bleak in the winter, but in the summer it was very nice, really lovely.

When I saw it that first time it made up my mind: I didn't want to go to sea any more, I wanted to stop there with her. But we hadn't been in it very long before she took very ill; I couldn't look after her and do a job as well, so she had to go back and stop with my sister again for a while. I'd got a fairly decent job as a site clerk with a small firm of builders in the locality; I used to go up to London to see her every week on the Saturday. But the rest of the week was awful, down there in that place on my own without her, I never knew what to do. And I did the very thing that was worst for me: I started to drink.

I used to spend all the Sundays drinking, not eating, not caring about anything at all except trying to forget how lonely I was. Not in pubs mind you, I was never one for that. Instead I used to buy one or sometimes two bottles of the very cheapest wine there was, British stuff which was made out of I don't know what, rough and raw tasting, but it had a terrific kick with it, you could get yourself almost unconscious on a couple of bottles of that.

There were several boys from round the district, you know, from the village and other houses scattered about, and they took to coming along on Sunday afternoon, giving me a hand with the garden, doing odd jobs for me for a few coppers or a drink of lemonade, something like that. I knew it was wrong of me to encourage them to come there, they were upsetting me, I could feel it: but that only made me drink the more, to try and suppress these feelings that I had.

But it was no use, it didn't make me feel better, it made things worse; in fact it got to the stage I was doing things I'd never have dreamt of if I'd been sober. I suppose you could say it was weakness on my part; well it was, I should have had more sense, more will-power, shouldn't I, told them to clear off and go right away. But I didn't. There was things went on, childish things, really stupid, no way for a grown man to behave at all. I don't know what it was, why I should want to carry on with them as I did. Sitting them on my knee, playing silly games with them, you wouldn't believe anyone could be so stupid as to do it. On and on, these boys coming, bringing their friends with them; they talked about it among themselves I suppose, they knew where they could go and get a sixpence anytime if they wanted one.

So that was it again, exactly the same thing; one of them must have told his parents about it eventually and they brought in the police. I was really for it that time, a second conviction; and up at the Assizes too, in front of a judge. He didn't say much, there wouldn't be much he could say, would there? Two years, I think that was all he said when he'd heard the evidence, just 'Two years' like that.

I felt dreadful about it. All that time, you know, that I'd gone away to sea to get away from it; the new home we'd made, a job I'd not long started with the building people. My mother, she was too ill to be told about it for quite a long while, my sister and her husband had to break it to her. Though once again, you know, she was marvellous; wrote to me regularly, said it would be all right again when we got back together in our own little house. I don't know how she stuck it, I honestly don't, it just shows you what kind of a mother she must have been, docsn't it?

Two years in Pentonville that time, a dreadful place; the only thing that kept me going was I'd made up my mind it was the very last time ever. I was forty-five, by the time you've got to that age you're no longer a young man. You know it's going to be the turning point, it must be. I put it all down myself to the drink. And while I was in prison I wasn't drinking of course, so I knew I could do without it if I really put my mind to it.

When I came out in 1952 I really thought things were going to be different. I got my mother back in the little house, for a short while I thought it was going to be all right, I'd turned the corner. Well, I have to admit it to you – I wasn't better, in fact I was worse. That same year when the autumn came on and mother was still ill, I took her back to my sister's again – and then I was back straight away in the same thing, down at the bungalow, drinking and having boys in at the weekends.

I don't think I was out a year that time before I was caught. I thought it was going to be a really long sentence then, at least double what I'd had before. But the police were quite decent, they put in a word for me that time, said the boys had made things difficult for me – which they had. Hardly left me in peace at all they didn't, Sunday after Sunday they'd be round. Well to cut a long story short I was back inside again, as I say, but this time for twenty-one months in Wandsworth. And I knew things were looking really black for me then all right, I didn't know what the future could possibly hold.

I came out about the end of 1954. My mother seemed much better then, in her health I mean, so we could start off living together again in our own little place. When she was there it made all the difference, naturally: there was boys coming round still, but I kept them out in the garden helping me, and I hardly touched a drink for months on end. But it wasn't all that long before mother started going downhill again, and eventually they took her into hospital. It was then they told me what was wrong with her, and I must prepare myself for her not having long to live. They let her come back: she wanted to come home, you know, I think she must have known she was dying. They often do, don't they, when it gets to that stage? Of course I was glad to have her, I'd have done anything, cut off all my arms and legs, anything at all to save her. But it wasn't to be.

I'd got myself a bit of a job, part-time at one of the local garages, so as to be able to spend as much time with her as I could. For a while she seemed to rally, I even began to feel there might be some hope. But soon the pills and things they'd given her to stop the pain, she'd had so many the effect of them wore off, they lost their strength. In the end, for the last few weeks she was in agony, it was pitiful to see. I told you about it, didn't I – how she used to be crawling about in the bed trying to get out; she'd no idea what she was doing at all. I stopped off work all together then, just so I could be with her whenever I might be wanted; I was scared even to go down to the shop for a packet of cigarettes even, in case she'd be calling for me while I was away.

It was no use and in the end she died. I suppose it was a blessed relief, really. But for days I just couldn't grasp it, you know; it didn't sink in what it meant, I kept thinking she'd be coming back somehow, she was only away at my sister's for a visit and any minute she'd walk in. Unbelievable to me, that's what it was – and when I finally did realise it, I didn't want to go on living myself at all. I kept everything in the house exactly as she'd left it, her slippers by the door in their usual place, all her clothes still in the wardrobe for her, the little ornaments she'd arranged exactly where she'd left them. Weeks it went on, months, and I was completely in a daze.

I tried a job or two, but they didn't last, there seemed no point in them, what was I working for? I'd get the idea of going out for a ride sometimes in the old Ford I had, on a day when the sun was shining. Then I'd say to myself, 'No, I couldn't bear it, I should be all the time wanting to talk to her as though she was sitting next to me.' And in the house I still did, I talked to her exactly as though she was there.

Then I really started drinking; I'd let days go by at a time without knowing where I was, what time it was, anything. And when I was drinking of course my mind started to turn again to this other thing. I knew it would, but I'd lost all wish even to try and fight it then. My own idea was to go down to the shop and buy two or three bottles of that cheap wine I told you about, and then sit in a chair and drink until they were gone. I used to see them on the sideboard, it felt like they were looking at me, beckoning me on. I had an idea I might even try and write a story about it once; I was going to call it 'The Blond Monkey'. That was what it was like; cheap white wine, well more a pale yellow colour really, and I'd be sitting there and watching it, and I'd know perfectly well what it was going to do to me, it was like an evil thing staring back at me. It was a monkey all right, a wicked one, very wicked: once it got inside you you were done for. If the shop was closed any time, I'd be washing the bottles out under the tap, can you believe it, trying to get out the last few drops? It was as bad as that.

I was notorious in the district by then; all the kids knew me, knew what they could get if they came. They'd be pushing notes under the door they would, if I was out. 'I'll be coming round to see you Sunday with my friend, will you take us to Brighton in your car?' All things like that, little devils they were; in fact they used to think I was funny, it made them laugh to see me carrying on. Some of them, even though they were so young, they knew all sorts of things, you know; used to recite dirty limericks they'd picked up at school, or tell jokes – stupid silly jokes with rude words. I'd get really annoyed with them I would. I'd say, 'You mustn't use words like that, it's not nice. Now don't you ever let me hear you using words like that again!' I've never liked that sort of thing, particularly in children, I always wanted them to be proper, not loose with their tongues; I don't approve of it at all, I never have done.

That's how it was then: drinking, not working, staying in the house on my own, and waiting for the boys to come round. Finding the notes pushed under my door, there's no getting away from it, as soon as I saw one I got a kind of a thrill because I knew it wouldn't be long before they were there. And that occasion, being perpetually drunk as I was, the police came in and actually found it going on, these boys running about half-dressed, and me sitting in the middle of it all in my chair. I can remember looking up and seeing the blue uniform and the brass buttons right there in front of my nose.

Well, it was impossible, wasn't it, it couldn't be allowed to pass any more? The judge was the same one I'd had in the previous case; he remembered me all right. He said, 'You're a menace, you are, I'm going to put a stop to your activities once and for all.' So he gave me seven years' preventive detention.

Seven years…I really did, I thought I might as well be dead, I couldn't imagine ever coming out again. I used to sit in my cell and think, 'What's the use? This is the finish, this is the only place for me now, it's all over.' Knowing my mother had gone for good this time, and all I could do was be thankful she hadn't lived to see where I'd ended up, because that would have killed her if nothing else did. But after a while, you can't help it, I suppose, you start thinking and feeling again. You say, 'Well, time's getting on, it is passing, perhaps somehow it won't be too bad, there'll be an end to it one day. I'm over the worst now, I must have done a good time of it by now, mustn't I?' So you go and look at the calendar to see how much you've got left – and you see that all you've done so far in fact is perhaps three months.

I think what saved me was I got sent to Nottingham prison. I hadn't been there long before they gave me a job in the book-bindery. The man in charge, what they call the foreman instructor, he was a really good chap. He gave me a proper training in it, taught me how to do binding, sewing, guillotining, hand-stitching, glueing, collating, trimming – every single aspect of it that there was. It gave me a whole new interest; I think I was a good learner, and after a while I really started to enjoy myself and feel it was worthwhile. I've always liked working with my hands, especially something you can take your time over until you've got it right. Tooling, blocking, lettering for the spines, it was all very nice. The years went by, I won't say without me noticing them, but at least with something for me to occupy myself with; and when it came to the end of my sentence the instructor said I was good enough to work at it outside, so why didn't I write to one of the big printing firms and ask them if there was any chance of a job. 'Go on,' he said, 'you compose the letter and I'll help you with it.' I wondered what they'd think, getting a letter like that from someone on prison notepaper. But do you know, they wrote straight away and said they'd take me on as soon as I came out. It was marvellous of them, wasn't it? I'd got a skill at last, hadn't I, something that would last me all my life; even though I was over fifty then, this firm said it didn't matter, they were still willing to give me a try even though I'd had a big sentence like eight years.

I beg your pardon? Oh did I, I'm sorry, I made a mistake then if I said seven; actually it was eight. It's like I was saying a few minutes ago, it's such a long time that you can't always think of it exactly, a year more or less makes no difference, you see.

After a long time in prison you forget other things too, you know, about how you came to be there and so on. Drinking – well I'd gone without it all those years, so obviously it wasn't going to be any problem for me to keep on the same way. And the other business, that was all over, I was getting on in years, I was sure it had all died away. It'd taken a long time, but there it was: all I needed to do was to keep on nice and steady just the way I'd been in prison. I couldn't help but be all right now. That was the way my mind worked.

And it was true, too, for what seemed like a very long time. This would be 1962 now. The firm I went to work for they were really excellent, they let me get into the work at my own pace, they didn't expect too much from me at the beginning. I went down to look at the bungalow, it was in a dreadful state with no one living in it all those years, I thought, 'Well this place is no good to me anymore, I might as well leave it.' So I went into digs near the factory where I worked – and I was very lucky again there too. A very nice widowed lady, middle-aged, I'd say in her forties, something like that; with two little boys of her own, one aged about seven and the other one nine. Do you know, I never even thought anything about those two boys, not to do with sex I mean. I'd no more have dreamed of anything like that with them than I would fly. They were lovely kids, we all got on well together; and there was another lodger in the house, he had a Hillman Minx, the five of us used to go out in it for picnics together or visiting different places. Like one big happy family we all were. The boys called me 'Uncle Wilfred'. I was so fond of them I wouldn't have let anyone touch a hair on their heads. Now why should that be, do you think, that there was no trouble with them, not even a thought of it in my mind? Life's funny sometimes, isn't it?

Getting back do you think we should be now? Yes, we don't want to be late do we? That'd never do, they'd never let me come out with you again, they'd think I wasn't reliable. I wouldn't like to let them down, not after they've been so good and taken a chance with me. Oh yes if you could keep on coming I'd be delighted, I really would;

I think it does me all the good in the world to have someone to talk to from outside.

★

On one of the roads back to the prison there was a public house called 'The George Borrow'.

—Now that's a funny name for a pub isn't it, I've never seen one with that sort of name before, have you? I wonder how on earth it came to be called that? He was a writer wasn't he, I read a book by him once, *Lavengro*, would it be, something like that? Gypsies, wasn't it, yes the gypsy people, he was very interested in them. Perhaps that's how it got its name; he stayed there once in the olden days, and he made a speech to the townspeople the next morning, standing out in front of it. What would he say? He'd tell them the gypsies were honest decent people, wouldn't he, just the same as they were only they preferred to wander about and not live in one place all the time. They had different ways, different habits, but they were good at heart and they ought to be allowed certain rights like any other human beings. He'd be a very good speaker too wouldn't he, a very passionate speaker, his eyes full of fire?

I expect it's something of that kind, don't you? There must be some story like that to it, mustn't there, to give it its name?

★

—I was thinking last time after you'd gone that it's only just under another year, you know, and then I'll be out. I don't know what I'll do, no: get a job, I suppose, try and make another start. I'll be sixty-one. I wonder if they'd have me back at that printing firm? There was nothing wrong with my work, they always said I was a satisfactory employee, good timekeeper, never took days off for sickness, nothing of that kind.

I did let them down, I can't argue about that. Two years I was with them, they must have thought I was all right; and then this offence occurred again. So no one could say I hadn't been given a chance, could they? It was nobody else's fault but my own. If only I'd had will-power. That nice woman I was staying with, the family outings and everything; I was well looked after, very comfortable. I don't know why I ever started, you know, going back to the bungalow again, I can't think what possessed me. Well no, that's not true; I can. It meant so much to me, it'd always been the home where I'd lived with my mother all those years. I couldn't keep away from it, I used

134

to go there sometimes and stand inside looking at it, at the state it was in; I'd break down completely you know, and start to cry. I used to say to myself, 'Whatever would she say if she could see what it looks like now, whatever would she say?'

What I ought to have done was get rid of it – sell it, give it away, anything. But I just couldn't. I started to go there now and again, trying to do it up a bit, repair some of the holes in the roof, get it into a decent shape. Then after a while in the nicer weather I'd spend the whole of Saturday afternoon there; and before long Sundays as well. Of course I knew what was going to happen, I knew it perfectly well; in a way I sealed my own doom about it through what I did. But I thought if only I could be left in peace to get on with the repairs it'd be all right. When some boys came round the first few times I told them to go away. Then there was a note through the door; and then another one after that. So I told one of the neighbours down the road that if she ever saw any boys in my garden while I was away, she was to phone the police and have them cleared out.

It was months afterwards, I'd forgotten all about it. She must have caught sight of them one afternoon when she was passing and that's what she did, just as I'd told her – and the police came down like a ton of bricks, they were everywhere, in through the front door, the back door, the windows, everything. And there we were, me and three boys: behaving indecently, we were, there couldn't be any argument about it. I thought with it not being an 'assault' charge it might go a bit better for me that time. Perhaps it did, perhaps that's why I only got five years and not another big sentence of preventive detention.

One of the boys was the younger brother of a boy who'd been involved the time before with me. It's not...well the police did say it themselves in one of my earlier cases, that it wasn't just me on my own, sometimes these youngsters had egged me on. What I've done has been utterly wrong, there's no question of it; there's no excuse to find for it, after all they're only children and I'm a grown man. But it's never ever been a case of me deceiving them, trying to get them into the place under false pretences and then taking them by surprise.

I...I want you to know everything there is to know about it, both the best and very very worst. There's nothing I'm going to conceal from you or try to hide. It...well I've got it here, I've brought it to show you; I've managed to keep it with me all these last years inside, just in case there ever came a time when there might possibly be someone I could talk to, and tell them the whole and absolute truth. This is just one of them; one of the notes that I've kept for if it was ever necessary to try and make this point. It's never been shown to anyone before, not to a soul in the world:

> Dere Wil, I hop I can com to see you Sat. I hop you will be in at yor hous an you wil hav som mor sweetes for me. I thogt abt you larst nite an it mad my dickey go orl hard. With lov from Jimmy. XXX.

—The ancient Greeks used to indulge in it, didn't they? Perhaps there'll always be people like that. Maybe it's something I got from my father do you think? He had a strong sexual side to his nature didn't he, only his consisted more of the attraction for women.

Yes, my thoughts are if I'm going to be honest, that it's true, it could, it could happen again. It seems to be something in your nature that you can't get rid of, it settles on you, it won't ever let you out of its grasp. Some kind of illness almost that you're suffering from, it descends on you, it's like a malady come upon you and you don't know what to do. Even some of the gentry have this you know, nicely educated people; you read about it, how it might happen to a vicar or a teacher, someone like that.

But you couldn't expect other people to understand about it, could you? They say, 'Well I don't feel like that, how can he?' They think it's disgusting, it's horrible, they don't want to know about it even, or consider it. And you'd never know with someone, would you, if you wanted to talk to them, just how they'd react? They all think it's something else, you see; their mind springs on to something else. Because it says it, doesn't it, when they read out the charge: 'Indecent assault'? It's only natural for them, people think it means more than it does. They think it must mean actually raping a boy, or trying to, an actual sexual act of that kind, and that you're dirty and horrible and cruel. But even the police you know, they told my mother about it once; they said to her, 'Your son's not one of these sex maniacs, don't think that, it's just this weakness he's got for liking to fondle little boys.' That was something at least; however awful it is, that's something that could be said.

MARRIAGE BRINGS PROBLEMS[1]

Harry Mills

Each summer evening twice a week he timed his arrival to coincide precisely with the striking of the clock on St. Hilda's Church as it was chiming eight away over on the opposite side of the deserted square. He would come in from the street and stride purposefully up the stairs, rap firmly on the door, and then push it open tentatively and enter with a hesitant smile and a hand extended in greeting, shyly proud of the small triumph of this exactitude.

—Hear that, well I've managed to make it right on the dot again haven't I? I like to be prompt for appointments whenever I possibly can, I think it's most essential people should be reliable over matters like that you know. Another lovely evening isn't it, and how are things with you? Good, oh yes I'm fine myself thanks, fine. Still a bit tired I must confess, it always takes me a little while to get used to the night shift: somehow I don't seem able to get off to sleep in the mornings properly you know, when I get back to my room. But my goodness when it comes round to six o'clock in the evening and I ought to be getting up, it's the exact opposite then, I feel I could go on sleeping for hours! I think it's only a question of practice though don't you, finding the rhythm of it again? After all I've been a night worker most of my life haven't I, most of my life, it's not as though I've not experienced it before. Shall I sit in my usual chair then here? Well yes now let me see: how far did we get exactly, last time?

*

His raincoat folded neatly and laid carefully over the back of another chair, he twitched up the knees of his trousers to preserve their creases;

1 *The Twisting Lane* (1969) London: Hutchinson, pp. 149–74.

folded his hands in his lap and blinked his eyes behind his horn-rimmed glasses, crossing one leg over the other and raising his foot, tilting his head slowly from side to side as he stared concentratedly at the toe-caps of his meticulously shined brown shoes. A tall, handsome man with neatly parted curly black hair, a long thin face and a pointed chin; straight backed in a smart green tweed sports jacket and grey flannels. His voice was quiet, restrained, firm; the dignity and deliberation of his speech never varied, however faraway the pained and puzzled look that came often into his eyes.

And every evening when he had finished talking and it was time for him to get off to the bakery where he worked, shaking hands again, Harry Mills always said, politely and calmly, the same thing.

—If I'm not here on the dot anytime, you mustn't bother waiting for me will you? You'll guess what's happened, and where I shall most likely be; and if that's so, I'll drop you a line as soon as I possibly can.

★

	Age		Charges		
1942	20	Conditional discharge	(2)	Sent to mental hospital	
1943	21	1 months' imprisonment	(3)		
1944	22	3 months' imprisonment	(4)		
1945	23	6 months' imprisonment	(7)	Broken engagement	
1946	24	6 months' imprisonment	(4)	Attempted suicide	
1947	25	3 years' imprisonment	(10)		
1948	26				
1949	27				
1950	28	Fined	(4)		
1951	29	Conditional discharge	(6)	Sent to mental hospital	
1952	30				
1953	31	18 months' imprisonment	(11)	Broken engagement	
1954	32	7 days' imprisonment	(1)		
1955	33	1 month's imprisonment	(2)		
1956	34	12 months' imprisonment	(3)	Attempted suicide	
1957	35	Conditional discharge	(6)	Sent to mental hospital	
1958	36				
1959	37	Fined	(1)		
1960	38	12 months' imprisonment	(16)	Broken engagement	
1961	39	3 months' imprisonment	(2)		
1962	40	4 months' imprisonment	(4)		
1963	41	Fined	(3)	Attempted suicide	
1964	42	Conditional discharge	(5)	Sent to mental hospital	
1965	43				
1966	44	6 months' imprisonment	(11)		
1967	45	3 months' imprisonment	(7)		
		(Total: 9 years, 3 months)	(Total: 112 charges)		

—She used to gad about with a lot of men, my mother did, a great lot of men. When she was young she must have been very pretty you know, very striking looking, always rather tall she was, and with long dark hair and brown eyes. Most of her life when she worked it was as a domestic servant in hotels, a chambermaid, that sort of thing. There was something in her of a wandering disposition, though; she never stayed for very long in the same place. Her mother and father, my grandparents, they were not like that at all: a respectable working-class couple they were, and they lived near Salisbury. I think he was a carpenter or something of that kind, and I lived most of the time with them after I was born: my mother didn't want me, I didn't fit in with the sort of life she wanted to lead.

Though there were times I was with her, there must have been because I can remember some of them. Exactly where or when or for how long I don't know. The only recollection I do have clearly is of her once taking me out shopping and keeping on telling me to hurry up, because I wouldn't keep pace with her. I was all the time stopping to look at things in shop windows you know, until eventually she said she wasn't going to wait any longer and off she went and walked on round the corner. When I got there I couldn't see her, there was only this street full of people; and I remember I kept running up and down it, crying because I was lost.

Somebody took me to a police station and they were all asking me who I was and where I lived and of course I didn't know. All I could tell them was that my name was Harry, but nothing else apart from that. They must have got me back to her eventually, but I don't remember the details of how; only the feeling of being lost and frightened in the street, I've never forgotten that. Then the next thing I remember is being in hospital; again I don't remember what for or how long I'd been there. When I left a lady came for me in a car and I didn't want to go with her because I liked being at the hospital, all the nurses were very kind and made a fuss of me, and I kept saying 'I don't want to go home, I want to stay here, please don't make me go home.'

The lady in the car was what would be called a Child Care Officer nowadays I suppose: anyway, she explained to me that I was going to be looked after by someone else who was going to take full responsibility for me and I needn't go back to my mother any more. Being put into care that would be called, wouldn't it? I was too young then to realise what it all meant of course, but from little bits I've been able to discover about it since my mother had never bothered to have much to do with me and she'd more or less left me to

139

my grandparents to look after. They were quite elderly people; apparently there'd been lots of rows between them and her and she'd taken me from time to time to live in different places with her for a while but had got fed up with me, until eventually the whole thing came to a head and the local authority took over.

I did hear once some years ago my mother was living as a sort of housekeeper with quite a well-known politician, but I don't know whether that's true or not. I've not seen much of her since I was small: a few times when I was fifteen, once in my twenties, and the last occasion would be about six or seven years ago. I don't love her at all and I don't think she can ever have loved me: whatever way of life she chose to follow, having a child certainly didn't fit in with it. She always wanted her independence, she's never been married for instance although I understand she's lived with several men.

For a very long time I'd no idea at all who my father was, but fortunately just at the period when it might have started to worry me I was taken by the lady Child Care Officer to live in this big children's home in Hertfordshire. There were about a hundred and twenty other boys there all like myself who came from broken-up homes: everyone would be more or less in the same boat as far as not having one or other parent was concerned. So I didn't think myself very much different to anyone else; and the other boys didn't question you about your own background or where you came from, because they were in the same sort of situation as you.

I stayed there from when I was six until when I was nearly sixteen. It was a private foundation run along Church of England lines, and fees were paid I suppose by grants from the local authority. I understand the only qualification to get into it was need, and there was always a pretty long waiting list so I gather my own situation must have been considered quite a needy one in order for me to be given a place.

Nearly all my childhood recollections consist of there. I can remember the first sight of the house when we got to it, like a great big country mansion with an enormous gravelled drive curving across the front, and at the side there were low stone railings looking out over a sort of sunken rose garden with old walls round it and a big pond with water-lilies in the middle. The sun was shining, there seemed to be mile after mile of lawns and trees, and inside there were polished wooden floors and staircases, big rooms with french-windows, and lots of sofas and chairs with bright cushions and covers on. I was quite sure it must be some kind of palace: I couldn't really believe I was going to be allowed to live there.

As well as being such a lovely place, it was also one of the best-run children's homes in the country in those days. The staff were chosen not only for their ability as teachers but also for their skill at dealing with the problems of young boys from deprived backgrounds. There was very great and constant friendship between the children and the staff. Everybody was on Christian name terms, and they took a real interest in you and tried to help you in every way they could, not only in lessons but at all other times too. They made a feature of discussions and debates about all sorts of subjects – sports, politics, religion, everything you can think of – and the emphasis all the time was on getting you to think things out for yourself and do them not because you were told to, but because you could see for yourself they were right.

Naturally a place like that had to have a very remarkable head-master; and it did have one nearly all the time I was there. I think it was about a year or so after I went there that he came, and he was still headmaster when I left, though I should think he's certainly retired by now. His name was, well we all called him by his Christian name which was Tom: nobody ever called the staff 'Sir' or 'Mr.' or anything like that because you looked upon them as your friends, which is what they were.

Such a thing as crime, even petty crime like stealing or not telling the truth, well it never existed in that place. I don't think it ever crossed our minds there was any other way to behave than the right one. For instance once at morning assembly after prayers Tom said there'd been a window broken in one of the back kitchens the night before, and he said 'Nobody's been to tell the cook yet that they did it. Would the boy responsible please hold up his hand?' And straight-away, you know, the boy stepped forward and put his hand up.

Another time I got into trouble myself once, for some very trivial thing like talking after lights out in the dormitory, and doing it about three or four nights in succession until eventually one of the moni-tors reported me to the Head. Tom took me into his study and said I knew very well we weren't supposed to talk after lights out, and if I went on doing it the only punishment he could give me was the cane. And he said he wouldn't like to have to do that, it would embarrass him very much, so he'd be very grateful if I'd do as I was told from then on. Which of course I did.

I suppose you could almost make that a criticism of the place; it didn't properly prepare you for what the outside world was going to be like, and when you left you found things could be very different from what you'd been brought up to. People did want to hurt you if they could for instance, and they'd be looking for an excuse to do it rather than for one not to. The other thing that was wrong with it as I see it now, was that it was for boys only, and I think it would have been better to have girls there as well. Certainly in my own case I've had great difficulty in getting on with them and felt shy of them for years, which I think perhaps I wouldn't have been if I'd had more contact with them when I was young.

But I don't want to criticise the place really, because I'm sure no one could ever have had a better upbringing in any other children's home, and there were all sorts of advantages I got from it which have remained with me all my life. Liking music, to give one example: we had a master there called Nick, who was very fond of playing the piano; about once a week on Saturday or Sunday evenings he'd give a recital in the hall that anyone could go and sit listening to if they felt like it. Bach, Brahms, Mozart, Beethoven, it was always good music of that kind; I got a great deal of pleasure out of it then, and I still do even though I've never been able to play a note myself.

Though I won't pretend it was a perfect life there; obviously it wasn't, because whatever they did for you and however hard they tried to make up for what you didn't have, it still couldn't be the same as a normal home background, could it? Every so often you were bound to feel lonely, and conscious of the fact that you were different from most other children. As I got older I became more and more aware of it; that I had no proper home, no parents to come and visit me, I didn't seem to belong in the world. It was then that I first got into my habit of going out for long walks on my own, all round the countryside, walking and walking, and feeling restless and unsure of who I was or where I fitted in.

One night, I suppose it couldn't have been long before I reached the age when I was going to leave, Matron was doing her nightly round of the dormitories and I remember she found me kneeling up at the end of my bed, looking out of the window into the dark. She asked me what I was doing, and I told her I was trying to imagine what life was going to be like outside, and looking at the stars in the sky and trying to puzzle out what life was all about. A few mornings later Tom brought this subject up at the end of morning assembly; he said Matron had told him she'd found one of the older boys looking out of the window at night and wondering what life was all about. Of course he didn't mention my name or give any clue as to who it was, but he said he thought it was a question everyone there ought to think about for themselves. He said 'I'm going to think about it too,

I'm over fifty myself and I must admit I still don't know the answer to it either.'

Well when I was almost sixteen, I had to leave the home. I was put to live in a hostel up in London and found a job in a hotel, a sort of bell-boy and general porter. I think it was chosen because it was a sort of living-in job so it settled the problem of both work and accommodation at one go. I might have been all right there, I think, if I hadn't been so – I think the word's institutionalised – by living so long in the home. But I was, I found myself not able to make friends or even talk to anyone very much; it was a very lonely life for a boy so young.

After about a year there I got into trouble; I was taken to court for stealing a radio set. It was quite true that I had stolen it, three or four months before, out of one of the guest's bedrooms in the hotel. I knew it was wrong to steal, so I've no excuse to make really. Only it hadn't been to sell, I'd no intentions of that sort, I'd taken it more or less for company in my own room at night; but one time when the manager came in to tell me about something, he spotted it and remembered the complaint there'd been. I believe the guest it belonged to insisted on it being reported to the police; anyway as I say I was taken to court. The circumstances were explained, who I was and where I'd been brought up and so on, and the court took a lenient view. I think I was bound over to be of good behaviour for twelve months or so.

The much worse part of it was when they read out the details about me in court. I knew I was illegitimate of course, I'd been aware of that since I was little; it'd gradually dawned on me while I was at the home that like a lot of the other boys there I had a mother who wasn't married, and I didn't have a father. What I hadn't realised though, until that day when I heard it said in court, was that my father had been my mother's brother: I wasn't just a bastard, I was the result of an incestuous union too.

—Not long after all that court business I left the job in the hotel and went to live with my grandparents again in Salisbury, and I got a job in a local hotel working in the kitchen. But living with them wasn't very satisfactory, they'd only a very small house and after a few weeks I moved out into digs on my own. Still a very solitary sort of character I was, but I did manage to get myself a friend who I went out with a few times. One of the chambermaids in the hotel, a few years older than me and from what I remember of her quite a nice girl.

There was nothing serious between us though of course at that age, it was more for companionship than anything.

After a time I heard that my mother had come down to my grandparents' for a holiday, so I went to see her. What I wanted to do was ask her about my birth, if what had been said about me in court was correct. When I tried she was very abrupt, she said of course it wasn't true and wouldn't talk about it. Though later on after she'd gone out of the house for a while, when I asked my grandma about it she didn't contradict it at all; she just started crying and said it'd be better if we didn't discuss it. So I've always taken it since as being true.

A few days after I'd tried to have the talk with my mother I took my friend along to my grandparents' house to introduce her to them. My mother was still there, and she and this girl didn't hit it off together. There was a bit of an argument, though I can't remember what it was about now. Anyway it meant I couldn't take her there again, and not long after she got another job somewhere else so I didn't see her any more. I felt very lonely after that, and I got in touch with the home who'd brought me up to ask them if they could help me find work in London again. They arranged for me to go and live at a Church Army hostel and be trained as a baker. I liked that, I liked that very much; I think it's a good way of making a living for a young boy to learn, and certainly the training they gave me was good. Altogether I should think it was just over three years I was there learning; and in fact when I was called up in 1941 I was taken into the Catering Corps in the same trade.

After the six weeks or whatever it was everybody had to go through of square-bashing to start off with, I was sent up to Yorkshire and worked in the camp bakery there. It was all right, but the big disadvantage from my point of view was that the work was divided into three shifts and I was put on the early one; I think it was from six in the morning until two in the afternoon and it meant that I had a great lot of time on my hands during the day after I'd finished work.

It was there that I first started my walking about round the town and so on, and getting into trouble. It all came to a head when there was a complaint from the wife of one of the captains in my own unit, and the result was I was put up in front of the local magistrates court on two charges. They gave me a discharge on condition I went to an Army mental hospital in Birmingham.

When I got there the doctors said there was no reason why I shouldn't go on working, I wasn't physically unfit or anything like that, so they gave me a job in the bakery while they treated me. Unfortunately the hours I worked were exactly the same as I'd been doing at the camp in Yorkshire, so I still found myself with a lot of time on my hands for walking around and I was constantly getting into trouble even while I was a patient at the hospital. The treatment they gave me consisted mainly of different kinds of pills: they'd try one sort for a fortnight, then try another sort and so on; but none of them seemed to make much difference.

In the end however they said I was all right, though I could have told them myself that I wasn't. I was re-posted to another unit over in Northern Ireland, and there I was put in charge of the catering for the officers' mess. The work was hard and the hours were very long, so I spent most of my time on the camp either working or sleeping and I kept out of trouble completely for about at least six months.

Then I was transferred again, to another unit down in Dorset, from where I was supposed to be going overseas, I think it was to the Middle East. Most of the time there seemed to be spent waiting and hanging about with nothing much to do, and before long I was in trouble again through my usual walking about, and this time I got a month's imprisonment for it. After that I was considered not suitable for sending abroad, and I was shuttled around between various camps and units for the next twelve months at a loose end until I ended up in prison again, this time for three months.

It wasn't until towards the end of the war in 1945 that I got much chance of settling down anywhere for very long. Then I got a fairly permanent billet at a camp in Sussex, on the coast near an anti-aircraft battery where there was a unit of ATS girls. We used to mix quite a lot in the canteens and soldier's clubs and so on, and I fell rather heavily for one of these girls who came from Scotland and was called Jeannie. We went out a bit together, and we seemed to get on very well; she was a quiet sort of person like myself and after a time I asked her if she'd like to get married when the war was over and she said yes she would, so we got engaged. Then almost immediately she was posted somewhere else; that sort of thing often happened in those days of course, but it upset me because she was more or less the only friend I had. Anyway, there it was: she went off to the East Coast right up into Northumberland, and for several months we got no opportunity of seeing each other at all.

So of course I got into my usual trouble again, and this time it was six months' imprisonment. I felt it was no use pretending to Jeannie, I'd better tell her all about myself. I wrote her a letter telling her everything, that this was the third time I'd been in prison and what for and all the rest of it – and I thought she might as well know the full story, so I told her about my birth too, who my parents were, everything. I got a letter back to say she was sorry but she didn't feel that she could possibly marry me. At the time I took it very hard indeed, because I did have the faint hope that she might just possibly react differently. Anyway, she didn't; she said she thought a marriage would be nothing without children, and obviously we'd never be able to have any, so she didn't see any point in going on with it.

When I came out of prison I was still in the Army, and I was sent then to a unit in Gloucester, but this time not as a baker. Instead I was put on a kind of toughening-up course, cross-country running, climbing up and down barricades, crossing rivers on ropes and that sort of thing, almost like a commando training it was. I was very physically fit, I'd be twenty-three or twenty-four then I should think, but I never really felt I'd make a very good commando, I'd much sooner be making cakes; and before long I got off that and back into my own trade again. Then I was demobilised, and once more I went to live in Salisbury. My first job there was in a shop, a kind of café and pastry-cooks combined; but once again there was the same old trouble with shift work, starting first thing in the morning and finishing early in the afternoon, and then having nothing else to do for the rest of the day but walk about. My grandparents were getting on in age and I couldn't go and see them too often, and I was living my usual lonely sort of life in digs. Eventually I was arrested again of course, and by that stage I was getting pretty desperate about myself. While I was on remand it suddenly came over me that the best thing to do would be to put an end to it all, so that night in my cell I tied one end of my tie to the window bars, stood on a chair and knotted the other end round my throat as tight as I could, and then jumped off.

I don't know what happened, I think when you try and strangle yourself you make a lot of noise while you're choking: anyway somebody came in and cut me down, so it didn't work; instead I got another six months' sentence. I served that one I think it was in Winchester; and almost as soon as I came out I started my walking about, it was only a week or two before I was arrested again. This time it was quite serious because there was an assault charge in it as well: a lady hit me on the head with her umbrella, and she kept on hitting me and hitting me in a corner, until eventually I hit back and in fact I knocked her down.

The police took a very serious view of that indeed; I was charged with more or less everything they could think of, and the outcome of it all was that I got a really stiff sentence of three years. In a way, perhaps this is hard for you to believe, but I felt a certain kind of relief, you know: I was going to be in prison for two years even with remission, and I knew that meant two years of peace and quiet with no possibility of trouble at all. Once you make your mind up, that there's no alternative to it, in a way you do feel relieved; you know that for a certain time at least your worries have been taken off your shoulders for you. And while you're serving the sentence you get the feeling too sometimes, that if you can live nice and quietly in there and not be any trouble to anyone, then surely you can do the same when you get out, and everything seems very simple to you.

When I came out I thought I'd be all right to try London again, so I came and lived up in the East End and worked once more in a bakery, this time for quite a big firm. The first few months passed off quite well, I thought perhaps being in prison for so long had quietened me down. But it was not to be, my trouble started again and I was as bad as ever over the next couple of years, though I did manage to stick in my job. In 1951, well obviously it couldn't go on and when I was next charged they decided they'd have another go at trying treatment for me. I was discharged on condition that I went as a voluntary patient into a mental hospital in Buckinghamshire. I stayed there a year, it must have been at least a year. I was given what they call 'aversion therapy', electric shocks and all the rest of it. It seemed to work, on the whole I think you could say it was a success, and I was discharged as cured towards the end of 1952.

Then I went to live for a while in Oxfordshire, round that part of the world; I got a job at one of the motor-car factories as cook in the canteen, and all went fairly well again. In my spare time I joined a club connected with old people's welfare, doing a bit of catering for them. It was while I was there that I eventually got engaged for the second time, to a girl called Joyce who I met there at the old people's club. She was rather like me, in some ways our backgrounds had been the same because she'd been brought up in an orphanage too. I had hopes that if I could really settle down and get a bit of money behind me we might make a go of things together. But that didn't work out either; after a few months she said her feelings had changed and she wanted to break it off. I rather got the impression there was someone else in the picture; however, there it was, whatever the reason she didn't want to go ahead.

I stopped going to the old people's club and I did what I've done before, came up to London and looked for another job. I think at that time I had quite a series of jobs of one kind or another, mostly connected with bakery work. In between times I was getting into a lot of trouble, a great deal of trouble, through walking about round different places. I went back to prison two or three times and everything seemed to be falling to pieces again, until it reached the stage in 1956 when I had another try at finishing it all. I'd been to the doctor for some pills to help me sleep, and one weekend I took a Green Line bus right out into the country, and went into a wood and sat down in a clearing and took the whole lot. I said a few simple prayers first and I can remember feeling very calm and peaceful about the whole business, not a bit frightened but in a way rather happy and relieved. I was right in the middle of this wood on my own, it was a beautiful sunny day, and I know I was thinking as I got drowsier and drowsier that this was the perfect way to die.

I was really very surprised when I woke up in hospital and discovered I wasn't dead after all. Apparently there'd been a man taking his dog out for a walk through the woods; this dog had found me and the man had sent for assistance, an ambulance and all the rest of it. One of the doctors who came round to see me in the hospital asked me if I believed in God: when I said yes I did, he told me the way to look at it was that God must have decided He didn't want me to die yet because there were still things for me to do. When it's put to you like that, it seems a reasonable sort of argument, I think. A few months later when I was in my usual trouble again, I asked the court if I could have another try myself at being treated for it.

This time it was a big hospital in Surrey that I was sent to. Their method was to give you drugs and medicine to keep you calm, and encourage you to join in group discussions and that sort of thing. They also gave you Pentathol quite a lot, that's an injection to help you talk about yourself to a psychiatrist. It was a very nice hospital, you were given a lot of freedom so long as you behaved yourself and co-operated with them. I'm afraid I didn't behave as well as I might have done, though; I used to go out walking about from there while I was still having treatment, with the result that for a period I was put in a maximum security ward where you're locked in and get no privileges at all. I had to stay there for about two months, to be taught a lesson I suppose would be the idea of it, and then I was let back on to the open ward.

When I was discharged from the hospital I tried living and working up in London again: I got a room in Cricklewood and had a fairly good job in another bakery. I met a nice girl and went out a lot with her, pictures and so on, and once more I felt things might be looking up if only I could get myself settled. Her name was Peggy, she came from a nice family, I really thought the world of her I did, you know. I told her about being illegitimate and she didn't seem to mind that; and then I took my courage in both hands and told her about who my father and mother were as well – and she seemed to take that in her stride too. When I asked her if she'd consider marrying me despite all that, she said she would, and the week after that we bought an engagement ring.

There was only one thing left to get over then; so one night I invited her back to my room and made a little meal for her, and after it I said 'There's still something else I've got to tell you, which is that I've been to prison nine or ten times.' I told her about the mental hospitals too and all the rest; and she said of course it made the whole thing different. Most of all she said what she resented was the fact that I'd been deceiving her, I ought to have told her long before we decided on being engaged. In the end she got really angry, she pulled off her engagement ring there and then and put it on the table and walked out.

This would be about 1960 now; and from then on things seemed to go steadily from bad to worse over the next four years. I was in a lot of trouble all over the place, in and out of prison, a whole succession of different jobs: it ended up with me taking another overdose of pills and being found unconscious in my room by the landlord who'd come round to see why I hadn't paid the rent. So it was into hospital again, out for a bit, and then after that back again to the mental hospital, altogether for about twelve or fifteen months.

Since then I'm afraid the pattern's gone on pretty much the same. If you look back on it over my record, for the last twenty-five years or so I never seem able to have kept out of trouble for very long. Every single year, almost, there's been something. Now I'm forty-six and that's getting on isn't it? I suppose the only way in which you could say things have changed is that six months ago I got married. Whether it'll work or not, I don't know: for someone like me it's bound to happen that marriage brings problems, really quite big ones.

—No one knows what to do with me; I have to accept that as a fact. I suppose it's a matter really of keep hoping, isn't it, try this and that and then perhaps one day something'll work, it'll die down, there'll be no more trouble. People say it's up to you to make an effort, and I think that's true, I do, there's a lot in that. But I don't think people know how much effort I have made, over the years; time after time, and for each occasion when I've failed, there's been perhaps half a dozen or more times when I've succeeded and stopped myself. They don't know about those of course, they only know about the failures there's been.

Up to now I think I've had every possible treatment that there is: imprisonment, drugs, aversion therapy, group therapy, psychotherapy – whatever you can think of, you name it and I've had it. And they all work for a time. Imprisonment's a success, it puts me out of harm's way for a while; but apart from that aspect of it I can't see it does much good really. It certainly doesn't alter my character or disposition in any way, and if there's anything in the idea of deterrence, I should think that's long lost any relevance it might possibly have had. I don't even consider it now; I don't think 'Oh I might go to prison' or worry about being caught. It never comes into it, when I'm walking about such thoughts no longer even enter my head.

The mental hospitals are good, they work too, they do a lot for me. But it's only while I'm there; and then as soon as I come out the effect wears off. This one I've been to the last two times, it's a very good place, they do everything they possibly can to get you to concentrate on what you might call the positive side of life: art classes, pottery, socials, dances. They have all those things, as well as the therapy sessions they give you either in a group or on your own, where you're encouraged to talk about yourself and your problems. I've had it all explained to me dozens of times; how it's something to do with my feelings about my birth and my upbringing, my sense of inferiority, my resentment towards my mother and all the rest of it. I think there's a lot in that, it's very probably all true. But understanding it and learning what it's all about still doesn't seem to make a blind bit of difference you know, when I get outside.

I think on the whole, the people who've been the most helpful of all to me I should say have been the police. One particular station, the one at Bone Lane, they know me very well, they've had to take me in dozens of times. The Inspector in charge there, he's a very nice man indeed. Last year there was an occasion when two of his constables arrested me in the street, and I must admit I lost my temper a bit. We had quite a fight really, because I didn't want to have to go with them. Well this Inspector, he came down to see me in the charge-room; and he gave me a really good talking to. He could have made a lot of trouble for me, you know, if he'd wanted to with my past record, especially because I'd resisted arrest. But instead of that he gave me a cigarette and told me to sit there until I'd calmed down; then he went away for a bit and when he came back he really laid into me.

He said to me 'Now look here Harry' he said, 'I know you and you know me, and I'm getting fed up with all the bother you're causing us. Don't you think we've got enough to do catching criminals and all the rest of it? We're very busy indeed, without you making a nuisance of yourself as well. And what's more' he said, 'we get lots of fellows in here who've been stealing and breaking into places, because they'd sooner do that sort of thing rather than work for their living; they're too downright lazy and dishonest to work. But that's not your case now is it? You can work and you do work; you're working now and you're making a living – but if I were to charge you, what'd happen to you? You'd go to prison again, that's what; you'd lose your job, you'd be right back at the beginning with nothing behind you at all. And that would be a complete waste of time and effort all round now, wouldn't it? So you go off home will you Harry, and let's forget all about it. And just bear this in mind for the future: you've not to fight any more of my policemen. If they pick you up you've to behave yourself and keep quiet and go along with them when they say.'

I've been in that police station quite a few times since you know, when I've been walking about at a loose end round that area. I've gone in and I've said to them 'Look, I've not done anything but I feel as though I'm going to; can I sit here for a little until I feel better?' And they'll let me do that, they give me a cup of tea and a cigarette, and then one of them will walk me to the bus-stop and see me on the right bus for home.

But of course they're not all like that, not all like that by any means. In fact that's the only one I know of where you can actually go in and talk to them and they won't pinch you for it. In some of them they'd be only too ready to stick every charge on you that they could, including any spare ones they've got waiting until there's someone comes along that they'll fit. I think perhaps there's more the police could do if they were allowed to, a lot of them; but they're under whoever's in charge aren't they, they have to follow the lines he lays down for his particular area.

My wife, she says we ought to go and live next door to Bone Lane and then I'd be all right. She says it half as a joke you know, but of course I have to explain to her it's not as simple as that. When I do go walking around I never know where I'm going to end up, quite often I haven't the faintest idea where I am at all. And anyway I seem to be all right more or less, wherever I am with her.

—She and I, we say that poem to each other sometimes, that one of Robert Browning's, 'Rabbi Ben Ezra',

Grow old along with me!
The best is yet to be,
The last of life, for which the first was made:
Our times are in His hand
Who saith 'A whole I planned,
Youth shows but half; trust God: see all, nor be afraid!'

Oh I learnt it at school I should think, originally. It's a long poem but between us we can just about manage to get through it together, all the way from beginning to end. She's the only person I've come across who likes it as much as I do; in fact that was how we first came to speak to each other. I was walking through the lounge and I saw her sitting over by the window with her back to me, looking out over the lawns. I didn't know who she was or what she might be thinking, it was just something about the look of her, I don't know what made me say it; but I went up and stood behind her and I said 'The best is yet to be.' And she said the first line of it straight off and then went on for about the next twenty or thirty lines, she knew it all.

Mary's her name. She'd been a patient there herself for six years by then, and very ill, she'd never been allowed out at all. She's what they call a schizophrenic, has to take pills every day of her life; they've told her she'll never be able to manage without them ever. We've known each other about three years now; after I was discharged I went back to see her regularly once a week, to take her out for a walk or to go to the pictures, whatever she felt like: or only sit in the lounge if she preferred.

Right at the outset we agreed we'd take each other just as we were, and what had happened to us before wouldn't come into it. I don't mean we hid anything from each other, because we didn't: she knows nearly everything there is to know about me, and I know the same about her. That ten years ago she was a prostitute on the streets for example, and a few other things besides. Neither of us is perfect and the other knows it: but what's done's done, and we love each other for what we are now, which is all that matters.

The big test to me really was whether she'd stand by me when I got into trouble again. I'd not pretended to her that I thought I wouldn't, but all the same it had proved too much for the others in the past. Mary's proved herself different: I've been in prison a couple of times since I've known her, and she just shrugs it off, she says perhaps one day when we can be together it might be all right. She's had one or two relapses herself with her own trouble, had to be confined to the ward for weeks at a time, hearing voices and all the rest of it. She always quotes that at me, she says 'We've both of us got excuses for giving the other one up if we want to, we've just got to take each other completely as we are.'

It was a risk getting married of course, but six months ago we decided we'd do it, we'd take the plunge. And even in that short time there's been a bit of progress; just a bit. She can come out nearly every weekend now, from Friday night till Sunday night, so that means we have two days and two nights together completely on our own. Sometimes perhaps on a Saturday afternoon we'll go out for tea or something like that, but most times we don't go very far away from our room since the time we've got together is so short. Mary doesn't like it much, going out, she always feels people are staring at her; she's very self-conscious because she's still a mental hospital patient.

Well I know what that's like, don't I, that feeling; I should do, I've had it often enough myself coming out of prison. That's just one of the many ways we understand each other. She understands my feelings about being a failure and an outcast, she feels exactly the same, and we can talk to each other about these things.

Only a couple of months ago she said she could never live anywhere except an asylum, that was the only place for her. And I told her it wasn't true, which it isn't: most weekends she gets through two whole days outside with me. Then I think it was only a week or two after that and the positions were reversed; she was cheering me up through one of my depressions when I said I couldn't ever see myself being cured, I'd end up one day for good in a prison cell. But Mary said I wouldn't, I'd end up happy with her in a house of our own, perhaps even a bakery of our own, where I'd have to work for ever and ever to earn enough money to buy her all the things she wanted. 'That's what you'll be sentenced to, Harry' she said, 'a life sentence of working for me!' She was laughing, you know; that's what we do, we laugh at each other for feeling so sorry for ourselves, and we can make each other cheer up like that in turn. But not when it's really serious; then we don't laugh, we talk to each other and try and help. I try and encourage her to feel that one day she'll be all right, and she does the same for me. So long as we talk to each other and can tell each other how we feel, then we think there's still a chance; and so long as we've got each other, that's the main thing.

Though I don't know how many men have got a wife like her who, when they tell her they've been out walking around all day in the street would put her arms round them and kiss them and say 'It's all right, I love you and I'll always love you; hold me in your arms Harry, so long as we stay together sooner of later we'll both be all right.'

The two of us are throw-outs from society, rejects, failures; and we know it. But together at least with each other we do sometimes seem to make a little kind of success.

*

Always the same posture, upright and neat in the chair; always the same level tone of voice, dispassionate and grave. Composed and calm he talked each night on into the fading light until often all that remained visible of him was the thin mask of his face, hanging disembodied like a long pale lantern in the darkening shadows of the sad and suffering air. Harry Mills, twenty times convicted in twenty-five years for over a hundred offences; with more than double that number of offences committed in addition, for which he had never been charged.

An indecent exposer. To some, a distasteful figure to be looked on with anger or contempt; to others, a sick person who ought to respond to treatment of some kind; and to some people perhaps someone to be regarded as a joke, almost with derision and as a figure of fun.

But not to himself; never, none of those things. To Harry Mills it was something he alone in desperation had to try and live with; a compulsion like an all-pervading blight, eventually and inevitably laying waste every effort hope or dream he'd ever had through the other greater agony of all his burdened guilty life.

—You can tell you're illegitimate; it's not a very nice thing to have to say, but on the whole it's something you can get over probably, it's not all that unusual. But the other thing, that your father and mother were…well you do have a terrible feeling, you see, that no matter what happens you couldn't ever really be normal, having been born like that. It's a feeling somehow of shame, that there's something different about you and there's no way round it, you are what you are and nothing's ever going to change it. It has been explained to me it's in no way my fault, that there's nothing in it for me to feel guilty about myself. But I can't help it, I do. I've never for instance in my whole life considered that it would be safe for me ever to have children myself in case I were to pass this, well, this hereditary taint on to them. I do not believe I could ever be the father of a normal child, and I know this feeling will always remain in my mind whatever anyone says. It's the only thing so far that I still haven't been able to bring myself to tell my wife.

You can't be as good as other people, you simply can't: not when you've been born like that. And I think that's been proved, because certainly I'm not normal, I'm not normal myself, and I don't think I ever will be. It's such a terrible, revolting thing to do. Oh yes, I think that too: not only other people, you know: I'm disgusted at it myself as well. I think it's right what they say in the charge, the wording of it, 'insulting behaviour'. That's what they usually describe it as; and it is, I don't think there's any doubt about that. I am insulting people, that is what I do.

Middle-aged women, smartly dressed, no one else. Someone who reminds me of my mother, a doctor said once, he pointed that out to me, and I think that might be right, that I'm still trying to insult her. No, it's not a prelude to a sexual assault, there's never anything like that in my mind. Just to shock. If a woman looks disgusted and turns away, then I'm satisfied. A woman smiled at me once, and came towards me instead; I ran away from her as hard as I could. I'm very frightened if someone makes an advance towards me like she did; all you want to do then is get right away.

I can't tell you why I do it; when it's happening I'm not conscious of anything except this feeling of being contemptuous towards women and wanting to try and give one a shock. I know when it's coming on usually; first there's this feeling of great restlessness and wanting to go out for a walk. In a way I walk to try and calm myself down, to tire myself out, and sometimes I get back to my room and I think 'Well that was all right this time, all I did was walk.' Then later it comes back to me, the memories come back, the incidents here and there, and I realise it wasn't all right, that wasn't only what I did at all.

Usually it's in the afternoon when I've got nothing to do except wander around. That's why I always try to get myself work on the night-shift because with that I'm so tired I stop most of the day in bed. The morning shift is the worst, six till two; after that I don't go home and go to bed like I ought to, I go walking around. So if I possibly can I avoid that shift and try to keep on nights.

You know you can never be cured, all you can do is try to come to terms with it somehow because you know you'll always have it. You've got to try and cope with it to the greatest amount that you can, and then you've got to live with the rest. It comes in spasms mostly, you'll have quite a few months when it never happens at all, you can't remember any more what it was all about. You think you must have faced up to it finally and fought against it and won; then suddenly it starts again.

There's been days when I've been out for hours and hours on end and never stopped, walking up and down, round and round, street after street, woman after woman I've seen and done it to every one. Over a hundred complaints in a month the police told me they'd had at one time; and of course not everyone even goes to the trouble to go to the police and complain. One woman was a magistrate, and I did it three times to her; she insisted the police catch me in this park where I happened to be each afternoon as she was walking home. They sent two women police in plain-clothes in to walk through it and that was it, I did it straight away to them. That was one of the times I got six months I think.

You see with a list of convictions like mine, you're always bound to get a prison sentence or sent to hospital, they've got to try and do something with you, haven't they? A very sick man, I've been told; but I can't understand that, because I can work and I do work, very hard, the full time that I'm supposed to, every single shift. I never pinch a day off or even an hour off or anything like that, I'm proud of my work and of being reliable. And a sick man, anyway what does that mean? First they tell me I'm that, and then when I've been in the hospital for a while they tell me I can go because I'm cured. But I never have been, after a few months it all starts again.

You sit in your room sometimes wherever you happen to be living at the time, usually with me it's a furnished bed-sitter some-where, and you think: 'What am I going to do, what's the point of it all, will I never be able to conquer this thing and stop?' Or must I accept that all my life I'm going to be in and out of prisons and hospitals for always doing the same? Am I always going to be a useless rotten man? This business, it's so futile, so meaningless, such a terrible waste of time.

I think all you can do is persuade yourself that life here isn't all, there must be an end to it eventually and something better to come perhaps in the next. I know Beethoven felt that, didn't he, when he found out he was going deaf? He wrote to his brothers about it, I read his letter once in a book. He was going deaf and he knew that as time went on he'd only be able to hear his music in his mind. Then he wrote his Third Symphony, the 'Eroica' they call it, don't they? When you listen to that, you know what he felt, that this world isn't everything, there are other things much greater and better beyond. Those who can't achieve worldly happiness can always listen to that music and learn from it; that man knew there was more to the world than what he was suffering then.

You never know, do you, when the end is going to be? You think everything's over but you can't tell, it might only just be the beginning for you after all. The last twenty-five years, they've been terrible. Perhaps the next will be better, but even if they're not, even if I go on exactly the same as I have done, perhaps just before I'm dying it'll all eventually come right and the last few minutes of life will have some meaning. If they do, those minutes to me will be worth far more than everything else all added up that's gone before.

I think that's the only way there is to look at these things myself, I can't see any other way. I'm a religious person and I believe in God, even though I don't go to church. I believe He's got a purpose and a way for you to follow, even though it might be one that you yourself will never understand. I think He had a purpose in bringing Mary and me together, I think it was for something: between the two of us we've got to try and work out what it was. He's set us problems to solve and put difficulties in our way, just like He does for everyone else; but I can't help feeling that He knows what He's doing and somehow, in some way, perhaps after a lot more things to go through yet for both of us, it will eventually come right in the end.

A RADIO IS A VERY GOOD FRIEND[1]

Norman

The most important thing of all, Norman was sure, was to keep yourself fit. While others were sitting at dinner tables after meals drinking endless mugs of tea and smoking and talking, Norman was away off up to his cell doing exercises. Step-ups, first with his right foot on a low wooden box, then with his left: a hundred times with each took eleven minutes. Then press-ups from the floor with his arms for another nine minutes; and after that five minutes' rest, before going back to the laundry where he worked.

And in the evenings while most prisoners slouched in chairs in a darkened room, watching television in an atmosphere full of smoke, Norman was not with them then either. Instead he was at his cell window doing complicated breathing rhythms, each one carefully worked out to strengthen the different muscles of the diaphragm; alternatively for occasional variety he lay on his back, supporting his hips with his hands while he bicycled his legs in the air. He could do that for fifteen minutes without stopping, and was hoping in time to get up to twenty.

He was thirty-one years of age. He had pale flaxen hair and deep blue eyes, and perhaps not surprisingly shining pink cheeks and a healthily-clear complexion. Small in build, he walked with a rapid twine-toed roll, springy and lithe. Not a great one for conversation, he said, when another prisoner first introduced him: but by all means if I'd like him to he'd be perfectly willing to come down to my room some time and have a try.

—Should I perhaps start by running through my sentences first for you; would that be the best? Right: well at the moment I'm doing life,

1 *The Frying Pan* (1970) London: Hutchinson, pp. 177–83.

plus a three years, another three years, a four years, and another life. I think. No, I'm sorry, that's wrong: it's two lifes, two four years, and a three years. Wait a minute though, I'm not certain I've got it right even now. Let me see; there were five charges, and another five cases taken into consideration, all of which I pleaded guilty to as well. I've forgotten exactly what he said, the Judge; which sentence was for what, if you know what I mean. There was a buggery and an attempted buggery, an assault and an attempted assault, a rape and two attempted rapes: how many's that? Five, six, seven: then there's three more somewhere but I can't remember them. I do know when he sentenced me he said a life to begin with, then the three years and the four years, and then he said another life at the end. I think the lifes were for the rapes: no, they can't have been, one of them was for the buggery, I do remember that. I would have to think about this more if you wanted it to be exact as to which sentence went with what charge and so on.

They were all concerning children between the ages of eleven and fourteen, or I think in one case it might have been a girl of not quite eleven, more like ten and a half, something like that. They were not children I knew, no. Yes, there had been some previous convictions; you do mean for this sort of offence, do you? Yes, well one previous one actually, a sentence of two years for buggery on a boy. The Judge referred to it at my trial; he said obviously it had no effect, so this time it would have to be a lot longer. He gave me these two lifes, and he said that meant the Home Secretary could only order my release when he thought it safe to do so.

★

—I was born in 1937 in a town in Somerset. I have three sisters and two brothers; then there's me, I'm the sixth, and after me there's a step-sister and a step-brother. My father is a man I never knew very well: to tell you the truth I couldn't say what he did or what he was like, because I don't remember him at all. He died I think, but I'm not sure; my first recollection is of my step-father being always there.

He was a very big man, my step-father, very aggressive and he did a lot of drinking. I was always terrified of him if I'd done anything wrong because he would thrash me with his belt. He liked his own children, that's my step-brother and step-sister, much more than he liked me. I remember once I was playing with my younger brother, my step-brother, in the garden of the house where we lived, and he threw a stone and broke the kitchen window. When my step-father came home he gave the hiding with the belt to me, because he said

159

I was the older one and should have known better than to be playing games throwing stones near the house.

When I was six I was put with another family, I believe it was called a foster-home; there were a lot of other children there, and a woman who looked after us all. I'm sorry, I've said wrong: the first home had two women in it to look after us, it was the second where there was only one. Then there were some others I was in as well; perhaps about five or six different ones altogether, I think. I know when I was young it seemed a bit of a puzzle to me sometimes exactly who I belonged to.

When I was ten I was sent to an approved school because of getting into trouble with some other boys at one of the homes. We went breaking into the backs of sweet shops and things like that. I didn't do any of the actual breaking in myself, I was their look-out to warn them if anyone was coming, but I know we were all charged with the same thing.

The approved school was away in the Midlands somewhere because of the war, and I was in it for six years. I didn't like it very much; I think all it did for me was to make me rather bitter, but I didn't learn anything else. I ran away from it once, I thought I'd go off somewhere else to try and live on my own. It was at night, and the police caught me hiding in a shelter in a park and took me straight back again. The headmaster said that running away was the most serious offence of all that there was, but he thought I'd been more silly than wicked so he was going to be lenient. He gave me twelve strokes on the backside with the cane: apparently he could have given me more for running away if he'd wanted to.

In my estimation the people who ran the school were wrong in the way they went about it. I think they should have had something like a married man and his wife at the top, who would understand children and try and talk to them. They only had masters there, and they were very free with hitting you when they got annoyed. In another prison I was in, a few years before I came here, a headmaster of an approved school came in one night to give a talk to the prisoners. He said as far as possible in his school, him and his wife tried to treat the boys as if they were their own. I thought that sounded much more right.

When I was sixteen I was sent home from approved school, I mean back to my own original home. I hardly knew my mother at all, because I hadn't seen her for so long. She hadn't ever visited me in the approved school because I think it was too far away for her to come. My step-father was the same as I remembered him from before, always noisy and shouting and hitting me for things. My mother was working as a cleaner in a cinema, and she used to take me along with her there when she went to work.

I never did any kind of proper job of my own, only gave her a hand now and again. In a few months I was in trouble with the police for trying to break into some cars on the cinema car-park; as a result of that I got sent for a period of borstal training. I hadn't actually succeeded in breaking into any of the cars, but I had been trying to.

Life in borstal was pretty terrible in my opinion. There was what they called a click of boys who were the hard and tough ones. If you didn't belong with them then you had to take a lot of knocking about if you wouldn't do things when they said. I was very small, and I was what was called a 'softie'. I also had a religious streak, which put me right out of favour with everyone. The Bible was my favourite book, and I preferred to read that to any other. I still do, I like the Bible very much: I always read something in it every night in my cell before I go to bed. I think what it says is true; everyone can be a good person and be saved in the end if they try. It doesn't matter how hard it is, it's up to you to keep on trying.

Excuse me, I'll have to go now, I was told I had to be back in the dining-room in time for tea. The officer in charge said if I wasn't he wouldn't keep anything for me. Would you mind if I stopped now and came to see you again tomorrow?

★

—Yesterday I was telling you of the borstal, wasn't I, how it was very hard and I didn't like it because I was the smallest one there? Then after about eighteen months, I think, I was let out from the borstal and somewhere had to be found for me to live. That was through my mother being dead. Oh I'm sorry, I thought I told you that yesterday. She'd died soon after I went to the borstal; I believe she had a cancer, so I was told.

I was put to live with a couple, a married couple who were very nice people. Something went wrong with that, I'm not sure what it was, I think they were removing from the district. Then I stayed in a boys' hostel for a while, and after that I moved on to some more people who had been friends of my mother's; they said they would have me and help me find a job. I worked for a bakery for a few weeks as an assistant roundsman, going out with a van driver and delivering the bread to different houses.

We started early in the morning, and we finished round about half-past five in the afternoon. I had a hobby, which was fishing, and I used to go to a reservoir near the town and fish in there on my half day. I should explain here I think that I had homosexual tendencies; I had indulged in homosexuality both at approved school and the borstal where it is more or less taken as the normal thing. One afternoon when I was at the reservoir a little boy came along on his own, he would be about ten or eleven, and I committed one of these offences on him.

I knew this to be wrong, and I made a special point the next Sunday of going to church and asking for forgiveness in my prayers. I felt this wasn't enough though, and that I ought to go and see the priest and tell him about it as well. On my next half-day, I went to the church in the afternoon, but there was no one there and the door was locked. Then I went back to where I lived and got my fishing-rod and I went to the reservoir again. Standing on the path exactly in the same place as I'd been the week before were two men in macin-toshes. They said they were police officers, detectives in plain clothes, and they asked me if I'd been there on the same day the week earlier. I said Yes I had, and they asked me if I had committed the offence and I said Yes, so then I was arrested.

When they took me to the police station they kept asking me if I'd done it before, and if so who had I done it to, and where. I said what was true; that I hadn't done it before to anyone. This was the offence for which I got the two years' imprisonment. I pleaded guilty but I didn't ask for any other cases to be taken into consideration because there weren't any. I served the sentence in a London prison. I asked for treatment or help of some kind, but I was told there wasn't any, it was up to me to go and see a doctor myself when I got out.

That's been one of the things I can't understand. When I did come out of prison, I felt alright. I thought I might do better up in the north again, and I got a job with a fairground, one of those sort that travel about to different places. For a long time it was true, I was better: there were none of these offences nor even any thoughts about committing them.

In one of the towns up there I met a girl, a very nice girl she was, who lived with her mother. I lodged with them. She already had a baby but someone had let her down; there was talk we might get married if I could find a decent job and we saved up a bit of money. I left the travelling fairground and went to work in a rag factory: it was hard but I was earning well, and everything seemed to be going along nicely. But then me and this girl started having rows, we were quarrelling more than we were getting on. It was winter time, and instead of going back to the house after dark, I started getting into the habit of going into people's gardens and looking through their windows. One man caught me and chased me away. He gave me a thump, so I went and reported it to the police; I told them I'd been assaulted in the alleyway by the side of this house, which was true. The police sent for him, and when he came he said I'd been trying to be a Peeping Tom. I hadn't, but they believed him. They told me to clear off, or else they'd charge me because they'd been having a lot of complaints from that area.

It was about a week after that incident that I went haywire. I was glad in a kind of way the police did catch me, because otherwise I don't know where it might have ended.

★

—The thing I like most about Grendon is that you're treated as though you were a human being and not just an animal. In other prisons you're always in danger from the other prisoners, but there's none of that here. I'm always spoken to politely and I always try to speak politely back. If I was treated like dirt, I don't think there'd be any hope for me. But I do think there might still be hope for me, if only a way can be found of putting me right. At my trial there was a medical practitioner who examined me while I was in prison on remand, and gave evidence he thought he could do something for me if the court would be prepared to let him try. The Judge said it was too late for that, I had to be punished and put away for the protection of society.

I don't know what the doctor had in mind: I've never seen him again. I think it might have been along similar lines to something called an 'implant', that you read about sometimes in the paper. I expect it would be rather like that; I would certainly be agreeable to them trying it on me if they wished. If there was any chance of a parole for me any time under conditions like that, perhaps they would consider doing it then.

But nobody seems able to say exactly what my chances are. So I think the best thing I can do is make sure I keep myself fit, get on with my work, and try and occupy my mind with work and the various activities which go on, such as helping with the scenery for the plays or going to the hobbies classes. About three years ago they were giving me a lot of drugs because I was getting so depressed; but they only seemed to make me feel worse. I think it's much better to keep yourself off them if you can. At the moment I've no trouble about sleeping or anything, and I think that's because of the exercises.

A man who went out last year left me his radio; he said I could have it for in my cell if I wanted. I've got very interested in listening to the various programmes for half an hour or so each evening before I go to sleep. Light music or records I like best. I think for someone in prison a radio is a very good friend.

No, there aren't any friends who come to see me; I have no visits from anyone, no. No, I don't get any letters; no, I've never had a Christmas card or a birthday card while I've been inside. No, not from anyone. No. I don't know anyone, you see.

STUCK[1]

Stanley Hart

'He's max max security,' said the guard, 'so I have to accompany you all the while. I won't be listening in but I'll be in earshot if you holler, OK?'

The windowless white-walled room was divided into two in the middle by a blue-painted floor-to-ceiling metal grille with an open wicket gate in it; a small table with two plain wooden chairs was on the other side. A small man with fair curly hair and rimless glasses, wearing overalls and a black sweatshirt, he came in through a door in the back wall. He had a firm handshake and a gentle smile, and his voice was low and quiet; he rested his elbows on the table while he talked.

★

—I'm doing two life sentences and three fixed sentences of fifteen years each, all of them running concurrently. Theoretically every one's a sentence which carries an opportunity for parole, but I think that's very unlikely for my type of case and it's not worth thinking about. I'm thirty-three years of age and so far I've put in six years and six months; no I beg your pardon, this week it's six years and seven months now. The earliest I could apply to be considered for parole would be when I've done thirteen years; like I say though I've no expectations of being given it, I shouldn't think I'd get out in anything less than twenty-five years if at all. Since it could be that I'll be incarcerated for the rest of my life there's no point in me speculating about it at this time. I try to keep it completely out of my mind. I'm successful at that, I do keep it out of my mind; whether it'll ever come back into it and what stage that'll be at I guess I wouldn't know.

---

1 *The Violence of Our Lives* (1996) London: HarperCollins, pp. 98–108.

I don't know whether you'd be interested to hear about my background at all? I come from a middle-class white-collar family and I have one sister, Marianne. My father I don't know about: I think he was a land surveyor, and when I was three and a half and my sister was six, my mother left him because he was continually physically abusive towards her. She's never talked about him much, so I don't know what became of him or really anything about him at all. Sometimes I think I'll ask my mother to give me more information but so far I never have. He's kind of like one of those secrets a family keeps in the closet: a lot of families have them, things they don't ever talk about, not even between themselves. I guess it might upset her if I did ask her about him: she's a terrific person and I sure wouldn't want to do anything like that. She comes to visit me twice a year all the way from New York, and a couple of times I've thought of asking her to tell me a bit about my father if the conversation went that way: but it never has somehow, so I've let it go by.

I'd want her to know as well that it's not I want to find him. I'm not one of those people who feel they must know where they come from or who they come from, and whether it's good or bad. You hear about children turning up and saying to their parent 'Hello, I'm your son' and then finding out they're drug addicts or if they're a woman they're a prostitute; afterwards the child wishes he didn't know. I don't have any fantasies about my father, whether he's a successful man and a millionaire, or possibly a drunk and a hobo: nothing at all. What it'd probably be anyway is the other way round: it's him wouldn't want to know about me if he knew my crime. I'll leave it like that, I always have done up to now: I can live with it that I've no mental picture of him of any kind.

My chief memory of my childhood, my young childhood that is, is of a lot of lonely times. My mother wasn't home mainly during the day: she had a job and worked because she had to have money to bring up my sister and I. All I have in the way of early childhood memories of people apart from my mother is of a woman who was our child minder for a time and used to come in to look after me and Marianne. I remember I didn't like her, I didn't like her at all, but I can't now say why: I don't recall she was cruel or hit us or anything like that. I know I was afraid of her though, perhaps afraid of her character or personality, the way kids sometimes are. I used to hide under my bed if I knew she was coming and hope she wouldn't find me: I think I hoped she'd think she'd lost me and feel bad about it, and my mother would take on someone else in her place instead. I expect she was quite a nice woman really, and my feelings were no different from the irrational ones lots of kids have. Kids do have those kind of fears: they don't understand adults, and often wonder what the hell's going on.

I'm not sure of the date or exactly how old I was, but my mother married again; and I distinctly recall my stepfather was someone I absolutely didn't care for at all. I remember him as a very remote kind of a guy who never spoke much, either to me or my sister. For a long time all I knew was I didn't like him without knowing why: but I gradually sensed in the way kids do that my mother wasn't all that happy with him either. I never saw him physically maltreat her but it was obvious I was right, because sometimes I heard her crying on her own when he wasn't there. It seems like she wasn't too good at choosing men for husbands when she was younger, because that marriage ended in divorce too. She's a very nice warm and caring person, but she sure did seem to have bad luck with men.

I guess it can't have been too easy for him either, having a wife who had two children already: I remember I myself gave him a hard time. Whether Marianne did or not I wouldn't know, but I do recall I deliberately made the effort not to be friendly towards him, and on top of that I cut up and behaved badly at school. I suppose a child psychologist might diagnose it as me trying to get my mother's attention or something of that kind. I know it reached a point where my stepfather said he couldn't cope with me any more and what I needed was the kind of discipline which he couldn't exert. So I was sent away to a military school then, where I was for a year. They taught you things like marching and weapon handling at a junior level, the idea being you'd go on from there when you were old enough directly into the military. That idea never appealed to me; and when my mother gave up on that marriage too and divorced him I was glad, because it meant I could go back and live again like normal at home.

She married for a third time eighteen years ago when I was fifteen, and this time she got it right. They're still together and he's a nice guy who treats her well; and I know he's been a lot of support to her all through the grief I've brought her, so he must be OK. I can't say I know him well or know much about him except through her, but he sounds to be a good guy, which is the least she deserves.

To go back on my background a bit more, I was never any good at school, either in my lessons or in sport. The reason for it I put down to the fact they taught nothing at school about the only subject in the world I've ever been interested in, which is motor cars. Right from when I can ever first remember, my ambition and my only aim was to be a racing-car driver. On my sixteenth birthday I got my driver's licence, and though I went to adult education college for a while after high school, still my unchangeable idea was the same. I don't think it was an unrealistic ambition either: I think I'd have made a very good racing driver if it hadn't been for what I did and where I now am. I was always crazy about automobiles: all I've ever read in my life has been magazines about cars, and I'm still the same. My mother sends me a couple of titles every month and I read them and reread them from beginning to end: I don't miss out on one single word, including the small print classifieds which tell you the latest prices of second-hand cars, and what people are offering which of them privately for sale.

When I left college, or rather when I dropped out of it, it was because I wanted to strike out and live my life on my own. I worked at several different garages as a mechanic to earn myself a living, and whenever I could find the time all I ever did then was practise driving. I wasn't crazy enough to think of myself as an Indy driver, I was just happy in auto-cross or track racing at a local level, everything of that sort. Now and again I won some local contest or small championship, and I know if I hadn't come to prison I'd have made myself a good career. The secret was hard work and practise practise practise all the time, developing your skills and identifying your weaknesses and improving your control of them at both ends of the scale.

One special interest I had as a mechanic was in foreign cars, especially British and European ones. I had a little green MG I was very proud of, and I also enjoyed Volvos, Renaults and Volkswagens, and I specialised in repairs and maintenance of those. Anything that was a bit out of the ordinary and different from our American cars always fascinated me: I'd strip down an engine and then very carefully reassemble it again to make sure I knew every detail of it and exactly how it worked: I always bought and read every manual about every make and model of foreign car I could find. In automobile engineering it doesn't greatly matter what your high school grades in conventional subjects were: what counts is how much you know about the insides of engines and how much experience you've had of handling them. I got so I could tell just from listening to one while it was running whether it was OK or not, and if it wasn't OK where the likely trouble was. Places I worked, other mechanics used to joke with me about it: a guy'd come in and he'd say there was something wrong with his Beetle, it was going 'whurr whurr', and I'd say 'Is it going "whurr whurr" or is it going "whurr whurr whurr"?' He'd say

'Well, "whurr whurr",' and I'd say 'Yeah well it sounds to me like you've got carburettor trouble' and usually I was right.

One big problem I had though was that being a good specialised mechanic and knowing that I was, I had what might be called an unfortunate tendency to always tell whoever the foreman might be in a repair garage where I worked that if some particular foreign engine was concerned, he didn't know what he was talking about. The thing is he usually didn't, and I did; but I'd put it across to him the wrong way and make a monkey out of him in front of everyone. That sort of thing didn't make me well liked, and usually a foreman'd take the first opportunity that presented itself to get rid of me.

I had trouble of the same sort with driving too: I'd no problem with the basics like keeping my head and waiting till the last split-second to brake or make a gear change, and I never lost my cool. But I was very impatient and argumentative with officialdom, and I was always ignoring rules and regulations about how many practice laps were permitted and doing more. When I was reprimanded about it, my usual response was to go back and do the same thing again the next day, so I was perpetually getting into quarrels with the organ-isers and officials of events I'd entered for. This did nothing for my reputation: more than once I was refused application to register and compete. One time I got a year's suspension from racing throughout the entire state where we lived and got around it by travelling long distances to go to meetings elsewhere. But often before long I'd get into the same sort of trouble there. I was never ever barred because I was a bad or dangerous driver; I wasn't and no one could ever say I was. But several places I wasn't allowed to compete because I wouldn't obey the officials and their rules.

Both these factors made life difficult for me: I was a good mechanic but always getting fired for speaking out of turn, and I was a good driver but one who wasn't allowed in an increasing number of events. Finally the solution was to start my own business, so I bought a big truck which I converted into a mobile repair shop fully equipped for servicing at a level very few other mechanics could offer. I drove around the country in it, stopping off any place I could find where there was an event. I'd tune engines and service vehicles, and also when I could I'd sneak into races, driving under an assumed name. I wasn't bothered about winning, or whether I came third or tenth or seventeenth: all that mattered was the joy I got from driving. That was a very good life and I was on top of the world. I was my own boss, I was doing what I wanted to and nothing else but what I wanted to, it was absolutely terrific. And it lasted for all of six years, the happiest time of my life it was: but then I was arrested and came to prison.

—In court I faced five counts on indictment, all of the same kind: forcible homosexual sodomy with boys of nine, ten and eleven years of age. I drew two life sentences plus three fixed ones of fifteen years. The boys concerned were all boys I'd known and been sexually active with for some considerable length of time, and I'd been friends with their families and parents and so on. I pleaded guilty to all the charges.

I'm honestly in no way trying to excuse myself about this, but the word that did sadden me very much in the indictments was that word 'forcible': it was completely unjustified. The boys were my friends, I liked them and I never ever in any way compelled any of them to perform the acts. Unfortunately though, the law says anyone who's aged thirteen or under isn't able to make a responsible decision for himself, so therefore any adult involved has to have used force. You can't put up a defence they were willing or at least didn't object to having it done.

My first sexual experiences in life were when I was six or seven, and they were all homosexual ones, that is they were all with other boys. From what few people I've ever been able to talk to about it, I don't think this is unusual at all. As a small boy, if you're a certain type, you not only don't understand girls but you're scared of them: they always seem to stay in groups whispering and sniggering among themselves, and when you hear and see them doing it you usually think it's about you. At least I always did. You're very shy and vulnerable and unsure of yourself, particularly with a subject as intimate and embarrassing as sex: the only people you can talk to about it with are other boys, which is because you know their feelings will be the same. Boys are people you feel safe with, you don't feel safe with girls.

I guess what I mean by safe is that you can fool around together, you can even touch one another's sexual organs; but as a boy you can't do that and you mustn't do that with girls. It's a fairly safe bet no other boy's going to go running to complain to his parents if you try to put your hand inside his shorts: he'll either tell you not to if he doesn't like it, or if he does like it he maybe'll try to do the same to you, with perhaps both of you doing it to each other at the same time. Either way though it'll be part of joking around and it's more likely than not that you will both be laughing about it. But try and do it with a girl, try and get your hands inside her panties and make out it's a joke, and she'll straight away tell her parents or a teacher you were trying to touch her up. Her parents'll tell your parents or your teacher will, and right there you'll be made to feel you've done something terrible you ought to be real ashamed of yourself for. I've never tried myself to do it to a girl, but that's how a kid would think about it I feel: it certainly wouldn't be something you could take a chance on.

I guess it's a subject I've been mixed up about as long as I can remember, because sexual playing around with other boys my own age was something I had no problems with, ever. I enjoyed it, and it never seemed like it was doing either me or them any harm. And I've always stayed that way; and from what I can gather that's the main difference between me and other men. As I understand it they undergo a complete change in their early teens. Whether it's gradual or suddenly overnight or what I don't know; but apparently they lose all interest in getting their hands into other boys' pants and want to get them into girls'. I don't know the right word to use about it, but I didn't change or develop or whatever the word is: I just stuck where I was and continued the rest of my life to only want to do it with boys.

The other additional way I didn't mature, but I'm not so sure that's a correct word either, again is as I understand it your liking and your sexual desire for physical contact grows along in parallel with your age. Mostly the people you want to indulge in sexual activity with, give or take a few years either way and in the usual run of cases, are the same age as you are. But that didn't happen with me either. I've always stayed stuck on liking little boys. In my late teens and early twenties I wasn't attracted at all to boys or young men of my own age. If I had been I'd have been OK, because of the age of consent: but I didn't and I wasn't, and that brought down on me not only contempt and despising from most of society, but also the full wrath and retribution of the law. So that makes me stuck again: I'm stuck in two ways.

I'll say one other thing as well, though it's a tricky area to talk about: most people can't bear even to think about it, least of all give it houseroom in their ideas. If you sound like you're even getting anywhere near getting around to it, it makes people nearly burst a blood vessel or have a major heart attack or something of that sort. I'll try and say it carefully: it's that if you're a grown man and you have a predilection for sex with little boys, you don't have to search the length and breadth of the United States to find some who're not too reluctant about letting you indulge. Some of them might actually quite like it as well.

There's a book I believe was a big best-seller and a film too, about an elderly guy who met an eleven- or twelve-year-old schoolgirl who didn't mind all that much at all when he had sexual fantasies about her, she almost once or twice gave him a come-on. I haven't read it, it was called *Lolita* I think; and after the first fuss died down the author won some big award. He certainly gained a lot of respect and kudos for it, I do know that: I think it's studied in universities as an English text too. That book was published all of twenty years or more ago; but no one's dared risk writing a similar sort of thing yet about a man and a little boy.

This whole thing's a big no-no of a subject even to try and talk about, because like I say if you try to start in on it people absolutely don't want to know. They think you're trying to excuse yourself or justify yourself or whatever; only me, I see it as a very interesting subject, naturally, and one I've felt often I'd like to express my feelings about. From very young my sexual orientation and desires have been only for young boys, and because I am what I am and who I am, it seems natural and normal when I express that in a physical way. But no one accepts that: yet I can't feel any different, even if I wanted to, which I don't. It's part of my whole personality and nature, and a very important and solid part. But I've truly never forced myself on anyone.

When I came to prison I had some psychiatric tests and counselling, and I was passed on to a man who told me if I co-operated I could be treated and cured. That made me very angry: he was talking of my homosexual behaviour with boys as though it was some kind of illness I could recover from and be like everyone else, which to me meant I should agree that in some way I was abnormal. I can't do that, I can't change a whole slice of my nature that seems perfectly normal as far as I'm concerned. In early Greek civilisation, which was one of the highest forms of society that's ever been attained, love for young boys and the physical expression of it was accepted by everyone. I think the boys were called neophytes, I'm not sure; but I've never found a dictionary yet that'll admit that definition to that word. Only this is another instance where as soon as you start to talk about it, everybody thinks what you're doing is special pleading on your own behalf. So I'm stuck that way too, because I don't accept there's anything wrong with homosexual feelings towards young boys.

There's one thing I do have to accept, I know, which is that whatever way I might look at it myself, society doesn't agree with me; and rather than compromise about it, society's prepared to put me to death, which is what it's done in incarcerating me here for ever, or until I'm too old and feeble to raise even a walking stick, never mind an erection. And although I know it, I don't see how I'm ever going to be able to do anything about it, because it would be like betraying myself. But there was one guy, he came to see me last year, I think he was a psychiatrist; and he did manage to engage my brain about it even though he's nothing like yet won my heart. He said OK he could accept me as a homosexual who was attracted to very young boys, he had no problems with that, and he was very insistent that I shouldn't have either. I said to him all this stuff about changing my nature and my character that I've been saying to you, and he said to me 'Listen to me now Stanley,' he said, 'you don't have to change at all. You just stay right like you are and don't let anyone persuade you your feelings are wrong or evil or any of that. They aren't, they're really not: for you they're entirely normal, just like you said.'

But, he said, there was a very big 'but' I should remember too: and I should work on it and try to bring myself around to it in my own good time. It was that what I said was all fine, but society didn't agree with me – as far as they were concerned I should be locked up and I could rot for ever in hell. So what was the answer? I said 'Go on then tell me, because I'm sure I don't know.' He said the answer to the whole situation could be summed up in one word, and that word was 'control'. There was no reason I should give up having my feelings, but what I had to find a way of doing for my own sake if nobody else's, was how to control them so they wouldn't bring me into such violent conflict with society that I might as well resign from life right here and now. I thought he was quite a guy, he was the first person I'd ever really met who seemed to have the smallest insight into the way I felt about things. He could even joke about it too: he said the ideal would be for me to be transported in time and space back to ancient Greece so's I could start a new and enjoyable life there. But when we'd had a smile about that, he went on further: he said since how to do that kind of time travel was something we hadn't cracked yet, the next best thing was to think about the alternative which we'd been talking about, which was control. He gave me details of what very few prison programmes there were, and where, which would take me in on them and start the long slow process towards achieving it, so's I reached the point where other people didn't control me by locking me up or injecting me with hormones or threatening me with dire retribution, but where I controlled myself on my own.

That did sound like sense to me, so for several weeks I gave it a lot of thought: in the finish I decided there was nothing else for it, I might as well give it a go. I applied through the official channels to three prisons before I found one which said they'd accept me, and when they did as you can imagine I was quite pleased. I thought well even if I went on the programme and the end result was failure, at least I'd have found it interesting; and in some ways it'd have confirmed whether I was right to look at myself the way I did, or whether who knows I might even change my mind.

In the stupendously bureaucratic penal system we have, you don't get a reply to a letter or written application till several months at the earliest after you've forgotten you wrote it; but I did hear eventually somehow or other that it could all go ahead. Which brings me to the dilemma I have now. The programme which'll take me runs for four years: and it's designed in such a way its end coincides with release, only under supervision of course, which they provide. That's the only way they can properly test whether it's worked. What they won't do is take someone on the programme and then put them back into prison again at the end of it. So they said what I had to do was apply to the Parole Board to set a release date: it wouldn't matter if it was ten years or twenty years from now, but the programme had to know it so the date I was put to start on it synchronised. The answer I got from the Board when I wrote that to them was they weren't prepared to give a date unless the programme director told them definitely when my treatment would be completed successfully. He wasn't prepared to say that: so here I am between the two of them, and neither will agree. What will happen now, I've no idea: nothing, I suppose. It's the same thing again though: what am I? Stuck.

The guard accompanied me across the compound back to the search room in the administration block. I thought it worth a try.

'What's max max,' I said, 'and why's he in it?'

'A classification,' he said. 'It means he's in a special maximum security unit which is inside a maximum security prison. I only came here three days ago from North State Correctional Facility so I wouldn't know why he's in it though. You from England? That's a place I'd really like to go. Do you have hot weather like this there?'

Part V

FRAUDS AND FALSE PRETENCE MERCHANTS

Frauds have always been widespread. Historically the law has been rather feeble and the police have rarely given quite the same attention to what is loosely termed as 'white-collar crime' as most other criminal activities. Certainly those few persons who are convicted of major fraud are generally treated leniently compared with offenders from the 'criminal class'. However, most of the frauds and the false pretence merchants whom Tony Parker interviewed seemed to straddle – with a greater or lesser degree of success – between the 'straight' and 'deviant' worlds. They are in both worlds but are not fully 'captured' by either world.

Parker describes his own antipathy towards offenders convicted of fraud and false-pretences. Yet he fails to clarify the reasons for this antipathy. It is probably because one can never be very confident that one has probed below the surface when one talks to men and women whose criminal livelihood is predicated on impression management. Has one also been fooled?

Bernie produces a bravura performance for the microphone, insisting on being dressed in a clean pair of prison overalls for the occasion. In contrast, one senses that talking to Miss McDonald over a much longer period was a much more enjoyable experience. Interestingly, though, Tony never reached the familiarity of first name terms. Frauds and false pretence merchants seem to want to keep part of themselves hidden.

THE F.P. MERCHANTS[1]

Everyone, I suppose, has his own idea of what constitutes 'the worst crime of all', and what type of 'criminal' he would least like to have to do with. For many years to me the worst crime has always seemed that of fraud and false-pretences, and the sort of offender I have had the least enthusiasm to try and get to know and possibly to write about, has been anyone referred to as 'f. and f.p.' or 'an f.p. merchant'. Murderers, rapists, child-molesters, embezzlers, ponces, drug-pedlars, parents guilty of cruelty to children – none of these cause my blood even faintly to stir; abhorrent and dreadful though their actual crimes may have been, offenders in any of these categories I have met have invariably been likeable and easy to grow fond of.

Unavoidably over the years I have had some contact with a number of false-pretenders, both inside and outside of prison. Many prison governors develop a particularly soft spot for them, and have sometimes tried to arouse my interest in certain individuals they had in their prisons at the time. 'He's a most fluent talker', or 'He can go on spinning the most fantastic tales for hours' have been the most common recommendations. Of course, prison governors do not find much entertainment in their daily routine, so that anyone who provides it is understandably regarded with some affection.

A typical example of such an experience was told me a few years ago by a governor who was and still is a great friend; he was trying once more to arouse my interest in this type of offender and repeating how intriguing it would be if someone could get behind their impenetrable façade and really discover any indications in their life stories of how they possibly came to be what they were. There

1 *The Frying Pan* (1970) London: Hutchinson, pp. 100–2.

was at that moment in his prison, he said, an absolutely perfect example of an 'f. and f.p.' who was shortly to be discharged.

An elderly grey-haired man of distinguished appearance and impeccably restrained manner of speech, he had behind him a long record of previous convictions for fraud and false-pretences. During his time in prison he had, typically, been no trouble to anyone; and his education and intelligence suited him for a fairly responsible clerical position in the prison administration office where, like so many others of his type elsewhere, he functioned as a kind of *maître-d'hôtel* without whose efficiency the day-to-day running of the prison would probably disintegrate into chaos. He had been there for years giving no cause whatsoever for complaint nor ever making one.

The governor had therefore been somewhat astonished to see him appearing in front of him in his office one morning during his daily session of adjudicating on prisoners' applications for changes of labour, for additional letters to assist them in trying to straighten out their domestic affairs, with allegations of minor infringements of what few rights they had, and all the other usual matters which prisoners insist on 'putting in to see the governor' about.

White-faced with fury, and in a voice agitated so much by suppressed anger that he could scarcely control himself to speak when he was invited to, the distinguished-looking elderly gentleman stood to attention before the Governor's desk, looked him straight in the eye and said: 'I wish to register a protest in the strongest possible terms about the decline in discipline which you are responsible for upholding in this prison, and the general falling-off in standards in the type of prisoner you are now accepting here.'

'Do you?' said the Governor, hoping he was maintaining that impassivity of countenance for which Prison Governors Class One are rigorously combat-trained both by years of experience and training, and even, it is sometimes suggested, by specific breeding. 'Really? Why?'

'Because' said the distinguished-looking elderly gentleman, his voice now better controlled because he was at last face-to-face with the one other person in the prison who could be relied upon to meet integrity with integrity, 'I regret to have to inform you that last evening when I was in the "Quiet Room" on K Wing during the free-association period, sitting there alone and writing a letter to my older sister, I had occasion to leave the room for a few moments to go to the toilet; and when I returned, I discovered that some prisoner had been into that room and helped himself to my fountain pen. I searched high and low to see if by any chance it could have fallen off the table and rolled out of sight somewhere on the floor, but I assure you it was nowhere to be found. I regret to have to make this accusation, Governor', he ended in tones of scandalised pain, 'but the conclusion is plain. There are thieves in this prison.'

The Governor lowered his eyes for a moment or two's contemplation of the blank blotter on his desk; then, when he was absolutely certain they would not reveal even a momentary indication that he failed to appreciate the truly hideous seriousness of the situation, he lifted them again.

'I am very sorry indeed to hear about this' he said. 'And I assure you I will have exhaustive enquiries made, in an effort for it to be recovered for you and the guilty person suitably punished.'

'Thank you, Governor' said the distinguished-looking elderly gentleman. Entirely satisfied that such words from so eminent a person could be relied upon, he turned to go.

'Erm – just one moment' said the Governor, anxious to savour to the last every element of the true delicacy of the situation: 'Had this fountain pen any particular personal, should we say "sentimental", value to you?'

'Certainly not' said the elderly gentleman, now on his way out of the office and more anxious not to waste another moment of the Governor's important time than to add anything further to trying to create an impression. 'It was a perfectly ordinary gold Schaeffer, that's all.'

WHITE-SLAVE TRAFFICKING[1]

Bernie

Bernie was possibly the least 'prisonised' inhabitant of Grendon; his whole demeanour and the manner of his talk unfailingly hinted that it was really an unfortunate error on the part of the judiciary ever to have put him in prison at all. Short, plump and middle-aged, his entirely bald head made him look much older than he actually was. He claimed to be 'just turned forty', but on the other hand, his life's experiences had been so extensive and varied that you couldn't help wondering how, by that age, he had managed to include them all.

There was always a kind of sweep and grandeur about even the most casual of his autobiographical reminiscences. In conversation against the subdued background noise from his radio of one of the endless and apparently eternal programmes of records played by disc-jockeys, he would suddenly break off and turn up the volume at the voice of a female singer. 'Know who that is? I'd recognise her anywhere; it's Edith Piaf. Haven't heard one of her records for ages, I wonder what's become of her? Mmm, Edith Piaf, well, well: do you know, I once travelled all the way with her from Istanbul to Paris on the Orient Express...' It meant no more, and probably considerably less, than the fact that at some stage of the journey he had perhaps been on the same train as the famous *chanteuse* and cabaret star; but the way Bernie threw it off, it conveyed instantaneously the suggestion that the two of them had made the one and a half thousand mile journey in its entirety, alone throughout in the same compartment.

Whereas other prisoners made merely parochial comparisons favourable or unfavourable, between where they were now and Parkhurst, Dartmoor, Wandsworth or Durham, Bernie's judgements were always on an international scale. 'Some of the French gaols are

1 *The Frying Pan* (1970) London: Hutchinson, pp. 117–19, 121–6.

unbelievable,' he would say: 'you should certainly try to get a look at one or two of those. Or even the Swiss ones; however high their reputation might be for having a clean and civilised country compared with the rest of Europe, you can take it from me that their prisons are at least a hundred years behind everyone else's. And if you ever see the inside of an Australian prison, like the one in Sydney for instance; well, it simply defies description.'

His wry cynical humour enlivened any occasion he was present at. One of the monthly features of Grendon was known as the 'Any Questions' Meeting. When these were held, outside visitors who happened to be in the prison on those days were expected, as a mark of reciprocal politeness, to attend an hour-long free-for-all in which any prisoners who felt inclined to do so could ask them whatever they wished or say anything to them that they chose. The average attendance figure of prisoners was about thirty (considerably higher however on the days when visitors included any young female). For the first few weeks while I was there, and until the men had grown accustomed to my presence, I was submitted to a regular barrage of queries such as 'What exactly is it you're here to do?', 'Whose side are you on?', 'How many copies of your books are sold in a year?', 'How much money do you make from writing about prisoners?', 'What do you think of this place now you've been here a few weeks?', 'What does you wife feel about you being here all the time instead of at home?' and similar questions.

After the initial period of interest in me and my presence had subsided, and all prisoners' questions had been answered either satisfactorily or unsatisfactorily, thereafter I used to attend the meeting primarily for the pleasure of hearing one of Bernie's occasional interpolations, or watching the skill with which he and a few of the other regulars quickly tied up some earnest young social work student in knots.

On one occasion one of the visitors present was a rather (to me at least) frightening-looking lady magistrate with formidable poise and *sang-froid*. After a short time she hit upon the stratagem of retaliating against everyone who asked her something by following her own answer with a sharp: 'Right, I've answered one question of yours. Now you answer one of mine. What are you yourself in here for?'

The answers came back briefly, almost laconically: 'drugs', 'housebreaking', 'taking and driving away cars', 'larceny'. Knowing what they could expect to be asked themselves if they said anything several who might have spoken remained silent, apart from a couple of the renowned 'hard-nuts', who positively enjoyed the opportunity of being able to toss back at her off-handedly their response of 'robbery with violence' or 'armed robbery and using a firearm to resist arrest.' But discussion inevitably began to flag for want of contributors. Then one public-school-accented young man asked her something, and as soon as she had answered and then followed up immediately with her standard query as to why *he* was there, replied blandly: 'Because of an overflowing pen.' Before she could open her mouth to ask for elaboration he added: 'It kept writing "Pay Bearer" on dud cheques.'

There were only a few sniggers, since most of the prisoners had heard it before. But up at the top of the room, Bernie put his hands on the arms of his chair and leaned forward magisterially. 'If you'll forgive me for saying so, I consider that damned effrontery on your part, Roger', he said. 'Have you forgotten that it was *I* who originally cracked that gag? I don't mind you using it, but at least if you do, you might have the courtesy to acknowledge where you got it from, especially when I'm actually present.'

He then turned to the lady magistrate himself. 'There is one interesting question I'd like to put to you, madam', he said. 'Could you explain to us how it is that every single one of the magistrates who ever comes here, including yourself, is of the enlightened, reasonable and totally unprejudiced kind? Aren't there any of the other sort left these days? Or is it just that in my own experience I've been peculiarly unlucky with those I've come up in front of? Oh and by the way' he added, 'to save you the trouble of enquiring afterwards, I'm in here myself for white-slave trafficking.'

★

When I eventually asked him if he would care to come and have a few tape-recorded conversations with me, and suggested the following Wednesday as a suitable first day, Bernie said with his usual poker-face and only an unsuppressed glitter in his eyes to make it clear this was a joke: 'Could we make it Thursday? I get my weekly issue of clean overalls that morning, and I know you'd expect me to look my smartest for the occasion.'

—Well as I believe I've mentioned to you once or twice before, I'm in for gambling. I'm an addict, what's known as a compulsive gambler, I have been nearly all my life. I don't know why it should be, but I'm completely incapable of resisting—

—Just a minute Bernie; I'm sorry, but would you mind making a fresh start? You know and I know, and you know that I know, that there's no such offence as 'gambling' which you can be convicted for. So could you possibly begin again please?

—Oh yes of course, I do apologise. Please forgive me; but you know how it is, you get into the habit of saying something and you come out with it automatically without thinking. It's cheques actually; cashing dud cheques, getting money by false pretences. What I meant though was that it was always to obtain ready cash for gambling; that was the reason perpetually at the back of it. But you're perfectly right to pull me up about it; as you said when you asked me to come and talk to you, it would be no use unless we stuck absolutely to the facts.

Right, now then, I'll begin again. My offences are fraud and false pretences. How do you mean, the largest single cheque that I've ever cashed that was a dud: do you mean here in this country, or abroad? Well in England I wouldn't say it wasn't for more than three or four grand at the outside. Pardon? Look, I thought you were supposed to know all the prison slang, where've you been all your life? Yes, a 'grand' does mean a thousand. No, of course there was no trouble in passing a cheque of that size: you've got to remember I was in a good class of business, textiles and jewellery, sums like that are changing hands every day, every hour almost.

Abroad, honestly, I couldn't tell you, because it was always francs or marks or dinars, I've forgotten all the correct conversion rates now. I would think it was probably about the same sum or somewhere near its equivalent in English money.

The largest single bet I've ever had? Hmm…you mean as one bet? I should think it would be perhaps eighty-five, nine hundred pounds; I can't remember any four-figure bets, not as a separate stake. I've won and lost much more in total in an evening's play in a casino, of course. I'd say about three thousand pounds at roulette in one night is about the biggest sum I've ever won; and I promptly lost it all and more, the next day when I went back again. Gambling debts? My God, if it was those, I'd be doing nine-hundred and ninety-nine years. As a bookie I'm officially warned-off every racecourse in the country, and as a gambler I'm known anywhere you like to mention, from the smartest casino in Beirut to the crummiest basement in the Euston Road.

Well, you're by no means the first person who's asked me that question, believe me; I only wish I knew what the answer was. What can I tell you? Wherever I am, northern hemisphere or southern, when I get into my car and switch on the ignition, all I need to do after that is sit back; it drives itself to the nearest point where there's gambling of any kind going on. I'm only a short chap like you; but when I'm at a table or on a course, I feel as though I'm ten feet tall. I never get depressed about losing, if I go down I'm instantly thinking what I'm going to make the next bet. I just persevere and persevere and try to win; and then if I do get onto a good streak I'll carry on until every penny of it's lost. And if they'll give me credit, I'll go on until I've lost that too.

Once in a while, yes, I do say 'That's enough, I'll stop now' when I'm winning. I say it, but I don't do anything about it; it's true as you say there is almost a compulsion to lose. Perhaps I'm not very imaginative; but at the time it honestly never strikes me I'm inevitably going to end up with nothing, anymore than it does that I'm not going to be able to meet a cheque. I can convince myself in a split-second that by the time it's presented I shall have won more than enough to cover it.

I've all the time got this feeling about the sands running out, do you know what I mean? Everything has to be quick; the money has to be actually in my hands, the bet has to be placed, another one to recoup it has to be on its way before the first one's even come unstuck, another cheque's got to be cashed for money to cover the first one. It's like that, on and on without stopping, as though there's only a few hours of my life left.

Perhaps it's because I was so late in starting, do you think? I never took to crime of any kind at all until I was thirty.

★

—My family background is absolutely respectable, utterly ordinary upper middle-class Jewish. I was the only son, for that matter the only child, of a successful textile wholesaler in the East End. By which I mean that's where his business was; we ourselves lived in a big house in one of the posh 'dormitory' towns as they're called, outside London. I think I was terribly spoilt as a youngster, certainly I wanted for nothing, and I had a good education at a private school.

There was never any lack of love and affection: I don't know if you know it or not, but Jewish families are very close-knit, there's always a big group of uncles and aunties and relatives all round. And there was never any doubt either about my future. I knew that when the time came I'd join my father in his business; that was the expected and natural thing to do. I'd no feelings of resentment about it; I thought myself what I was when I was twenty, a very lucky young man. Perhaps I was a bit lonely and solitary in that I never went out with girls much, they didn't greatly interest me. But that doesn't mean I'd any homosexual inclinations; as far as I'm aware I was then, and still am, normally heterosexual. As often happens in thousands of other families, I was content to wait until a nice suitable Jewish young lady from a good background came along.

Perhaps things would have turned out differently if one had, but I rather doubt it. If I'd been married with a home of my own by the time I was thirty, I expect I'd have lost that too, in the same way as through my activities my parents eventually lost their home and my father's business had to be sold to pay off some of my gambling debts.

The onset of the fever, as you might call it, was gradual and began when I was around twenty-nine. First it was dogs and horses and football pools, then it was casinos and gambling clubs; anything and everything that anyone was offering to take odds about, I was there. As I said, soon it was bouncing cheques all over the place to get hold of cash, going abroad to escape the consequences, gambling there and then having to move on to somewhere else.

I've had nine months, twelve months, eighteen months, two years, three years, all under my own name in this country. In addition I've done a fair bit of time elsewhere abroad, France, Switzerland, Sydney and so on. I honestly couldn't add them all up for you Tony, really I couldn't. I wish you wouldn't keep asking me to do these sums: you don't have to be a mathematical genius to be a gambler, you know.

Incredible though it is after all I've done to them, my parents still keep in touch with me and visit me occasionally. Jewish people are usually very devoted to their children, you'll find as a rule; and mine are no exception. I'd like to tell them, just as I'd like to tell you, that from now on I'm giving up gambling for ever. But it's not true, I've no desire to stop it at all. What I would like to do is moderate it, keep it within limits, so that it doesn't get me mixed up in frauds and false pretences charges all the time, but – I say, excuse me, but is your watch right? Then would you excuse me if we broke off here? I've just got time to get back down to the Wing and hear the result of the Jubilee Handicap at Kempton Park: I've got two packets of Spangles on it with one of the officers.

★

—The thing I detest most about this or any other prison for that matter is what is called 'nick culture'. I won't have any part of it. Crime, I don't know, it's the only subject of conversation most prisoners seem to have. They talk about 'doing your bird', 'being banged up by a screw' and all the rest of it. I don't want to know, I don't like to hear people talking like that, it annoys me. I'm not anti-authority, I don't call the officers 'screw' even behind their backs; it wouldn't worry me if I saw three hundred outside my door when I opened it every morning. They're just people, and very nice people some of them, not symbols of some authority I'm setting myself against, just because they're wearing uniforms. I think no differently of them than I did in one of the Swiss prisons where I was once, where all the officers wore civilian clothes.

I think this is quite a good place: it's certainly a very interesting one, because you get such a wide variety of different types of offender here. You hear them talking at meetings and even though most of what they say is rubbish, they're not the type of person you'd come across outside; or at least if you did, they wouldn't be opening their mouths quite so wide about what they've done as they're prepared to do here.

I meant to be more reserved when I first arrived; but now on occasions I do actually join in if the discussion's on a fairly sensible level. So it does have some effect, this place, in drawing you out of yourself a bit. For instance I very much doubt whether I'd even have been prepared to sit and chat with you if you'd met me in some other prison.

Perhaps that might minimise the chances of my coming back. What improvements would I like to see, what do you mean? In the running of the prison? Well, on the whole I think it is very well run; we've got to remember it's a maximum-security place, it has to be because of some of the people they've got here. Perhaps a little bit more freedom inside; but not too much, I'm not one of those who doesn't believe in a bit of discipline, in fact I think they tend to be a bit too slack about that here.

On the other hand they've a fairly high standard of staff, which I think is good. And it's not all male, which is an excellent idea; I think it's nice to see one or two women around the place. Apart from what I said a few moments ago about a bit more freedom, I don't think I've any serious criticisms at all. Give you a concrete example of what I mean? Yes, all right: I've got a very nice silk dressing-gown locked up in my personal property which they took off me when I came in. That's the only thing that slightly irritates me: I really can't see any reason on earth why I shouldn't be allowed to have it in the evening to wear while I'm having a read before going to bed, alone in the privacy of my cell.

★

Only once did I know Bernie in any way more than 'slightly irritated'. It was when, after he had been talking about his Jewishness at some length, I asked him whether in view of his own wide experience and knowledgeability, he could throw any light on the curious fact that there were proportionately fewer Jews in prison, compared with their incidence in the country's population, than of any other group or denomination. That was not correct, he said quickly: there were no grounds at all for assuming that crime occurred less among Jews than anyone else.

Yes there were, I insisted: every year the official figures issued by the Home Office in the Prison Department's Annual Report showed it. Complete bloody nonsense, he told me flushing bad-temperedly; I had misread them or I hadn't understood them properly. In fact he hoped I would forgive him for saying so, but it was astonishing that any apparently intelligent person such as myself shouldn't immediately suspect, when faced with figures of this kind, that the totals must be wrong, if not actually deliberately fabricated in order to mislead.

By then his equanimity was re-established and his humour began quickly to reassert itself. Perhaps I might find if I went into it very carefully and without letting anyone know what I was doing, he suggested with a glint in his eye, that all the officials in the department at the Home Office responsible for compiling and issuing these particular figures were themselves Jewish.

I laughed, and shook my head. Oh well, he volunteered finally, he was correct in his assumption, wasn't he, that my knowledge of prisons outside Great Britain was very slight? Quite so: and he could assure me from his own much wider experience throughout the rest of the world that in all other countries there were proportionately as many Jews in prison as there were distributed throughout the population outside. Even while he was propounding this, the final clinching argument had already struck him. He ended with a smile: 'And look at Israel. I understand that there nearly ninety-nine percent of the prison population is Jewish. Isn't that correct?'

I'VE BEEN VERY LUCKY[1]

Miss McDonald

FRAUD
AGE: *40*
NUMBER OF CONVICTIONS: *9*
TOTAL TIME SPENT IN PRISON: 7 *years* 4 *months*

'Thoroughly spoilt', 'spineless', 'weak willed', 'easily led' – pejoratives like these have been used liberally and frequently, since the early days of her long history of law-breaking, in assessments of Miss McDonald's character by the judiciary and penologists.

The primary source for this aetiology of a criminal career, however, is not impersonal insight. It is Miss McDonald herself: and she had used and repeated these and several other similar phrases within the first quarter of an hour of our meeting. She has said them and heard them said about herself so often now they have become an almost spontaneous response to questioning, used to construct a self-perpetuating explanation of the inexplicable. For to Miss McDonald, life has always been too difficult and complex to deal with. Some of her attempts to do so would make subjects for high comedy if their results were not so inevitably and disastrously self-destructive.

She lived with a cheerful chubby and hard-working man, whose wife deserted him some years ago, in a small neat house in an impeccable suburban road. Tall, with slender long legs, beautiful auburn hair, large brown eyes and a pale and flawless complexion, she carried herself with a willowy grace and dignity that complemented the gently undulating cadences of her quiet Lowland Scots voice. She talked happily about herself, often with animated and enthusiastic

1 *Five Women* (1965) London: Hutchinson, pp. 108–38.

denigration, in sentences which were at times as elaborately tautologous and labyrinthine as any of Henry James'.

Perhaps it is this habit, more than any true characteristic, which has earned her the appellation 'spineless'. Certainly at many times she is unsure what course of action – if any – to commit herself to: out of a desire to please she agrees with all the good advice, however impossible of attainment, which she inspires others to give her freely. Then to their exasperation she does the opposite of what they have suggested and she has agreed with. And she feels absolutely wretched and inadequate, always, about it.

Behind stiff white lace curtains over the windows of the polished and immaculately tidy front sitting room, beneath a flight of five china ducks going up the wall, we had afternoon tea three times a week. After it she smoked one cigarette. Then she tidied away the cups and plates, we concluded the proper observances of social enquiries about health and relatives, and conversation became less casual.

*

I hope you'll nae mind, Mr Parker, switching off the tape-recording machine if Mr Hardy pops in any time for a wee chat, until he's away out of the house again? He doesna mind ma talking to you, but it's just that I havena ever said anything to him about ma being in prison and things like that, and it might upset him a bit if he haird me describing it on the tape. I always seem to be so busy looking after him, doing his washing and mending and feeding and keeping the house nice, somehow I havena found the time ever to mention it to him yet.

I tell him you've come to talk tae me about ma childhood in Scotland and that. And that's true right enough isn't it? Och though if I was a stronger person I'd have told him about it by now. I expect mebbe I will too, when I get the opportunity. But it's nae an easy thing to do tae introduce the subject, I can't seem able to lead round to it.

Well now, I promised I'd show you the photographs today, didn't I? Here they are, I got them all ready for you last night when Mr Hardy was away down the public house. This is ma mother first of all – you can see what a fine woman she is, can you not, a fine big woman? I'm not as big-boned as she is, but I take ma height from her, and my lovely complexion. But a terrible disappointment I've been to her, that's true enough what she always says. Her only child, and I've nearly broke her heart many a time, I have.

Now this here is a picture of ma grandfather; my mother's father he was. He died before I was born, but I haird ma gran and my mother talk about him often enough. You see him there in his station-master's uniform, taken outside the station just before he retired; look at his wax moustache and his cheese-cutter collar and all those gold buttons and braid on his cap! He was a fine man too. My gran used to get this picture out of her trunk and show it to me when I was young, and the gold watch he got when he retired, and some certificate or other he'd won for a brave deed once. He was a very well-known and respected person in our village, my grandfather, he was the stationmaster there for over twenty-five years.

Now this here is my gran, her I did know of course, because we lived with her. I was very very fond of my granny. She died when she was 81, and her hair still brown, not a touch of grey in it anywhere. She used to let me take the pins out of it and brush it for her, it came right down her back to here.

She was only very small, not like the rest of the family, but she was one of the best women there's ever been, she was. She used to teach me things when I was little; she'd say to me 'If you learn now, child, it won't be so hard when you grow up.'

We had an outdoor wash-house, and she used to take me in there and show me how to use the tubs and the big wooden washing-boards. When it came to Monday washday, I always used to try and get off school by saying I was feeling poorly so I could help her with the washing, I loved doing it so much. I still do, ever since I can remember I've always loved doing the washing; I'll take other people's washing and do it for them, I just like squeezing things in the warm suds and wringing them out and making them all nice and clean and fresh.

And ironing I like, and housework, dusting and polishing and scrubbing floors, I really enjoy it. And cooking – anything to do in the house, sewing, darning, mending – whatever it is, I'm happy all day long doing it. I'm always cleaning Mr Hardy's shoes for him, even when he says they're already clean, or pressing his shirts twice over, things like that. He says he ought to clean his own shoes at least, but I say Why, if I enjoy doing it for you?

And my granny taught me how to do embroidery as well, how to make tray cloths and dressing table sets and covers for chair backs, all things like that. She was really the best gran a child could have, she was. Another thing she told me was she was a great believer in the Co-Operative; she said wherever you went in the world, you should always shop at the Co-Op, you get value for your money there.

673465 was our number, you never forget it, do you, it stays with you all your life.

I haven't any pictures of my father at all. He died when I was three, and I don't remember a thing about him. He was the porter at the railway station: my grandfather got him the job before he married my mother. And he was no good at all; my mother had a terrible life with him before he died, he drank a lot and was always gambling and things like that. She was very very unhappy with him indeed, and in a way I think it must have been a good thing when he was killed like he was, on the railway, run down one day by a train.

Of course it meant my mother had a very hard life looking after me and bringing me up on my own. That's why I had such a lot to do with my granny: she looked after me while my mother was out at work earning the money to keep us. She worked on a farm near by, and in the evenings she used to go to one of the big houses in the district where two sisters lived: they were noble people and had a lot of banquets, my mother used to help out with the catering arrangements.

All through my childhood there wasn't much money, but I had a happy life, I was very happy as a child indeed. I think in fact I was too happy. I was spoiled, my mother's always told me that she was inclined to just let me do what I liked, because I was her only child and she wanted to do too much for me.

All round where we lived in this village were beautiful woods and hills, a river and an old ruined castle. We had this little house of my grandmother's, just the two rooms downstairs and two upstairs, my gran slept in one and me and my mother in the other. My mother and I used to go out together quite a lot, to church on Sundays and then to see friends and relations. I was always very shy I remember, even when I was thirteen or so, just used to sit on the edge of the chair and not say anything, and I blushed bright red if anyone spoke to me. I was very tall and thin too, and my mother was very young-looking for her age, so everyone used to say we were just like two sisters out together.

When I was 14½ my granny died and I left school so I could help out with the money for the family. I went to work in a Woolworth's in the nearest town. I didn't like it a lot because they didn't keep you on one counter, they moved you around. I liked the cosmetics and the jewellery, but not the electrical equipment and the household goods. After a while I got another job in a drapery store, it was much more boring but the money was better.

I didn't go out very much even then as a young girl. My mother didn't like me to, she preferred me to stay at home in the evenings and listen to the wireless with her and do embroidery together. She kept most of my wages and gave me pocket money out of it; but of course by the end of the week I'd had it all back and more, as she pointed out, because she spoiled me so much, buying very good food and keeping me comfortable and giving me everything I could want.

I moved on from the drapers when I was about 17, I think, and went to work in a factory in the town. There were a lot of girls there I got friendly with, and just sometimes I could go to a dance with them on a Saturday night. I met a Polish boy called Janeck at one of the dances and wanted to bring him home, but my mother said he wouldn't be suitable so I didn't. Then I met another boy whose father was a big man on the local council: he was called Stanley and he was 24, seven years older than me. My mother thought a lot about him, and when he asked if we could get married she said 'Yes' straight away. We got engaged, and his mother made a big fuss about it: he was her eldest boy and I think she wanted him to do better for himself. They were that sort of people, my mother said, and she told him he could come and live with us when we were married.

I became pregnant while I was engaged, when Stanley and I were in one evening and my mother had gone out. I think if you're really in love with somebody that kind of thing can happen, and I was very much in love with him. So the wedding had to be a very small affair. I'd wanted a white one, but in view of what had happened my mother said she couldn't approve of it. Instead we just had a few close relatives and friends, and I wore a plain suit, and hat and gloves. I looked very nice, I wish I had a picture to show you but I haven't got one down here in the south.

Afterwards we went on a 'bus to the seaside and we stopped at a hotel for the weekend, then my husband had to get back to his job. He worked as a site manager for his father who was a builder. Only a few weeks after, he started saying he had to be working late at the different sites he was on. He got to coming in later and later, sometimes it was after midnight; he just didn't seem like the same person at all. One day my mother was talking to a neighbour who remarked on how often he came home late and said she'd seen him in the town one night with another woman. My mother was flabbergasted, when she came in she just sat down and couldn't speak: she wouldn't tell me what was the matter or anything, I had to beg and beg her before she'd tell me what it was. I didn't believe it when she did tell me, but my mother said she didn't think the neighbour was the type of woman to say a thing like that if it wasn't true.

We neither of us said anything to Stanley when he came in that night, but a few evenings later after he'd come in for his tea and got up and went out again my mother said 'You follow him, try and find out what he's up to.'

It was dark and I went round the back of the house and down the road to the next 'bus stop; when the 'bus came along I went downstairs on it, because I knew he'd be on the top where he could smoke. When it came into the town and stopped in the market place he got off, and I jumped off too behind him. He went straight over to the picture house, and there was a blonde lady waiting outside, and he took her arm and they went in. She looked very common, really she did.

I just felt like I was in a trance, I went back to the market place and got on the next 'bus back home. When I walked in my mother took one look at me and she said 'It's true then. Well, what did I tell you?' We sat up waiting for him until quarter to twelve when he came in, and then my mother said to him that he couldn't stay on in the house if he was going to behave like that, it would have to be one thing or the other.

He said he wouldn't do it any more, and soon after that I had the baby. When the pains started my mother went for the midwife and she came and delivered me. My mother rang up my husband at work and told him it was a boy, and he said he was going to be late home because he'd have to go and tell his parents about it on the way. He didn't seem to be interested in the child at all, and he started staying away from the house altogether because he said he had to go and work on sites that were right over on the other side of the Clyde, and I didn't see him for days at a time.

One day when the baby was about two months old I was in the house on my own, my mother was out at work and my husband was away somewhere I didn't know where. I felt I was short of money for make-up and things like that, so I took one of his suits from upstairs and went on the 'bus into the town and pawned it for £2.

He came in that same night and started looking for it to go out in. He asked me where it had gone, and what had happened to it. When I told him what I'd done, he lifted his hand and smacked my face and then he went out. He stayed away for about a week that time.

A few weeks later I'd gone into Glasgow to do some shopping one day while my mother was at home to look after the baby and let me go out, and I went into Burton's and said could I have a suit on approval for my husband, who wanted it for a special function he was going to and he couldn't get in to try it on for himself. They said yes so long as I gave them my name and address, and could show them a letter or something to prove where I lived. I did that, and they gave me the suit, and I took it straight away down a back street and sold it to a dealer who gave me £3-10-0 for it. Then I went and bought myself a jumper, and a few things for the baby.

I didn't say anything to my mother when I got back, and a week later I went back over to Glasgow and into the Burton's shop again, to tell them my husband would be coming in shortly to pay for the suit. Another week or so went by, then they sent someone to the house to enquire what was happening. I wasn't in, and my mother didn't know anything about it, so they came back again later in the evening when I was home, and asked me what I'd done with it. I told them, and my mother was in a terrible state. They said they were going to put it in the hands of the police, who came the next day. I was charged and taken to the magistrates' court. I was just 20 then.

The magistrates said I must either pay a five pound fine, or go to prison for 30 days. I couldn't pay the five pounds so that was it, I was taken to Glasgow jail for a month.

But your mother – she could have paid the fine surely, couldn't she?

I think she did try to raise the money but she couldn't; anyway she said she was sorry, but she hadn't got it, and she thought it would be a lesson to me never to do anything like that again.

The magistrates didn't suggest a conditional discharge or probation – just prison right away?

Well I think perhaps they thought the fine would probably be paid. In Scotland they're generally much stricter than here, especially where women are concerned; they're very strong on women defrauding men, they don't like it at all. And of course it was a good lesson to me – I was crying all the time I was in Glasgow jail, worrying about my mother and what she'd be thinking, whether she'd have any more to do with me or not. No one else in the family had ever done a thing like this, and one of her brothers was in the police force too, oh it was terrible.

She came to see me in prison and said I'd really have to think about myself while I was in there, and make up my mind never to do anything like it again. She said my husband had been to the house and taken the baby away to live with his family; and she couldn't stop him because of course she had to go to work herself and couldn't look after it. But she said when I came out perhaps I could get the baby back again.

When I was released my mother took me to a solicitor but he couldn't do anything about the baby. I got in a very bad nervous state then, so she took me to the doctor and he said he thought I ought to go into hospital and have a course of that electrical treatment, the ECT it was called. I went in as a voluntary patient in Glasgow in the September or the October, and stayed there for eight weeks.

Twice a week they took me down to the basement and gave me this electric shock; they lie you down on a bed and put these things on each side of your head. I was very frightened of it. You feel you're falling down and down in a big pit, and when you wake up you've got a terrible headache and you feel awful. But I did feel better for it, and I came home in time for Christmas. But it was a very depressing Christmas for both my mother and me, that one was. Neither of us could enjoy it very much, we just sat and talked quietly together.

In the three months at the end of that year you − a girl of just over 20 − had been in prison; in a mental hospital; lost your husband; and he'd taken your baby?

Yes. Like I say I think it got my mother down a lot, she seemed to grow much older round about that time too. After Christmas I went to work in the local brickworks, lifting bricks onto trucks. It was shift work and hard work, but at least I was earning a bit of money and trying to get myself straightened out. One night I said to my mother I think I'll go to the pictures down in the town, and in the market place there I saw my husband standing waiting for a 'bus on his own.

I went up and asked him could we have a talk, and we went and had a cup of tea. I asked him how the baby was and he said I wasn't to worry, the baby was fine. So then I said was there any chance of him taking me back again, and he said there wasn't at the moment, he'd have to wait and see how things went with me. When I got back I told my mother about it; she said I'd have to be very careful, I shouldn't really have anything to do with him in my position, otherwise it might create difficulties in the future.

I found the brickworks too hard really, and after a time I stopped working again and stayed at home looking after the house while mother was out. But I got very restless, and one day I went to Glasgow again, into a different men's shop, and this time I got two suits and sold them, and went on a bit of a spending spree doing shopping. I did the same thing a week later with another two suits, saying they were for my husband like before.

Of course the police came to the house again, and this time my mother was really angry about it. She said in court that whatever it was was wrong with me, I must have inherited it from my father, it wasn't from her side of the family, they were all good; but he was bad, so it must have come from him. And she said 'If she's no intentions of doing what's right herself, then there's nothing I can do for her.' This time I got six months.

She wouldn't come to see me in prison or even write to me, so I asked the chaplain what I should do and he said I ought to write her a really nice letter, and he'd put a word in for me too. I remember exactly what I wrote: 'Dear Mother' I put, 'This is to ask you if you will please forgive me for what I have done. This is really going to be the last time, and all I want is for you to forgive me. I know that what I have done is really a terrible thing, not only for myself but also for you being outside and having to meet people who know. But if you will only come to see me, I will pull myself together, I promise I will.'

The chaplain put a letter in with it like he'd promised, and about a week later she came. She was talking to the warder who was supervising the visit more than to me, telling her how they'd had nothing like it ever in her family and she couldn't understand why I did it and brought such a lot of shame on her. She said to me I'd have to leave the house, I couldn't go on living there any more.

I did feel sorry for what I'd done, and I said if she'd only give me one more chance I'd make up my mind I was going to be good. The chaplain did a lot for me, he had a talk with her about it too, and eventually my mother said she would reconsider her decision. So at the end of my sentence I was able to go back home again.

A few days after I'd got back she said she was going out to have a cup of tea with a friend, and she wanted me to go too, so over we went to this house in a village not far away. There I was introduced to the man whose house it was; he was a widower, and he had three grown-up daughters. He said to me 'You're going to be just like one of my own girls, you can come and live here and be one of us.' On the way home I said to my mother 'What does he want me to go and live there for?' and she said 'Well, he wants me to marry him, and if I do I shall be living there and selling our house of course.'

He was only a little man, much smaller than my mother, and the next weekend he and she went down into England somewhere to see his relatives. On the Monday I was at home and a telegram came, it said 'Got married today.' I shut the door and sat down, I was shocked, I felt really terrible about it, that I hadn't even been invited. To tell you the truth, it's an awful thing to say but I think I was really jealous about it and being very selfish: I wasn't thinking about my mother's future at all, and what a hard life she'd had.

The next day they came back, and then on the Wednesday a furniture van came and took away all our furniture; some of it was sold, and the rest was taken to my step-father's. I had to share a bedroom there with one of the other girls, Edith, she was the youngest one, and his favourite.

I got a job, this time in another shop, a furniture store, and I was there for quite a long time, nearly a year. Then I started getting into trouble again, taking suits from shops again and selling them; I got another six months, and then I got nine months, and then I got a year. Usually it was suits, and one time it was some blankets and bedding. My mother and my step-father were getting really ill with it, I think. I was getting really depressed about everything too; so I decided one day I'd just give in my notice at the job I was in and go like that, off down to London and have a holiday. I had about £40 altogether in savings and holiday money and back pay, so I asked for my cards, went back to the house, packed a few things in my case, left a note for my mother and step-father, and caught the 'bus to Glasgow and then a coach to London.

I came out at Victoria coach station and went in the first hotel I saw and booked a room there, then I had a few days looking round at all the places like Buckingham Palace and Westminster Abbey that I'd heard about. And would you believe it, in St. Paul's Cathedral I think it was, I walked right into one of the girls who used to be at the factory with me before I got married. She was living down here with her husband but they were separated and she was earning a living as a waitress. She wasn't really a very nice girl, I think; she knocked about a lot with American soldiers and used to go in pubs drinking. Of course I thought she was very daring and exciting, I was easily impressed by all her talk, and when she asked me if I'd like to go to a dance with her one Saturday as a partner for a friend of her friend, I said I would. Both these two men were American soldiers or airmen, I'm not sure which, and me and my friend got separated quite early on in the evening.

I had a lot to drink and felt awful sick and dizzy, and this American gave me something which he said would make me better, he said it was a kind of aspirin. But it just made me worse, I really felt half unconscious with it. He said he knew somewhere where I could sleep it off, and we went to some back street hotel place where we spent the night. In the morning he said he was going out to get a paper, and I waited hours and hours for him but he never came. When I went downstairs the manager said he'd paid the bill and gone straight out, and I thought Well that's funny, it really is, I was quite sure he'd be coming back. His name was Harry, I think.

When I saw my friend again the following day she said he'd probably had to go back to camp in a hurry: she thought it was somewhere up near Cambridge. So I decided I'd go there and see if I could find what had happened to him. When I got to Cambridge on the train someone at the station told me there were a lot of American camps round about, which one was it? I'd no idea at all, so that was the end of it.

I booked in at a hotel in Cambridge because it looked a nice town, and I thought I might have a few days there on holiday. But then I realised I'd hardly any money left at all, not really even enough to pay my hotel bill. I was walking down the street worrying about it late in the afternoon, when I passed an antique shop and I saw a beautiful French clock in the window. So I went in and asked if I could have a look at it, and the manager showed it to me, it was £65.

I said a friend of mine was going abroad, and I'd like to give it her as a present, but my husband wouldn't be back in Cambridge until late that evening – could I possibly take it overnight on approval and show it him and see if he thought it was good enough? I told them the name of the hotel I was staying at, and the manager said that would be quite all right, so out I went with it. Then I walked right over the other side of the town until I saw a second-hand jewellers, and I went in and asked if they bought antiques. They said they did sometimes if they were good enough, so I showed them the clock and said it was my mother's who'd just died and I didn't want it in the house any more.

They said they'd give me £20 for it, and I said that would be fine and took the money, and out I went. I stayed in Cambridge a couple of days, did some shopping with the money, buying a suitcase and some clothes, and then just as I was walking along Trinity Street at lunch-time a police car pulled up and they asked me to go with them to the police station. The hotel had given them my description, I think. I was taken to court and remanded, then I was put up at the Sessions and I got twelve months for it and sent to Holloway.

After I'd been in there a little while I knew there was something wrong with me, so I put down for the doctor and she examined me and told me I was pregnant. I didn't know what to do, whether to write and tell my mother or not, but finally I plucked up my courage and did. There was about three weeks' silence and then I got a letter from her, she said she was really disgusted with me, she said not only being in prison again but being pregnant as well, she thought it was awful. She said I was well old enough to know the difference between right and wrong. It wasn't as though I was too young or anything, and she thought it would be much better if I stayed in the south and had no more to do with her.

I saw the welfare people in prison about the baby and we agreed that I'd have it adopted when it came. But it was such a lovely little boy I didn't want to part with it, I said I was going to keep him. They asked me how I was going to manage outside with him, but I said something would turn up. He was called Michael, and when I left prison he was only a few months old and we were put in a sort of hostel place. I got friendly with a woman there, quite elderly, who'd been left by her husband. She got a flat from the LCC, and asked me if I'd like to have a room there with her. I said Oh yes, I would, and went with Michael to her for a while.

She was a very Christian woman, very nice, with a lot of pictures of Jesus up on the walls. She did a lot of praying and grew a beard. She used to come into my room in the dark in the middle of the night, and say 'Don't be afraid, God is in this room.' I got a bit uneasy about it because of the baby, and she started having epileptic fits as well, so I went to live with a lady called Mrs Robbins who lived in another flat and said I'd be very welcome with her. She had a baby of her own, so I left Michael with her and went to work in a café as a waitress.

This woman Mrs Robbins whose flat I was living in, I had to pay her £3 a week for my rent and looking after Michael, and it was very hard to do sometimes, especially if I'd been off work with a cold or something like that. I got really fed-up of scraping along living that way.

When I was in Holloway some of the other people there, they'd asked me what I'd done. When I'd told them they said twelve months was an awful lot to get just for a clock that I'd only got £20 for, and if I was going on with that sort of thing, I ought to do it for the sort of money that would make it more worthwhile. So one day I put on my best outfit, and I went off to Regent Street. I looked very nice, very smart, I had a pale blue suit, a big white leather handbag and white shoes, white gloves, and one of those umbrellas with a long straight handle, and my hair all done very nicely in long waves down on my shoulders.

I looked in the windows of the jewellers and the silversmiths: Mappin and Webb's I didn't like the look of, it seemed a bit frightening, but I chose one of the other big ones, and said could I look at some silver tea-services? The man at the counter said what price was I thinking of, and I said it didn't really matter, but I wanted something decent. He put this big piece of velvet on the counter and then he got one set out of a glass case, it was really beautiful, a three-piece one, a Georgian design and figured all over, oh it was lovely. He said it was £195. Then he showed me another one, a four-piece but much plainer and a bit cheaper, I think it was £170; and then there was another one at £230, only I didn't like it, it wasn't anything like so dainty as the Georgian one. So I said to him I liked the £195 one very much, I was very tempted but I didn't know if it was going to be suitable for what I wanted it for, which was for me and my brothers and sisters to give to our parents as a silver wedding present. I said of course they would want to see it first, would it be at all possible to have it on approval for 24 hours? He said he'd have to ask the manager, but he thought it would be all right; and after a few minutes he came back and said it would be all right so long as I could show them some proof of identity. So I said How about my driving licence, would that be all right, he said, of course; then I made a big fuss about having come out without it, but I had an envelope with my name and address on it, and he took a note of that. He packed it up for me very nicely in a box and I said I'd definitely be in the next day, either with the money or bringing it back, but I was quite sure my brothers and sisters would think it was beautiful and we'd keep it.

I hadn't much money on me, and I thought there was no point in going all the way back to the flat with the parcel: I bought a shopping bag off one of the street-sellers in Oxford Street, then I went in a ladies toilet, locked myself in and unpacked the tea-service from the box, and put it in wrapping-paper in the shopping bag. Then I came out, caught a bus along Oxford Street to Marble Arch, and started to walk along the Bayswater Road, quite a long way along to a pawnbrokers and second-hand silver shop I knew was there.

I went in and asked them if they'd like to buy a very good silver tea-service which was in beautiful condition, it'd never been used because it had been given to my parents as a silver-wedding present but they'd been killed in an accident. I took it out of the bag and he said Oh yes, it was really beautiful: he asked me to sit down, and went away in the back somewhere with one piece. I was feeling a bit shaky, wondering if he was going to get in touch with the police or something, but then he came back and said How much did I want for it? I was really very stupid about it, I said Well I'd been thinking of £50. He said Well it was very nice, and in lovely condition, but by the time they'd sold it that was about all they'd get for it themselves, so he could only offer me £45. I let it go for that, I was silly, and he gave me the money all in £5 notes and I signed a receipt for it and gave him my name and address.

I remember coming out and thinking Oh isn't it marvellous,

£45 – I've got all that money just like that. As I was passing a kiddies'-wear shop I saw a little blue coat with fur on the collar in the window, and I thought That'd just fit my Michael, so I went in and bought it. Then I went into Selfridges and bought a present for the lady who was looking after him for me, one of those lovely vases that change colour as you look at them. Further along Oxford Street again, I went in another shop and bought myself a lovely black skirt: then I thought I'd done enough shopping for one day, and I got on another bus and went straight home to the flat. When Mrs Robbins saw all the parcels she said 'Have you come into some money then?' and I said well strangely enough I had, just a little bit, and I gave her her present and we put Michael's coat on him; he looked lovely in it.

The next day at work I slipped out and rang up the shop where I'd got the tea service, and I said my brothers and sisters would be deciding that night about it, could I leave coming in till the next day? They said Yes, that would be all right. Well the next day was a Saturday, I didn't ring them up or anything, and all the following week I kept worrying and worrying and wondering what to do. Then one night when I got home from work Mrs Robbins said two men had been from the shop, and they said they were coming back later. I felt awful about it when they came back. One of them said 'We're not making any accusations against you, Miss McDonald, but please either pay us for the tea service or give it to us back.' I said well I was awfully sorry but I couldn't, and I told them what I'd done with it. Then they said they were very sorry about it but they'd have to tell the police, which they did, and came back again with two CID men who took me down to the police station and said the best thing would be for me to take them the next morning to the Bayswater Road shop where I'd sold it.

I did that, and then I was put up at Bow Street and remanded to Sessions. While I was in Holloway on remand different detectives kept coming, did I know anything about this that and the other case, would I ask for it to be taken into consideration and so on. They were hoping to get me to admit some that they wanted clearing up, but I wouldn't because I knew nothing about them at all.

When I came to the Sessions the judge was an old thin-faced one, I've forgotten his name: he said he reckoned I'd done this deliberately and he was going to double what I'd had before, so he gave me two years this time. I didn't have anything to say, just pleaded guilty and I didn't have counsel or anything because there was nothing for him to say either.

Mrs Robbins said she'd keep Michael and look after him for me, and she had him all the time I was in Holloway. When I came out I didn't really want to go back living with her because of the neighbours, so I got a little room of my own in Acton and went to work in a transport café. After a few weeks one of the drivers who came in regularly and I'd got friendly with said why didn't I get a bigger place, a flat where he could come and have his meals and things, and if I did he'd pay half of it for me although he was living with his stepfather in another flat at the time. I said I would, I'd try to find somewhere, and I did – just a small place, two rooms and a sort of kitchen place. He told me to tell the landlady that he was my husband, and he was a long-distance lorry driver and was away a lot.

He used to come about two or three nights a week, his name was Alf and I really liked him. When I went to see Mrs Robbins she said You're not going to take Michael to live, are you, I've got so fond of him, so I said Well you can keep him a little while longer if you like. I was paying her £3 a week for him, and £3-10-0 a week for the flat, and I was only earning £8 and Alf wasn't giving me anything for the rent – so all in all, it just wasn't working out and after about three months I was really in a mess again. Alf was talking about us going up to Scotland for a holiday together, and I knew we'd never be able to afford anything like that if the situation didn't improve.

So I thought Well this time I've got to do something really good. I made an appointment to have my hair done, and I put on a very smart black suit I'd got through a catalogue that Mrs Robbins had, white blouse and white gloves and a little black hat, and off I went up the West End again. It really is a bit exciting, you know, it's like going exploring in a way, setting out on something that you're trying to succeed at, and not knowing what you're going to find.

I tried two big jewellers but they both said they didn't ever let things out on approval, and I was beginning to get depressed, thinking my luck was right out. But the next one was all right, it was a really gorgeous place, it had the Royal crest on the door and carpets that you really sank into when you walked across them. A middle-aged man in a morning suit came up to me, Good morning madam can I help you?

I said I was a teacher at a well-known school, I told him which one, and the staff wanted to give a present to the Headmistress who was retiring, what would he suggest? Had they a very nice silver salver or something like that? He said Yes they had, and he brought several out to show me, including one really big one at £125 with handles on it. I told him I wanted one a bit cheaper because we were getting a tea-service to go on it as well, and finally I chose one at

£65. Then he said Had we got the tea-service yet, and I said Well no, actually we hadn't, so he said Could he show me some? There was a very nice one at £135, quite plain, which I liked: I asked him could it have engraving done on it, and he said Oh yes, easily.

Then I said I thought the salver and the tea-service together would be about right, and I'd have to ask the other members of the staff to come in over the next week or two and look at them – unless he could possibly let me have them on approval for a day, could he? He said Yes certainly, of course they could, and he'd have them packed up for me straight away. While that was being done, he saw me looking at a marcasite bracelet at £55. He took it out of the showcase and said would I like to put it on my arm to see how it looked? I said oh yes I would. It was really lovely. I told him I was very tempted by it, I must think about getting it at the end of the month. So he said Why not have it put down on your account, madam? I said well yes, all right, I would. He wrote everything out on a bill, he was going to put it for the school but I said since I'd got the bracelet it'd better all be put down to me at my private address.

He asked should all the things be sent, but I said it was all right, one of the other teachers was meeting me for tea at Swan and Edgars and she had her car so we'd manage. So he said Well he would get one of their delivery boys to carry it up to Swan and Edgars for me, which he did. When we got there I told the boy thank you very much, he could just leave me there now: when he was out of sight I got on a 'bus quick, and got off again at a jewellers along Oxford Street.

I went in there and I didn't mention about the silver, only the bracelet which I said I wanted to sell. I told the man a fib, I said it'd cost £65 not £55, and I wanted £45 for it. He said he couldn't manage that, but he'd give me forty, which he did.

Then I got on another 'bus and went home. I didn't unpack the silver, just pushed the parcel under the bed. When Alf came round that evening I told him I'd drawn some money for our holidays and I'd got £40. He said that was marvellous, we'd go very soon; but then the next day he said he couldn't get the time off work, we'd have to wait. I knew it was no good waiting, and I tried to talk him into going for the week-end at least, but he said it couldn't be done because he couldn't afford it unless I drew some more money to see him over.

So that meant I had to go out the next day with the tea-service and the salver, which I'd really wanted to keep a little while. I put them in my shopping bag, and the tea-service I sold down near

Victoria for £50 to a little shop where they bought it without any hesitation, just like that: and the salver I took to the silver department of one of the big stores, but they only gave me £42 for it. Still, that was over a hundred pounds in all with the bracelet the day before, and I was quite thrilled about it really.

I went back and told Alf and I said Now we can go to Scotland this weekend. But first I did a lot of shopping, I bought all sorts of things for the flat, masses of tinned food for the larder, everything I needed. Then the next day I thought I'd better 'phone up the shop where I got the silver, just to tell them why they hadn't heard from me – but when I started to explain, the man said 'I'm afraid you're too late, we've put the matter in the hands of the police.' I think they must have got on to the school and found out like that, they were certainly very quick.

I ran straight out of the phone box, I didn't dare go back to the flat, instead I went over to Mrs Robbins to see Michael, and asked her if I could stop the night there. Next morning when I went into work I felt quite sure something was going to happen, and sure enough round about half past nine two detectives came in for me and took me to the police station. In my handbag there were the bills for the silver marked 'On approval', the receipts for the money from the people I'd sold them to, everything.

So there it was again. Alf came to see me on remand, he was really shocked, he said he'd never have taken money off me if he'd known where I got it from, he thought it was dreadful. When I came up at the Sessions, it was the same judge again, and he said to me 'You've got no intention of going straight, have you? Well, I doubled it last time, and now I'm going to double it again. This time I'm giving you four years. And if you come here any more, you know what you can expect, don't you – eight years, do you understand?'

I went back into Holloway again, and because I'd got a long sentence I had a good clerical job in there that I was more or less permanently on; quite a responsible job it was too. I got it because I'm always so good in prison: in all my time I've never ever once been punished or even put on report for doing anything wrong. A lot of the officers say I'm the very best prisoner they've ever had, because they know I'll give them no trouble at all, and I was so quiet. I didn't mix with the other prisoners, they're not very nice and they use such awful bad language, you wouldn't believe it.

I wrote to my mother again while I was in, asking if I could go back there when I came out, because that's what the welfare thought I ought to do. But she said No, her husband wouldn't be able to stand it, all the worry and that. Alf came to see me and he was very good, he said I could go back with him afterwards and we'd get married; and Mrs Robbins said she wanted to adopt Michael if only I'd let her. I told the welfare I didn't think she was suitable, she was not very good at keeping herself out of debt and things like that. I said to the welfare I'd really like to go to see my mother on my release, and they were very good, they got me a travel warrant for Glasgow; but I went back to Alf instead, and stopped with him and his step-father for a while.

One night he took me to the pub for a drink, and while we were there Mr Hardy, who knew Alf, came up and started talking with us, and asked us back here afterwards for some coffee, and put some records on so we could dance. Alf had had rather a bit too much to drink, and he went to sleep in that chair; while he was dancing with me Mr Hardy said 'He'll never be any good to you, you know, he's no intentions of marrying you. Why don't you come here and look after me, you can walk straight in tomorrow and everything here's yours, you'll have nothing to buy, and we'll get married as soon as my divorce comes through.'

So that was what I did, and I've been here ever since.

★

Talking to Miss McDonald was always an enjoyable experience. We never, of course, reached the familiarity of Christian name terms; and there were certain subjects which were by unspoken agreement only touched on very briefly, as detailed discussion of them would have been obviously improper.

When she spoke about her visits to the West End shops where she obtained the silver tea-services and the jewellery, her enormous brown eyes seemed to light up, her voice grew firmer and her back straighter; it was as if in reliving the experiences she was becoming a real person and personality in her own right for the first time. And when she described how she chose one tea-service, or one silver salver, rather than another, it was clear from her enthusiasms that what guided her choice was not merely the monetary value: it was personal taste, as though she really were choosing the article for a present. Perhaps that was why she was successful, at least in persuading the shopkeepers that she was genuine and could be trusted with the goods on approval: for, incredible though it seems, they really did, as records of her court appearances confirm.

Yet every time she performed her frauds, she ensured disaster for herself by giving her real name and address. Did it never occur to you, I asked once, at least to gain a little time for yourself by giving a made-up name and address? She looked at me in astonishment at the suggestion. Mr Parker, she said reproachfully and with great dignity, I am not a liar.

On another occasion she mentioned in passing that she was not a thief. What are you then, I asked? Well, she said with quiet reproof, You may think of me what you like, but I have never taken anything from anybody that they didn't willingly give me of their own free will and to my face. I've never stolen from anyone's house, gone in and taken their purse or anything like that, and I've never even shoplifted – I couldn't ever do things which are just stealing, I think it's dreadful.

Could she, I once asked her, think of any reasons why with the kind of background and upbringing which she had had, she could have changed so quickly into someone who indulged in regular criminal activity, and was not put off at all by being caught and repeatedly sent to prison?

Back came the usual answer – 'Because I was spoiled I think, as a child, and that made me weak-willed and...' I asked her not to go on with that, to leave it for the time being, to think and to come back to the subject again another day.

When she did so, her interpretation of her own motives was at least a little less self-condemnatory; but only little more illuminating.

—You know you asked me to try and think why I went on and on doing all those things and getting into prison so often? Well one of the reasons I think was that when my husband left me as soon as the baby was born, I wanted to get him back so much I felt if only I could get him to pay some attention to me I'd do anything.

So the first thing I did was to pawn one of his suits; and he just hit me, that was all. Then I went into the Burton's shop and I gave my real name – well, it was his name wasn't it, really – so that I made sure I'd get into trouble. I kept hoping and hoping the first time when I was in prison that he'd feel sorry for me and that he'd left me. I suppose another woman might have started drinking, or going with other men, but I did this instead. I hoped when he heard he'd take pity on me, and start writing to me or come to see me.

But of course it didn't work. It just went on and on, and the more I went into prison the less it seemed to matter to me, the more pushed away from decent people like him and my mother I felt, until in the end I really didn't care at all whether I went into prison or I didn't. Perhaps if I'd been put on probation in the early days, under somebody who could have told me what to do and kept a firm hand over me, that might have worked. To tell you the absolute truth, my mother did go on about it a bit too much, I think, and I don't think it did me much good really.

Do you blame your mother for how you became?

Oh good gracious me no, it wasn't her fault was it? She did her very best for me in every way.

Your husband do you blame at all?

No, no, I don't want to give that impression. You see really and truly I think it was my own fault he left me, because when we got married I wouldn't let him touch me until after the baby was born, I thought it might harm it. I think that was why he went with that blonde lady. Sometimes even now I still think about it all, long ago though it was, twenty years now. If ever I was up there near home and I bumped in to him, I'd have to speak to him...

What would you say?

I suppose I'd be stuck for words at first, I'd have to try and say 'Hello' at first, and then to start with I'd ask him how he was getting on and how the boy was. I'd ask him if he was married again or living with anyone else, and if he was happy and being properly looked after; and if...and if...

And you'd be wanting to say—

Please, please Stanley, will you take me back? Please forgive me and have me back, I'll try so hard to be good, I really will, if only you'll have me back and give me another chance...Oh well, it's all too late to think about now, it's all over and gone. I heard once a few years ago that he'd married that blonde lady, so I suppose that's it.

Miss McDonald, since that first time you went into hospital for the electric-shock treatment, have you ever had any further psychological or psychiatric examination or treatment, either while you've been remanded in custody before sentence or during the long periods you've spent in prison?

Oh no, there's been nothing like that, I've never needed it, you see. That shock treatment was because I'd got so depressed and unhappy at that time, but I've never had that trouble again. I'm a very happy person, and always have been ever since – because I think on the whole I've been very lucky and had a good life and an enjoyable one.

All the prison doctors who've ever examined me have all said the same thing, that I'm a fine, fit, healthy woman and there's nothing wrong with me at all, and no reason for me to go on getting into trouble either except that I'm weak-willed because I was spoiled so much when I was a child.

I mean, I can't say it was anyone else's fault at all except mine, can I? I've always got myself into trouble, no one else has led me into it. After all, nobody makes you do things, do they, except yourself?

Did you say you thought you'd been lucky and had a good and enjoyable life?

Yes I do, and I have – everything provided for me always right from being a child, a good mother, a nice home. Of course going to prison wasn't so nice, because you meet so many rough types of person there. And if I get sent there again – well, next time that old judge said it'd be Preventive Detention for me, so let's hope it doesn't ever come to that, eh?

Part VI

AT DEATH'S DOOR

Tony Parker was passionately against the death penalty. At the time he first started writing, the death penalty was very much on the political agenda. Telling the world what it meant to be in the condemned cell, especially for an innocent man, was an important contribution in challenging the use of the death penalty. Today those same accounts are useful reminders of what imposing the death penalty actually means when in many parts of the world the death penalty is being re-imposed or the frequency of its use is increasing.

Thirty years after talking to Michael Davies, who in 1953 in England had stood trial at the Old Bailey charged with stabbing to death a young boy in a gang-fight, Tony Parker was speaking in the United States to Guy, still incarcerated after forty-five years. Guy's reprieve was a chance affair and he is determined to 'find a place in the scheme of things'. However, it is in returning to his beginnings where the sadness of a life spanning nearly three score years and ten is highlighted. Social circumstances are important for some offenders and is a theme which underpins so much – though not all – of the work of Tony Parker. For Guy to say quite simply 'I believe I'm the child of poor whites who lived in Tennessee: that may or may not be true but it's what I've been told by social workers over the years' reveals a world which we need to try to understand.

IN THE CONDEMNED CELL[1]

Michael Davies

Well, while the jury was out I was taken into a big room at the back of the court; very bare, gloomy, dark panelling walls, an enormous round table in the middle, and some like high-backed dining chairs round it. We just sat there, me and the prison officer who'd been behind me in the dock, keeping an eye on me during the trial, we just sat there and chatted a bit. Not saying much, you know, just sitting and smoking – well, I didn't smoke, I don't smoke, but he did, he was more or less smoking all the time. The only thing we talked about that I remember was the, you know, the length of time it was taking the jury to arrive at a verdict. It seemed to be dragging on but then the door opened and someone said 'They're coming back', so back we went in the court. But they hadn't come back to give a verdict, they'd only come in because they'd got some query they wanted further direction on from the judge. It was about how they ought to look at Lawson's evidence, some point about that, and the judge dealt with it and then we had to go back in the big room again and sit and wait.

And this screw then, I remember him trying to keep me going, and saying 'Well, that's a good sign, boy – they must be…arguing, it's a good sign.' The longer we had to wait, the more he kept on telling me it, saying the longer the wait was the better it was for me because it could only mean they were having differences and arguments. I was trying not to be nervous and jumpy, but you can't help it, naturally you do feel it because you're waiting for something that's going to mean so much to you, it's going to be, well, life or death, isn't it, just that. But I kept thinking, well, perhaps the screw was right, the longer it went on the better the chance I'd got, obviously they

1 *The Plough Boy* (1965) London: Hutchinson, pp. 187–97.

couldn't be all that confident about it if it was taking them so long to make up their minds. After all, I knew the previous jury had disagreed, at the first trial when it was me and Coleman, so there was obviously going to be just as much doubt again, I thought.

Mind you, I knew the judge this time hadn't exactly showed what you might call a lot of partiality my way, I knew there was a lot of animosity there, he'd all the time seemed to have it in his mind he'd got a young thug here that he was going to teach a lesson to, and if he had anything to do with it he was going to see that I went down for it, right or wrong. All the way through he'd kept looking at me and talking to me as though he wanted me to know he'd got me right there in the palm of his hand and he was going to keep it that way.

I knew there'd been a lot of trouble about youngsters and teenage hooligans and gangsterism and that sort of thing, and I thought they were doing this to me as a sort of, well, as a sort of example to others, you know, put the wind up them properly so they'd think about the way they were carrying on. But I thought they wouldn't carry it too far, they'd acquit me after they'd put the show on for everybody to see, and that would be that. I felt obviously they must acquit me, there couldn't be any other result; they couldn't very well find me guilty because I hadn't done it, and they must know I hadn't done it, so that was all there was to it.

Well, after what seemed like hours they came again and said the jury was ready, so back we went once more into the court. I remember then, looking at them all, looking at the jury and wondering what they were going to say, whether they'd say they couldn't agree again, or whether they were just going to acquit me straight off.

But they didn't say that. When the bloke at the end, the foreman, said 'Guilty' – it just didn't register, it didn't seem to mean anything, I couldn't grasp it, I couldn't understand somehow that I'd really heard it. Then somebody said 'Have you anything to say why sentence of death shouldn't be passed on you?', and I said 'I'm not guilty of murder, sir', and then they put that black square thing on the judge's head and he said – well, I don't remember what the exact words were, something about being taken to a place of execution and there to be hung until I was dead, and ending up with 'And may the Lord have mercy on your soul', which I think was a bit hypocritical on his part, but still.

It didn't sink in at all, I didn't realise at first what he'd done. Then the screw tapped me on the arm, and I turned round and walked down the steps at the back of the dock, and I was taken down to a cell underneath the court somewhere. I sat down there with him on a bench for a bit, and neither of us said a word. Some other officers come along and took my things – personal things, keys, wallet, money; they took those off of me, and I still didn't say anything, I didn't say a word, just sat there and looked at the wall. But after about ten minutes or so, or perhaps a bit less, then it suddenly hit me what he'd said, what the words had meant. He'd sentenced me to death. I was sitting there on that bench and I was, well, I was a dead man.

I was choking, trying to choke it back, you know, but it seemed to hit me all of a sudden just like that – I was a dead man. I think it was only a minute or two that I broke down for, but I did cry, I put my face down in my hands and I sobbed. This screw, Mr Wilkes was his name, I remember, he put his hand on my shoulder and he said: 'That's right, boy, you get it out of your system, that's right, boy, just you let it go.' He wanted me to have a cigarette, he said it'd make me feel better, but I didn't have one because, like I've said, I don't smoke.

He was really doing his best that bloke, he was a nice man, he was trying to console me and after a bit he said: 'Now don't give up yet, boy, there's always hope, isn't there, you can go to the appeal court, don't forget that.' I was just nodding, I couldn't think of anything to say, I was just nodding my head, but I couldn't really take in what he was saying because I felt numb.

Then after a while some more officers come along and they put me in a van and took me to Wandsworth. When we got out of the van inside the gate in the yard we were by some iron steps; we went up them, just a few steps they were, and then we were in a funny little room with nothing in it, almost like a little cloakroom it was. Off-of it there was a door to the right, and we went straight through there and then we were in quite a big room that had been made out of three cells knocked into one. And that was the condemned cell. There was three lights in the ceiling and a wooden table in the middle with some chairs at it, and a couple of other chairs like small armchairs, and then opposite where we'd come in, over on the far wall, there was a bed.

But I couldn't take much of it in, in fact I could hardly take any of it in, because the first impression I got as soon as I went through the door was how full of people the place was. There was loads of them all milling around – the officers who'd brought me, some more offi-cers who were receiving me, the chief officer, and the doctor, and the governor, and heaven knows who else – it seemed like there were about twenty people there, all jumping around and talking, pushing me and pulling me about, someone saying 'Get your shirt off', someone else saying 'Put this on and take that off and put this on', and the doctor examining me and screws putting bits of paper in front of me and saying 'Sign your name there' and the governor reading out the regulations about calling the officers 'Sir' and having special visits and privileges – it was all so noisy and packed with people I just didn't know where I was.

Then suddenly it all seemed to calm down, and everybody went out, and I was left with just the two screws who had to be there all the time to watch over me, and everything went absolutely quiet. The screws tried to get me talking to take my mind off the case – would my family be coming up to see me the next day, how was my mother, that sort of thing, but not forcing it, just making the odd remark now and again. Something was brought in for me to eat, an egg sandwich I think it was, and some biscuits and some cocoa. I didn't feel like eating, I drank the cocoa, but I couldn't touch the food.

On the table there was a few magazines and a couple of books and some jigsaw puzzles in cardboard boxes; oh yes, and a chess set: one of the screws asked me did I feel like a game, but I didn't, so after a while they started a game of chess themselves, but not concentrating on it very much and trying to keep on talking to me. I didn't feel like saying anything much.

The clothes they'd given me to wear were very loose and sloppy, a shirt that had no buttons on it, just sort of knobs of cloth that went through the button-holes, no tie, of course, no belt, no braces, you're not allowed anything like that, nothing you might try to kill yourself with: and carpet slippers on your feet.

I walked up and down for a bit, sat on the bed, went and sat back at the table watching the chess game, then walked up and down a bit more. I'd no idea what time it was, I could see it was dark outside through the wire netting and bars over the windows. There were three of them because of the original lay-out of the separate cells. Over the middle one there was a kind of reading lamp on a sort of swivel, I thought perhaps it was for shining down on the table if you were sitting there reading, but it wasn't – it was to be shone on the bed like a kind of spotlight while you were asleep.

I still wasn't feeling anything, it all seemed unreal as though it wasn't really happening. After a while I lay on the bed just sort of looking up at the ceiling, then I got up again and walked around, then I lay down and stared at the ceiling some more. I was trying to puzzle it out in my mind, what had gone wrong, how it was that it'd happened, turning it over and over and thinking it couldn't really be true, could it, this wasn't really happening, I couldn't see how it could. I don't know how long I lay like that, I kept hearing the screws talking quietly to each other, one of them came over to the bed and said 'All right, son?' and I nodded and he went back to the table: I kept dozing then waking up again and trying to think, then dozing some more. I was tired, so eventually I dropped off.

The next morning they let me sleep on for quite a bit. When I woke up there was two different screws there who'd relieved the ones that'd been with me through the night. The doctor came in to see me early on after I'd got up. He asked he how I'd slept and how I felt. I said all right. Then the governor come in and started telling me about visits and letters, what I could do about this and that, did I want anything like cigarettes or sweets or chocolates. After he'd gone the new officers started to chat with me, then I was brought some breakfast, something to eat and some tea. I got through some of it.

It went on like that – the day to day happenings, I don't remember very much, because no day was any different from any other day as far as that went. You had a complete change of clothing each day and a complete change of bedding, and you were taken out twice a day on exercise on your own in the yard, while all the other men in the prison were kept out of sight so they couldn't see you. When you were out they searched your cell from top to bottom every time to see if you'd managed to hide anything there, anything you could kill yourself with. They were always very careful you shouldn't have a chance to do it yourself.

As I say, one day was very like another. Every day there was a visit from my mother and sister. They were a strain the visits, it was killing my mother, I could see that. She looked terrible. I didn't know it at the time, but she'd cracked up altogether, she was in bed all day and the doctor visiting her, giving her pills and drugs and things to keep her going. Then each afternoon she got up when it was time to come for the visit with Joyce. I tried to pretend I was cheerful and hopeful for her sake. I didn't know all it was doing to her, but what I could see was pretty bad.

November the 11th was the day they'd told me they was going to execute me on. November the 2nd I had my twenty-first birthday. Then a few days later I was told the execution date had been postponed, because my case was going to come up in the Court of Criminal Appeal. So I told Mum it was going to be all right and she mustn't worry, because they were sure to give me the appeal. When they had a look at the case they were sure to, so it was going to be all right.

The 1st of December the hearing was going to be, and the nearer it got the more hopeful I was, until by the actual day itself, it's funny, I really was, I was quite cheerful. Then when the appeal court dismissed it I went right down, I couldn't believe it. How could they just chuck it out and say they found 'no substance' in it, or whatever it was? Anyway, after that they come in and told me they'd fixed up a new date for the hanging – December the 18th, a week before Christmas.

I went on doing the jigsaw puzzles and trying to read the books, and the days and nights went on again like I've said, one very much like another. I was losing a bit of weight; the meals weren't too bad, I had more or less the same food as the other prisoners, but mine had to be cooked separately, so it turned out perhaps just a bit better.

One or two people as well as my family came to see me. The solicitors, of course, and the Roman Catholic priest at the prison – a very nice old man he was, very kind and very sincere, I think his name was Father Daly, he was a really good man.

Joyce, my sister, she was terrific, she'd got Mum to try and keep going, and she was pregnant herself, but she was fighting all the way, trying to get new evidence and also dealing with a big petition for my reprieve. She kept telling me all the time I mustn't give up, I mustn't stop hoping, it was going to be all right, everybody was praying for me, and a lot of outside people were interesting themselves in the case too.

But it was wearing me down all right, I'd got over the stage of thinking it was a nightmare and I was going to wake up. I knew I wasn't going to wake up, I was wide awake and I was right in it.

On two occasions they moved me out of the condemned cell for the night, because they'd got another couple of chaps in the cells further along who were lined-up for topping. They put them in my cell, which was the one next to the execution shed, so they could take them straight out in the morning and do it. One of these fellows was twenty-four and the other one was twenty-five, and they topped them both after a night in my cell, and then moved me back in again.

I wasn't giving a lot for my chances then. I was a bit younger than those two, but I started thinking about Derek Bentley, and how he was younger than I was, he was only seventeen or eighteen, and they'd topped him though he was completely innocent, and they'd got far less reasons for doing it to him than they had to me.

It didn't look as though I was going to make it to Christmas, but one day the governor came in and said they'd postponed it again because my case was going up to the House of Lords.

So then my hopes started building up again. I knew it was only very rarely people on a murder charge ever got up as far as the Lords, and I thought, well, that must be what they're doing, they're going to take it absolutely as far as they can, right to the end of the line. I thought, yes, that must be it; they were going to work it that way, when they were absolutely certain in their own minds they'd made a big enough example of me to frighten everybody else.

I talked about it with Joyce and Mum on the visits, and between us we managed to persuade one another that was how it was going to be. And the more I started to think about it, the clearer the whole picture seemed to come into my mind, you see, because there was another point which began to dawn on me as well, which seemed to confirm my estimation of the thing, which was this: I knew that when you went up to the appeal court, they could – if they wanted to – substitute a lesser sentence for the one you'd been given. They could have knocked out the death sentence and given me something else instead – something like fifteen years for manslaughter, if they'd wanted to, or something like that. But when you went up to the Lords, well, there was no chance of that. They either had to confirm the thing, or else quash it altogether – and if they did that, well, that was the end of it, you walked out of there an absolutely free man. So that, to my mind, was obviously what they were going to do; they hadn't wanted to do it in the appeal court where I might have got a big sentence even though it was reduced. They were saving it for the Lords so that I could be set free right on the spot.

That was how I'd got it worked out. The Lords hearing wasn't going to be until the beginning of January, so that saw me over Christmas all right, and I was really beginning to get quite cheerful again. I remember at Christmas time saying to Mum and Joyce: 'Well, next Christmas we'll all be together again, all this'll be forgotten long ago by then. Early in the New Year it'll all be over and finished with, and they'll let me come home.'

Christmas passed, and the New Year, and I felt really, well, almost in a kind of way pleased about the whole thing by then, full of confidence, quite light-hearted and happy, you know, that things were obviously going my way at last.

When we went to the House of Lords the copper who'd been in charge of the case all the way through, he was there that day, to listen to the appeal get turned down. When they took me out we went past him, very close, and he just stood there giving me a long cold look, when I got level with him. It seemed to hang on and on, the seconds going past and him and me there, separate, looking straight back and forth at each other. Then one of the screws behind me gave me a slight push along and that was the end of it, it was gone.

They took me back to the condemned cell, and it all seemed to be winding up very fast.

It really began to sink in at last. I'd got it all wrong, I'd had it all wrong the whole time. They weren't playing. They were going to have me. They really were going to execute me. They really were going to take my life. I could feel it, it was ebbing away from me. It was my turn. They'd topped the other two fellers, and I was going to be next through that door.

Each morning when I opened my eyes it was the first thing I saw, right opposite from me in the other wall, bang in the centre of it. It was the door I'd come in through on the first night I arrived. That little room I'd thought was some sort of cloakroom was the execution chamber, or half of it. It had a sort of movable wall like a shutter which they could draw back for an execution so that it became a fair-sized room.

The door was absolutely plain, metal covered, perfectly flat. No handle, no keyhole, nothing like that. Just a blank piece of metal. Just to the side of it there was a cross. As you step through that'd be the last thing you'd see.

I used to lie on the bed and try not to look at it when my eyes opened. But somehow or other it was always the first thing I saw.

Joyce and Mum, when they came, it was terrible. 'Petition', Joyce kept saying, 'thousands of signatures, don't give up, don't give up, Mick, don't.' But Mum didn't say anything, she just sat, her mind didn't seem to be there.

I don't think mine was either. You're off the ground somehow, floating, swimming, trying to move and connect, and you don't. February the 2nd, that was all I could think of. That was the final date.

Thursday, Friday, Saturday, Sunday, Monday...I don't remember the days. Monday, Tuesday...I can't remember them, which was which.

All I remember is the door.

Then the governor come in. He had a piece of paper in his hand, and he started reading it off, very quick, I couldn't get what he was rabbiting about, only something about 'respite' or 'reprieve' or something like that. Then he said 'Do you understand what I've said?' and I said 'Yes', and he turned round and went out.

I saw one of the screws was smiling at me, and I said 'What was that, was that a reprieve he just read out to me?' and he said 'Yes, that's right, son, you've been reprieved', and then he put out his hand and shook hands with me, and so did the other one, he did the same.

I remember feeling very light-headed and dizzy, I couldn't properly take it in or grasp it, you know what I mean? You see I'd been living with this thing so long it'd become well, it'd become a part of my life...that's a funny thing to say, I suppose, 'it'd become a part of my life', because it was my death, wasn't it, my dying that'd become part of my life...but that was how I felt when they gave me my life back again, it didn't seem as though it could be true at all.

Then a few minutes later some more screws came in and they took me straight over to the hospital block, took me into one of the wards there and told me to get into bed. I did, and I just lay there for a bit. Then after a while, the man in the next bed had got earphones for a radio over his bed, so I asked him what time it was and he said it was just on six o'clock so I said 'Could I borrow your earphones, please?' and he said 'Yes'.

So I listened to the six o'clock news, and they said on it that the Home Secretary had recommended a reprieve for me, changed the thing into a life sentence and I'd been reprieved. And I thought: Well, they've said it on the wireless now, they've told everybody, they can't go back on it now, they can't do it to me now after giving it out like that, they can't go back on that, they can't, that's it.

How long were you actually in the condemned cell altogether?
Ninety-two days.

MY STORY[1]

Betty Drew

—My life as a young girl, being in the sanatorium and how I met Janet. Up to and including killing her.

I didn't have much education, I spent a lot of time off school because I wasn't a healthy child, when I was fifteen I was diagnosed as having tuberculosis. In those days they didn't have all the drugs for it that they do nowadays, it was very serious for you if you'd got it, and a lot of people died from it. You had to go into a special hospital called a sanatorium where there were a lot of other people who all had the same thing. The only treatment there was was that you had to lie still and rest all the time. You were coughing and spitting blood and so were all the other patients and a lot of them died. It was very frightening to be a young girl in a place like that. The only thing everybody always talked about was dying. It was an enclosed world, and you didn't feel anyone else understood you except the other patients. They'd got the same illness and they were the only ones you could talk to, not people from outside at all. It was a bit like prison, nobody who hadn't experienced it really knew what it was like.

They had education classes there but they weren't very good and I missed out on a lot of things. Either you felt too ill to go to the lessons, or often they couldn't get teachers because they were frightened of coming into contact with people who'd got tuberculosis. So that did make it a very enclosed world like I've said.

You formed very intense friendships with other people because you had this threat hanging over you all the time, that you were suddenly going to get worse and die. Sometimes they'd let you go home for a weekend but that wasn't very successful. You felt your family were holding you at arm's length in case they caught it too,

---

1 *Life After Life* (1994) London: HarperCollins, pp. 174–81.

and people didn't come to see you for the same reason. I never minded going back to the sanatorium, I preferred that to being at home.

My special friend among the other patients was Janet who was a girl who was two or three years older than me and very pretty. We used to go for long walks together in the sanatorium grounds, and sometimes we held hands and a few times we kissed each other. We were both very innocent and there was nothing more in our relationship than a very big affection for each other. We read the same books and played gramophone records and danced together in the recreation room. I had a big crush on her and she had a crush but a smaller one on me. In those days there was a lot less frankness about such subjects than there is now, and you didn't talk about such things as lesbianism because hardly anybody'd ever heard the word or knew what it meant. Nobody even thought of ever doing anything physical together. So I should describe what we had as a close lesbian relationship but without sex.

From time to time you could be discharged from the sanatorium for a trial period and go home and see how you were Janet was married and her husband sometimes came to see her but they weren't very happy together and she said she didn't like living with him but she'd nowhere else to go. She said he didn't like living with her either because he was frightened he was going to get TB. Sometimes she was at home when I was in the sanatorium and she came to visit me. The other way round, when she was in there I'd visit her. And of course sometimes we were in there together. It went on in this way for between two and three years, and then it came to one day when I was out and she was coming out, and I asked her would she like to come and live at our house. I'd spoken to my mother and sister about it, and they were agreeable and we had a spare room.

We were both having what they call a long remission of the illness and we used to talk about what we'd do to start a new life together in the future when we were both completely better. But we also quarrelled a lot and this was chiefly my fault because I was very jealous. She was a very quiet person but I was very noisy and aggressive and used to physically attack her. Then I'd burst into tears and say I was sorry, and she always put her arms round me and we made it up. From time to time she would go to see her husband for a day or two and I was always miserable and unhappy when she did, and worried in case one day she didn't come back.

Then one time she told me she'd been and he'd demanded his rights and she'd had to give them to him. This was the same phrase my mother had used that time I told you about. I didn't know what it meant so I asked Janet, and when she told me it made me feel sick. I didn't want her to go, but I told her it was disgusting and she must leave the house. She packed her bag and said she was going to her mother's, and she left.

I was in a state of fury, and I told my mother and my sister I was going to her mother's house to kill her. They tried to prevent me but I went, and I took with me a hunting knife with a deer-horn handle that I'd bought the year before. I really intended it for if I ever met her husband. I went to Janet's mother's house and her mother opened the front door, and then Janet came out and we stood on the front path and I was shouting and screaming at her. Her mother tried to drag Janet away but I lunged after her and stabbed her in the chest with the knife. I stabbed her just the once but very hard, and they say it went right through the breastbone just about here.

At that moment my mother and sister arrived in a taxi because they had been worrying about what might happen. Then the police came as well and they took me to the police station and charged me with attempted murder. This was because at that stage Janet was not yet dead but she was dying.

While she was in hospital before she died she made a death-bed statement saying what had happened, and that I'd threatened to kill her before, which was true. Then she died so the charge became murder, which in those days was a capital crime, that is one you could be hung for because there was still the death penalty.

While I was in prison awaiting trial I became seriously ill again with tuberculosis and had to be kept in the prison hospital. A QC came to see me and he said he'd do his best for me but he didn't give much for my chances, the police had got a lot of love letters I'd written to Janet and they were going to read them all out in court. A doctor came and examined me and he said he didn't think I was going to live very long anyway. I felt very ill in the hospital wing of the prison but I didn't feel they treated me very kindly. I'd murdered somebody, I'd written the sort of letter that one woman wasn't supposed to write to another one, and I'd got TB, so everyone treated me as though I'd got three things they didn't want to come too close to, and they kept their distance.

By the time it came for me to go to court I was coughing up a lot of blood. They told me I was to lie very still all the time, and when I said I was going to plead guilty they said that was good because it meant I wouldn't have to be cross questioned and move about, and they could take me into court on a stretcher. Which was what they did and they got two packing cases to lay it across in the well of the court.

SENTENCE OF DEATH ON 'DYING' GIRL

Sentence of death was passed yesterday at Devon Assizes by Mr Justice Pilcher on twenty-year-old Elizabeth Anne Drew for the murder of twenty-six-year-old Mrs Janet Margaret Jones of Plymouth. The jury, who included three women, took seventy minutes to reach their verdict. Drew, who was said to be suffering from a severe illness which was probably incurable, heard the verdict apparently without emotion from the stretcher she was lying on in court, and was afterwards taken by ambulance to the County Gaol.

Prosecuting Counsel said that Drew fatally stabbed Mrs Jones with a dagger because she refused to return to live with her and that this was a premeditated act. He said, 'It was clearly a case of cold-blooded callous murder.'

Principal Prison Medical Officer Dr R. Brown said that while she was in custody on remand, Drew had refused to be interviewed by him. But he had studied all the evidence and documents carefully, he said, and in his opinion the accused was sane 'when she drove the dagger into the dead woman's body'. He did not agree when questioned by Drew's counsel that she did not know what she was doing. He agreed that he had no qualifications in mental disease except experience.

Defending, Mr J.C. Maude, QC, submitted that Drew had a disease of the mind and at the moment of the murder did not know the difference between right and wrong. He also referred to her serious physical condition, and said it was not possible to estimate what effect long treatment including the administration of drugs could have had on her. He asked the jury to return a verdict of guilty but insane.

In his summing-up to the jury, Mr Justice Pilcher said the jury had only one short point to consider. 'She is guilty of murder unless you think that at the time of striking the blow she was insane within the meaning of the law.' He said it was quite clear that during their association, Drew and Mrs Jones had formed a perverted passion. The jury might feel disgust or sorrow that that sort of thing should exist, but no doubt the prisoner was 'passionately attached' to Mrs Jones. 'The state of her mind is a question of fact, and therefore is a question for you, members of the jury.'

(*From a contemporary newspaper report*)

—What the judge said to me when he sentenced me to death. I didn't need to write it down because I can remember it exactly word for word off by heart. He said: 'Elizabeth Anne Drew, you are twenty years of age and it is my duty to pass upon you the only sentence which the law can pass for the crime of wilful murder. The sentence of the Court upon you is that you be taken from this place to a lawful prison, and thence to a place of execution, and there you suffer death by hanging, and that your body be buried within the precincts of the prison in which you shall have been last confined before your execution; and may the Lord have mercy upon your soul. Take her down.'

—My story of what it was like the first time I was in prison.

After I'd been sentenced to death I was taken to the condemned cell in Exeter prison. The first thing they do is weigh you and make up a bag of the same weight as you are, and practise with it on the end of a rope so they can work out what the right length of drop for you should be. If it's too short it won't break your neck, you'll just hang there and slowly strangle to death, and if it's too long you fall too far and it can jerk your head off. The condemned cell is next to the execution shed with just a door in between so you have only to walk a few steps when they come to hang you, and you can hear them practising with the bag at night when they think you're asleep.

My mother and sister came to see me every day but there was always glass between us, and they were always embarrassed and couldn't think of what to say. I didn't really want to see them anyway. The other person who came every day was the prison chaplain. I told him not to because there was nothing to talk about, but he went on coming and kept asking me had I changed my mind about repenting.

Altogether I was eight days in the condemned cell and doctors kept coming to examine me. I felt as though I was dying from my illness and the amount of blood I kept coughing up, and I hoped I'd die before they came to hang me. Then one afternoon the Prison Governor came into my cell with a letter in his hand which he said he had to read out to me. It was from the Home Secretary and it said in view of my health my sentence had been commuted to one of imprisonment for life. After he'd gone the prison officers in my cell all shook my hand and congratulated me. I thought it wasn't very sincere of them because from the looks on their faces they seemed to be thinking I was so ill I was going to die anyway, and they were relieved I was saving them the trouble.

The day afterwards I was moved to Holloway prison where they had a proper hospital. A Scottish doctor came to see me and examined me, and he told me he was determined to save my life. I didn't like him, and I told him I didn't want to live, but he said he was going to do it whether I wanted it or not. He sent me to an outside hospital in Middlesex for an operation for the removal of one of my lungs. I was there for ten days and then I was sent back to the hospital wing at Holloway and I spent nearly two years there under treatment from this doctor. He said I needed rest and care and not to work. He was a very strange sort of man, very Scottish and very abrupt, and in all the time I knew him he never once smiled or gave me a kind word. Everything he said was very gruff: 'Turn over so I can listen to your back, cough, put your clothes back on', all the time like that.

Then one day he said he'd done all he could for me and I was as good in health as I'd ever be, but I was to look after myself and if I ever felt tired I was to go and lie down. He told all this to the prison staff too and said I was only to do light work, so they put me in the library. As I gradually got my strength back I became very aggressive again and was always arguing and fighting and getting into trouble. Stop it Elsa. The Governor called me into her office one day and said they couldn't do any more for me at Holloway, they were going to send me to Askham Grange where it would be up to me and how I behaved how long it was before I was let out on licence.

I didn't like Askham Grange any better than Holloway and I still kept getting into trouble up there. Elsa's getting restless because it's past her feeding time and she wants me to feed her and take her out for her walk, so I'll have to stop in a minute. In the end at Askham Grange they told me they were going to let me out on licence. I'd been in prison altogether I think it was between seven and eight years. All right Elsa shut up, now stop barking, I'm going to feed you in a minute. At Askham no she's not going to are you my beauty no you're not, all right then we'll have to stop and go on from there tomorrow.

HAPPINESS IS JUST A WORD[1]

Gus Webster

A small bald-headed man with a yellowed lined face and lacklustre eyes, he sat on a bench in the prison's deserted dining hall talking in a strained hoarse voice, smoking cigarettes one after another without pause and stubbing them out in an overflowing chipped white ashtray which he held in his hand.

—My name is Gus Webster and I'm sixty-nine. My crime was first-degree felony murder: I was sentenced to death for it at the age of twenty-four, but it was commuted to imprisonment for life. I've been incarcerated so far now for just over forty-five years.

To give you some kind of background I'll summarise my life for you as best I can. But all it amounts to really is one word, and that word's institutions. I'm a product of them, I don't know any other kind of life: as far back as I can remember I've been in one kind or another of them since the day I was born.

I believe I'm the child of poor whites who lived in Tennessee: that may or may not be true but it's what I've been told by social workers over the years. Occasionally they came across bits of information about me and passed them on. They say my father was an alcoholic who never stayed the same place very long, and my mother was a schizophrenic who was confined to mental hospital before I was born. She had me while she was in there, then wandered off on her own leaving me for someone else to look after. My last name, my surname as it's called, may be hers or it may not; or it could be my father's, which it is definitely I don't know. I'm told there was a patient registered with her name at that hospital, but nobody can find out much detail of how I appeared. She's obviously dead by now.

1 *The Violence Of Our Lives* (1995) London: HarperCollins, pp. 121–30.

At birth I was passed on to an orphanage, and I grew up in state homes for children for my first sixteen years. They were like my permanent base, but there were occasional fosterings out for short periods at different stages. They were all only for short periods because I didn't stay with any of them for more than a few weeks at the most and then I ran away. I was picked up by the police when I was wandering the streets or out on country roads, and then returned by them to one of the orphanages I'd come from. My impression of foster parents is that every one of them were people doing it for payment rather than they had a liking for children. No one made any lasting impression on my memory, I couldn't even tell you one of their names. My recollection's of a whole series of different men or women in different homes, periods in a whole lot of orphanages, and taking lessons at any number of different schools. Between times I rode freight trains, hitchhiked on trucks and generally bummed around.

You know, it was a blur of faces all the time. They wasn't attached to persons, it was like they were all passing on a reel of film projected on a wall. I never had no kind of bond with any one of them at all. Even with a social worker or someone of that sort I had no lasting consistent relationship I recall: they always seemed to be changing. Not with anyone at all did I ever have what might be called an exchange of affection: I never knew what it meant and I still don't now. There was no one I ever felt warmth towards and no one came across either as displaying it to me. It wasn't mutual dislike, just nothing between me and anyone, nothing at all.

I've often thought I'd try to write about how it felt in all of my childhood to be a cipher to people, no more than a name on a record sheet or a number on a file. I have this picture in my mind of the same thing happening every time: meeting someone in an office or some-where and them pausing a minute before we started talking while they read up about me and checked out who I was. I came across the word 'loner' in a magazine article not long ago: I looked it up in the dictio-nary to see how it was defined. It said a loner was a person with a preference for being independent and staying on his own. I was a loner all through my life; but it wasn't a matter of preference, I wasn't offered no choice, I never knew there was an alternative. Another word I looked up one time was 'happiness': it said it was a state of having or giving great pleasure or joy. That's something I've not expe-rienced either, for me happiness is just a word.

I've always had a feeling of not belonging anywhere, and I remember an instance that kind of confirmed it to me when I was thirteen or round about that age. I was placed in a state juvenile home in Nevada and one day a woman came who was a visiting social worker and she asked me into the office with her for us to have a talk. She said she'd been doing some digging around concerning me and she'd discovered the names and address of a couple in Tucson Arizona six hundred miles away who could possibly be related to me, maybe an uncle and aunt. She said would I like her to write them and perhaps enclose a letter from me also, asking if they'd correspond. I said sure I would, so she said OK she'd go ahead: but she warned me I shouldn't be too disappointed if we drew a blank. I wrote out a short letter for them along lines she dictated and gave it her to send on.

The juvenile home was one which didn't have strict discipline or many rules and they didn't bother too much about locking things up. So in the evening I snook back in the office when no one was there, and I took these people's address from the note she'd left in my file. I wanted to do more than just write them a letter, I wanted to meet with them and ask if they could tell me a little about my mother or father. Up till then I'd never come across one single person in my life who might be connected with them or could say they'd ever so much as seen them and what they looked like.

A couple of nights later I walked out from the orphanage and hitched my way into town. Then I took a long bus ride through the night and most of the day to Tucson. I slept in a derelict shack and next morning enquired of people back at the bus station where the address I had might be. Someone thought they knew it and told me it was a farm way out to the north. That involved me hitching another truck ride to find it and when I saw it at first it looked like a kind of wonderland. It was big and well kept-up, and obviously the folk who lived there must have been pretty prosperous, I thought. I walked up a long drive to the house and knocked on the door, and it was opened by a woman I remember was wearing a house coat of some kind of blue velvet material which looked very smart.

I asked did the people whose name I had live there: she didn't tell me, and her reply was very sharp, asking me why did I want to know? I didn't have no reason not to tell her: I said I was looking for them because I thought it could be they were relatives of mine. A look came on her face like it was set in concrete: she asked me was I the boy the social worker'd sent them on a letter they'd had the previous day. I said yes I was; and then she looked me straight in the face and said they didn't know me and they'd never heard of the people, the social worker thought could have been my parents. I was going to say something in reply but before I could she said if I didn't get off their land immediately she was going to call the police.

I've often thought about it since and I don't have any feelings of bitterness towards the woman. I think she probably could have been correct. If homeless youths were all people who wanted to find themselves a good niche in life, her farm she had there would be a good target for anyone to aim at. She'd maybe had people before, arriving claiming to be some kind of long-lost relative. Anyway, I didn't say anything else to her, all I did was turn around and walk away.

After travelling all that way I didn't feel like going back to the state juvenile home in Nevada; instead I made my way right over to Georgia, doing casual work on farms and I lived rough then for around three years. I never stayed in any one place long, not because I was restless but because I developed a liking for the fact I could live how I liked, not eat meals or go to bed when somebody else said, and I could please myself about everything. But one day I was walking along the roadside some place where by the side of it there was an orchard of orange trees. The fruit on them was like no oranges I'd ever seen, big and juicy and tempting; so I went in the orchard because it had no fence or anything round it, and I plucked about six and set myself down to eat them on a slope by the road. After no more than five minutes a sheriff's car came by, and when he saw me he pulled his gun and stopped, and came over and asked me what in hell I thought I was doing. I didn't react or anything to make him think I looked like I might be trouble: I only said I was hot and thirsty and the oranges looked good so I'd helped myself. He said that was enough for him, I was stealing; he made me get in the car and he drove us into town.

I couldn't understand why there was so much hassle about it, till then I'd never come up against the law. I was kept in a cell and the next day put in front of a court. I was charged with theft, wrongful entering of someone's property, vagrancy and I think other things too but I've forgotten just what. The end result was I was sentenced to two years in a juvenile correctional centre, which I think was because they didn't know what else to do with me. I've no reason for saying it, only my suspicion is they contacted the state orphanage I'd been in, and they'd said I was too old for them or something, and they couldn't have me back.

So there I was, another period in an institution: but now it was for offenders and it was specifically a criminals' one. There were around sixteen hundred boys there: I didn't make any close friends with any of them but it was the first place I'd been where I got partly acquainted with other youngsters of my own age. I remember I listened to the stories some of them told about things they'd done and I was amazed: in comparison my own life had been very dull and uninteresting. I wasn't attracted to the idea of imitating them and living a life of crime, but it broadened my knowledge of what went on in the world: drugs, thieving, guns, knives, sex, pornography, homosexuality, prostitution and everything. It was a real education.

When I was set free I continued living my life the same way as I'd done previously. A description of what I was when I was twenty would be to say I was a bum, with a slight tendency towards petty thieving which I hadn't had before. I didn't do house burglaries or anything big: it went no further than taking something if it was lying around when nobody was looking, and then selling it for what I could get. Pocket radios, watches from washrooms, wallets from coat pockets, all one-off casual things of that sort. I also worked too if I had to: digging, cement mixing, nailing up boardwalks, car washing, all sorts. The only one of any real relevance is I worked a few months in a diner as a short-order cook.

There was another young guy there who was also a cook: he was an ex-con from California. It takes one to know one is a saying I've heard: there's definitely some truth in that. I don't know why it should be but if you've done time you can usually tell about somebody if they've done time too. You don't have to ask them or speak even, all you need do's look at them, and watch the way they look back at you. Sometimes you might give a little nod to each other, to signify you know. It was like that with this guy from California, the first conversation we ever had when we were leaving one morning at the end of a shift wasn't 'Have you been convicted ever?' it was 'Where were you and how long did you do?'

One day we went out in the woods to shoot some wild turkey: I don't know where he'd got it but he had a gun, and I'd never handled one so he showed me how to. Before long our outings were on a regular basis once a week: and we started giving each other confidences about ourselves and telling each other our life stories. Mine was not very interesting, but he said he'd once actually pulled an armed robbery by breaking into someone's house. The next occasion we were out he mentioned he'd learned of a prospect and asked me how I'd feel about coming in on it: there'd be just the two of us, him and me. The idea scared me a little but I didn't want him to see that, so I said OK yes I would. We went back to town and had a drink on it and he told me what was in his mind.

He had information that there was a certain guy, a fairly small-time gambler who always had sums of cash in his house. They weren't big enough for him to start screaming about if he lost them, maybe not more than a thousand dollars or so at any one time; and he didn't take special security precautions, so it ought to be a pushover to go in and rob him. It was out of my class so far as anything I'd done before, but I thought about it and the excitement of it greatly appealed. Two nights or so later we set off, in an automobile we'd taken from a parking lot, and we drove out to this house. Because of his record the guy I was with said if anything went wrong and we were caught, we'd get a lesser sentence if I was the one who went in and did the hold-up: he'd stay outside in the car with the engine running ready for a quick getaway. He'd brought stockings with him for us to put over our heads, and I remember thinking this was what proper crime was about, and now I was heading for the big time.

I went up the steps at the front of the house and I did like you see in the movies, I banged on the door and I shouted 'Open up! Police!' We'd figured a small-time gambler like him would be scared by that approach and not put up too much resistance; and when the door was opened quickly without questions it seemed to indicate we were right. A middle-aged woman answered the knock and straight away I jumped in the hallway with the gun and told her to back up. Another woman came out from one of the side rooms very scared with her hands up over her head: she asked who I was and what I wanted, and I said where was Alf or whatever the guy's name was. The first woman started to cry: she said he didn't live there, he lived in the house next door.

She was right: we'd come to the wrong address. I was standing in the hallway thinking obviously from the way she was behaving she was genuine and we'd made a mistake, and I was wondering how to get out. At that point all the lights in the hallway switched off and somebody jumped on my back from behind. I didn't see any details of him. Later I learned he was the same age as me and he was the younger woman's son. There was a struggle in the darkness: he was trying to get the gun from me and my feeling's always been the woman joined in too and tried to help him. Then suddenly the gun went off, just a single shot, and the guy slumped up against me and then slid down to the floor. The older one of the women must have found the light switch because the lights came on again, and there the guy was, lying dead with the side of his head blown in.

I had a real sick feeling inside of me. I knew I ought to be trying to run away, but I couldn't move. The younger one of the women

231

looked like she was paralysed too; but the old one reached out with her hand to the telephone and took it off the hook, and then after a minute said very quietly 'Police'. The three of us in our different ways were all in shock I guess: my memory just blacks out from there on, and I don't remember more. Me and the guy waiting in the car outside were both arrested and charged with felony murder. We were held for a year before we came for trial, and the outcome was the only one possible: we were both sentenced to go to the electric chair.

—It was three years all told I was on Death Row waiting to be executed, and in that time I felt like I aged a hundred years. Nobody knew me or came to see me except my attorney: I was a sort of an unknown person to everyone, sitting there waiting week to week and from month to month. The attorney was what they call *pro bono*, he was paid for out of public funds, and I expect he thought my case was a lost cause. He said he'd contact the last juvenile home I'd been in but whether he did or not I don't know: nothing came back so far as I know in the way of a reply. It would have been ten years at least since I'd lived there: everyone who'd had any knowledge of me had moved away long since and my records had been lost or misplaced I suppose.

He didn't come to see me much, maybe once in three months but no more: all I recollect him saying to me was 'Don't worry' and 'It'll all come out good in the end' and other things like that. They didn't sound very convincing or inspiring and all round his enthusiasm wasn't very marked. If I was to say to you it was a lonely time that would be about it: but loneliness was something I'd always been used to, it'd been my constant companion the whole of my life and I didn't expect any different. After a year and a half I was told the news, I forget who by, that the other guy who'd been with me on the attempted robbery had been given a commutation to life imprison-ment of his death sentence and it'd been on several grounds. One was he'd been outside in the car all the time and not even in the house when the shot was fired; another was his attorney had put up a persuasive argument that all the way along the line the idea had been wholly mine. Most important though and what finally swung it for him, so I understand, was he had family and they kept writing all the time to the State Governor and asking him to show clemency.

There was no one to do the same for me, or had any interest in doing it. All that could be said on my behalf was I'd had no genuine intention to kill anyone when I went in the house, and the gun had gone off by accident in a struggle in the dark with at least three people's hands on it. There'd been mine and the young man who was killed and very likely his mother's too, and no one could say for certain whose finger it was had been on the trigger when it went off. They weren't arguments with much conviction to them: someone had died, someone had to pay the price, and the only person who could do that was me.

There's a whole lot of formulations that are gone through in the way of appeals against sentence of death, and a definite chronological order in which they're done. As far as I know my attorney went through them all in the right order, but none of them had a positive result. Dates for my execution were set and then postponed for the hearing of each appeal, but finally when they'd all run out the last date was fixed for five minutes after midnight on the first Thursday of April in I think it was 1952. As the time got nearer and nearer I was so scared I didn't eat or speak, and I refused an offer for the chaplain to come and see me the night before I was due to die. I didn't have any religious belief and nothing was in me that aroused any desire to make a last minute conversion.

They came for me at nine thirty on the Wednesday evening and moved me from my cell down into the execution chamber where I was to stay the last hours until the due time. It was very eerie because there were other people there such as guards and a doctor and prison officials, but none of them said anything at all to me or seemed to notice I was there: they were paying no attention to me, just kind of looking through me all the time. It was half an hour before midnight before anyone said anything to me: that was the prison warden. He looked at me, then nodded at the chair and said 'Time'. They strapped my arms and legs in it and from behind me I could feel them putting a heavy metal cap on the top of my head and fixing some electric wires to connect with it. The warden then went off into a kind of separate chamber in front and to one side of me: it was his responsibility to pull the switch, and I could see him through the window of it making a big show of concentrating on meters there and dials. I was numb: in my mind and my emotions I was dead already, and the only feeling I can remember is wishing they'd get on with it quickly and not wait for the hand of the clock on the wall to reach five after twelve.

In the room where the warden was was a telephone on a high desk. I couldn't hear that it rang but it must have, because the warden suddenly stopped what he was doing and went and lifted the receiver off the hook. He listened a few moments, then he nodded and put it back again. He looked at me through the glass window panel and he did a movement like this across with his hands in front of his face to signal it was off: then he came out back into the execution chamber and said 'You've got a commutation.' I closed my eyes and I completely blanked out unconscious.

—When I opened my eyes I was in a hospital bed: I was under sedation and didn't know whether I was dead or what. My consciousness kept coming and going: I'd fall off into sleep, then half wake up again, then go back into unconsciousness once more. I was fed on liquids a day or so but gradually I began to sit up and eat a little: I remember taking some plain cookies at first, and some milk. I was in the prison hospital where the nurses were all male, and one of them told me it was fifteen minutes before he was due to pull the switch that the warden had the telephone call. Nobody seemed to know why the sentence had been commuted to a life term, and it was about six months before I found out. Apparently the State Governor had only heard at the last moment I was due to die that night, and he'd acted off the cuff but not given reasons. If he hadn't I wouldn't have been here today talking to you, so the fact I'm still alive is only due to his intercession on my behalf. I believe he was supposed to have later said something about me having been brought up from birth without parents or relatives and I was therefore everybody's responsibility in some kind of way: because I had no one to stand and plead for me, that wasn't sufficient reason for me to die. He was against the death penalty too I think. I wrote him a letter telling him as best as I was able my gratitude; and twenty years ago when he himself died I wrote his widow saying I owed my life to him and I'd always do the best with it I could. I guess she must have thought there weren't many available possibilities for that, but if she did I like to think I've proved her wrong. I went on from there determined I'd try and find a place somewhere in the scheme of things for a convicted murderer who'd been reprieved.

Part VII

CONCLUSION

As Tony Parker became increasingly well-known, he was often asked about his technique. How did he manage to get such a range of people to talk to him? What was the secret?

While the interviews always remained confidential, Tony was happy to talk about how he went about his task. Over the years he had developed his technique thoughtfully, carefully and methodically. When someone wrote to him about his methodology, he would send a copy of his sheet on 'Some very basic principles of interviewing' or another sheet entitled 'Some notes on what questions to ask, and how'. Later he focused on the 'Principles of tape-recorded interviewing' which largely summarised his art. These short documents encapsulate many of the clues towards identifying what is particularly distinctive about the Parker approach. Hopefully, there is enough here for someone to carry forward the Parker tradition.

Lyn Smith met Tony when she came to interview him. They kept in touch during the last decade of his life. She suggested a book about his work and methodology. Tony modestly cast the suggestion aside: 'Who on earth would want to read it?' By the time he had come round to the idea, his deteriorating health and other writing commitments meant that it was never to be. Lyn Smith, however, can tell us more than most about Tony Parker's methodology.

SOME VERY BASIC PRINCIPLES OF INTERVIEWING

Tony Parker

1   Always remember the interview is about the other person, and not about you. However great the temptation, don't be led into talking about yourself, but tactfully guide it back to the subject in hand, i.e. the other person. (If anyone ever starts asking me about me – my wife, family or whatever – I always know that I'm not handling the interview right, because she/he should be thinking about themselves, not about me.) Be pleasant, but not too jokey.

2   Always use a tape recorder, and always one with an integral mike (a mike is too obtrusive). Put it in sight, but out of the sight-line between you and the person you're talking to. While you're talking, hold eye contact between you every single moment.

3   Before you go to the interview, check the recorder's batteries, and that you've got sufficient tape(s). While you're putting the tape in the machine, don't be too good at it. This stops you looking like the self-confident expert, which can be a bit frightening to the other person (and get them thinking about you: see 1 above).

4   Always take with you (but keep in your bag) a second, stand-by recorder, so that if for any reason yours doesn't work (tape snag, low battery or whatever) you can use the substitute instead without making the situation seem like a crisis.

5   Before starting, reassure the person you're interviewing that (a) no one else besides you is going to hear the tape, and (b) you're only using a recorder because it's easier for you, rather than taking notes. So: they don't have to bother speaking to the mike, 'ums' 'ahs' and 'ers' don't matter, and there's no problem about 'wasting' the tape. Tell them this.

6   Start by saying you want to check the tape recorder is actually recording (which indeed you must, to avoid getting home and finding you've only a blank tape). I always use the old BBC standby for this: 'What did you have for breakfast this morning?' This is unexpected and slightly comic, and helps put them at their ease. Their short answer will, together with your prior question, be quite sufficient for you to stop, rewind and play back the check. After you've done it, don't forget to go back into 'record' mode again.

7   Without drawing attention to it, make sure that for the interview you're sitting on the same level as, or preferably slightly lower than, the person you're talking to. This conveys subconsciously that they are on top of the situation, and are not the frightened rabbit being looked down at by the 'expert interviewer'. See 1 and 3 above.

8   At the end, ask two questions. (1) 'Is there anything on the recording that you don't want me to use?' If there is, give your word you won't use it, and don't. (2) 'Is there anything you feel you'd like to add on, or explain more fully?' I very often tell people before I start that I'm going to ask them these questions at the end. This serves two purposes: (1) it puts them more at ease, and (2) it's a useful way of indicating to them that the interview is ending.

9   After it's over, people very often say 'Could I hear a bit of it?' Agree instantly. Then, whizz back to about the middle (not the beginning or the end), replay about two minutes but no more, and then switch off, saying enthusiastically 'That was great, thank you very much.' Don't let it run on more than two minutes, or let them decide when that switch-off will be. This prevents them (and sometimes you) getting too fascinated by it and over-running in time.

10   Afterwards, at home, transcribe every word and pause and um and ah and er of it. It's murder.

SOME NOTES ON WHAT QUESTIONS TO ASK, AND HOW

Tony Parker

1   Remember they're doing you a favour (you're not the one who's doing them one) in giving you their time and attention. Tell them beforehand roughly how long you'll need (and overestimate it by 10–15 minutes, don't underestimate it). This prevents them getting irritable and wondering how much longer it's going on. It also allows you to finish earlier than you said, with the implicit suggestion it was due to their skill and helpfulness.

2   Remember it's a chat, not an interrogation that you're going to put them through. Tell them that if you ask them something they don't want to talk about, all they need to do is say 'I'd rather not talk about that', and you'll immediately move on to something else.

3   It's not at all difficult to reduce someone to tears. What *is* difficult is to put them together afterwards, and as you're not a trained therapist you won't be able to do it properly. So don't let it get to that stage in the first place.

4   There's no shortage of clever-dick interviewers who can't wait to make it plain to the person they're interviewing that they know as much, or probably far more, about the subject in hand than the person they're talking to. You are not like that. You are an ignorant but interested learner, most intrigued by what the person's telling you, and extremely grateful to them for doing it.

5   Never presume you know what someone means, and if in doubt, ask them to explain. For example: if they don't know what a brilliant musician you are, don't feel impelled to tell them. Instead you can ask a question such as 'What exactly *is* a "riff"?' This will also give you an idea of whether they know what they are talking about or not (but don't let it show if you discover they don't).

6   Similarly ignorance, real or feigned, can be invaluable to you. Very often someone will say to you at the end of a sentence '(Do you) know what I mean?' Instead of nodding instant agreement, say something like 'I'm not sure if I do, could you explain it a bit more?'

7   Whenever possible, avoid asking a question which can be answered with a straight 'Yes' or 'No'. For example: don't ask 'Do you like Eric Clapton?' Ask instead 'What do you think of Eric Clapton?' When they've said, follow it up with 'Why?'

8   Remember: you are there to listen, not to talk. Listen to yourself as well, constantly checking that you're not saying too much. Don't be afraid of remaining silent, giving the person you're interviewing time and 'space' to think before and while s/he is speaking. Don't rush in with another question until you're sure they've said all they want to say.

9   Never ask 'double' questions (i.e. two questions at once) such as 'Do you like Indian takeaways or do you prefer Chinese?' Rephrase into two parts: 'What do you think of Indian food?' 'How do you feel about Chinese?' (Neither of which can be answered 'Yes' or 'No', remember.)

10   The purpose of detailed transcribing of tapes mentioned in Part 1/10 is not only to get what the person said, but also to listen carefully to your own questions, to realize how poor they were, and to resolve to try to do better next time.

11   Finally. Never ask questions for the sake of asking them. Write down before exactly what you want to know, and memorize the list. Keep it out of sight, right until the end, and then say 'I'll just check I've asked you all I wanted to', and take it out and openly look at it. But *not* at the start, ever.

PRINCIPLES OF
TAPE-RECORDED
INTERVIEWING

Tony Parker

I am an oral historian who has had twenty books published in the last thirty years. I have recently been given an Honorary Doctorate by the University of Essex for my work in this field, and my methods are these:

1   Before I begin my tape-recorded interview I explain to the person I am talking to exactly what I am doing – what the interview is for, and how, if it is used, what the context is in which it will appear. I also explain it will take between 45 minutes and 1 hour.

2   My interviews are always conducted face-to-face and person-to-person. No recording is made without their permission and without them knowing the recorder is switched on.

3   I never interview anyone in the presence of anyone else.

4   I never use a person's real name or give a clearly identifiable physical description of them. Similarly, all locations mentioned are changed – for example, Birmingham to Leeds, and so on. Some people say they don't mind being identified: and if they wish to identify themselves in a published book, that is their prerogative.

5   I never discuss or even mention what anyone has said to me with anyone else, nor do I ever play back any part of a tape-recorded interview to other people, in public or in private.

6   At the end of the interview, I ask the person I have been talking with if there is any part of our recorded conversation they want me either not to use, or not use at all, and record their answer on the same tape. If there is, I give them an undertaking I will not use it, or alter it as they wish me to.

7   Finally, I explain that though I may not use all they have said (perhaps for example because others have said or will say something identical), I will not put words into their mouths or have them saying things they didn't say.

8   If anyone would like to meet me first, without commitment, before deciding whether they want to be interviewed or not, this can easily be arranged.

ONLY LISTEN...

Some reflections on Tony Parker's methodology

Lyn Smith

I first met Tony Parker in 1986 when I was sent by the Imperial War Museum to his Suffolk cottage to interview him about his pacifist experience in the Second World War. Like so many of those who have met Parker through his work, I remained in touch and we became good friends.

Over the years we had many discussions about our mutual interests in interviewing and the crafting of books from interview material, and I had often suggested a book about his work and methodology. Parker eschewed this proposal with his usual humility – 'Who on earth would want to read it?' – until May 1996 when he wrote saying that he was now more receptive to the idea. How about a collaboration?

> I'm getting such a steady stream of enquiries now about interviewing and transcribing and editing and 'How do you do it?' questions that it seems to me there might well be room for, and an interest in, a short(ish) book for oral historians *manqué* – particularly in schools where there's a growing interest in projects based on it...

We agreed that I should interview him on the different phases, transcribe and edit to a first draft, Parker would then give the final edit and I would write it up. His deteriorating health and pressure of his ongoing work – he was finishing his book on Studs Terkel and interviewing for the putative doctors' book as well as organising this anthology – meant that the project was delayed. His death put the seal on it.

Tony Parker did, however, set out his basic principles of interviewing which have been given in the preceding chapters. Oral historians, in the main, would accept these pointers as sound advice: the importance of open-ended questions, of listening and not interrupting, the total respect for the interviewee and so on. But this was only part of the process: his aims were always directed at producing books forged out of the interview material. These achieved critical acclaim and popular success. Parker would argue that there was no 'secret' to his success, that 'anyone could do it. Why *weren't* they doing it?' But this is to underestimate the sheer perfectionism he put into his craft, his meticulous preparation, interviewing, editing and writing skills, as well as an idiosyncratic approach and his level of motivation. These were the attributes of his work which led to the accolade: 'He was the greatest oral historian of our day.'[1]

Preparation was paramount, and Parker would read extensively about his topic. Working with offenders, for instance, he would obtain every Home Office pamphlet relating to a particular offence and he would know every statistic. Having identified key people in the field, he would contact them asking for their help or advice. The same was true of work he did in the United States or the Soviet Union. The important thing was that by having names and organisations behind him, he established his credibility as a serious writer with a serious purpose, not just another journalist wanting a sensational story.

Information was equally important as interviewing started. This was not only out of respect for the informant, but for getting the balanced view he always sought, or for following up clues and themes which had unexpectedly emerged and needed expansion. It was this concern with solid, meticulous preparation and ongoing research which made his books so comprehensive in the range of voices he presented.

Once the ground had been prepared, lists of would-be informants made out and permission obtained to interview, Parker would then if possible meet the informant beforehand for a preliminary meeting. If this was not possible – for instance, interviewing in American prisons, or working in the Soviet Union – then a well-briefed intermediary would prepare the ground. Parker made it clear from the start that no money was involved. His aim was to achieve a position of absolute trust and mutual respect between himself and the informant: also he felt that if people were paid they might be tempted to exaggerate, or invent. He needed to convince the informant, whether

---

1 Obituary, *The Times*, 11 October 1996.

an offender or otherwise, that he was coming to meet them on absolutely equal terms, in a spirit of openness with no preconceived ideas, and not judging him or her in any way. The moment that cheques or money became involved that was undermined.[2]

Parker would always carefully explain his procedure. Informants were always assured of complete confidentiality: no one but he would know their real names and that any description would be altered to avoid identification.[3] He also guaranteed that on completion of the book the tapes would be wiped clean. These assurances would be given on the tape at the start; at the end he would ask them, again on tape, if there was anything they had said that they wanted taken out or changed, or anything added. He would tell them that the interview would last just one hour and give some idea of how many times he would like to see them. He would also make it clear that until he had gathered all his material, he could not guarantee that they would feature in the book at all. As Margery Parker explained:

> His main concern was to put them fully in the picture and not take advantage of them – to use them and then disappear. He would give his address and telephone number and offer that if they wanted to keep in touch, he'd be pleased. This often happened and many of those interviewed became good friends. Others, the sex offenders, for instance, would telephone from time to time, especially when they were having a bad moment...It wasn't exactly counselling, but like a friend ringing a friend. He'd make cheering noises down the phone 'OK, do you want me to come and see you then?' or 'Shall we go and have a talk somewhere?' and off he'd go.[4]

Any potential problems were worked through before interviewing started. A major challenge for Parker was working through an interpreter for *Russian Voices*. Before leaving for Russia, he had worked out a setting whereby he was sitting slightly below the informant and with the interpreter standing behind him or her – the whole aim

---

2 An exception to this would be *The Courage of His Convictions* when Tony Parker insisted on equally sharing the fee of £1000 with Robert Allerton.

3 Once Margery Parker became involved with transcribing, Parker would qualify his promise of confidentiality by saying that 'only his wife and he would hear the tapes, but only he would know their true identity'.

4 Margery Parker, interview with Lyn Smith, 11/12 June 1998.

being that the informant should speak directly to him and forget there was an interpreter present. Interpreters were given strict instructions not to interrupt nor tailor what the informants were saying in any way, but must reproduce exactly what was being said. Margery Parker, who was in the room at one time during an interview, recalls 'It was very interesting to see how the man was turning round and referring to the interpreter to begin with, and then gradually as the interview went on you realised that he was responding directly to Tony and had forgotten the interpreter. He had worked this out right from the beginning.'[5]

Having meticulously laid the groundwork, Parker then started interviewing – a thrilling moment, as he explained: 'Studs certainly put his finger on it when he told me "You're Columbus, you're setting out into the unknown sea. There are no maps, because no one's been there before." '[6]

All manner of venues were used for interviews: prison cells, prison offices, army barracks, a Russian hotel room, libraries, people's sitting rooms. Like most interviewers, Parker preferred going into people's homes; apart from people being far more at ease in their own surroundings, he also found it gave him some ambience. If necessary though he would interview anywhere: when working on *Five Women*, for instance, he interviewed one woman in a car – the only option. Like all interviewers he was always worried about extraneous noise. Although interviews for his books were not used for purposes requiring high-quality sound, clarity obviously made transcription so much easier.

Care with seating arrangements has already been mentioned: he would always ensure that lighting was kind to his informants and was concerned not to dominate them physically, always choosing, if possible, the lower chair. Ever anxious not to appear as the slick professional, if he felt the situation called for it, he would fumble with the tape-recorder to evoke sympathy and put people at ease. It was also important, he felt, that his informants had some control of proceedings. He would therefore place the tape recorder next to them, show them the stop button, and tell them they could turn it off if ever they felt unhappy about things.

Although he had researched the topic thoroughly and had some idea of the informant's place in the scheme of things he eschewed

5 ibid.
6 Tony Parker, *Studs Terkel: A Life in Words*, London: HarperCollins, 1997, p. 163.

lists of questions; but he had these in his mind. Once the flow of talk started, he kept himself very much in the background, silent and watchful, slipping his questions in to encourage expansion of a point or to keep the talk on line – Parker was not an indulgent interviewer who let people ramble on. He had a good idea of what he was looking for and, without very obviously directing the interview, he was usually able to get it. The sessions were always stopped on the hour. His style was so relaxed that people often thanked him for 'an interesting conversation'.[7] But his interviews were more than this; he knew his subject inside out and aimed to give a voice to people who were never heard, social pariahs often who seldom had the chance to express what they felt inside. He was out to demolish stereotypes: of offenders, soldiers, Russians and Americans. He was looking for the *essence* of each person and to give them opportunity to express that essence. In order to achieve this, and to do them justice he *had* structured the interview – his virtuosity was the unobtrusiveness of this.

Anyone engaged in in-depth interviewing of this type will under stand the challenge of remaining fully engaged, attentive and sympathetic, yet at the same time keeping the necessary distance and objectivity if one is to perform effectively. Parker perfected this to a fine art.

Given Tony Parker's commitment to wipe the tapes, there are few left. I have heard the first few sentences of one surviving tape: this is a good example of his warming-up skills. The anonymous interviewee is young and nervous. He starts by asking her 'What are you doing?' She tells him. 'What were you doing before that?' and then 'And before that?' How long is this going on, one wonders. But it becomes apparent that the young woman is realising that he is *really* interested in her and what she has done right back to her school days. This is a *serious* interview and she has to think about it. And she does: the flow starts and it's going somewhere. Although you no longer hear Parker's voice, he is there: quiet, empathetic, just listening.

There is little doubt that being an excellent listener was one of Parker's great strengths. As for silences, he would say that the silences were often more informative than what was said. He would relish moments when people fell absolutely still. He too would stay silent, and this 'pregnant silence' would grow.[8] He would listen and watch

---

7 Tony Parker in conversation with Lyn Smith.
8 ibid.

their every expression and gesture and these would come back to him as he later listened to the tapes, and the silences would nourish the books along with the words.

The importance of Tony Parker's personality as a factor in his success as an interviewer cannot be exaggerated, as Margery Parker explains:

> Tony had this extraordinary ability to tune in very quickly to somebody and to strike up an affinity. I think he made tremendous eye contact – he had a very direct look – and was able to convince people that he was seriously interested in them and what they were going to talk to him about was of value. He convinced them that they could trust him absolutely if the revelation was going to be in any way intimate, and that he would not be shocked whatever they said. I always thought he had a lot of the Quaker concept of 'concern'. There is no doubt that some of the appalling things they had done left him feeling very sad and upset, and he would feel concern for the victims, but beyond that he felt profound compassion for the offenders. Somehow by sheer force of personality, this was conveyed to those he interviewed.
>
> He would say that his greatest asset was his ordinariness: he wasn't very tall, he wasn't all that strikingly good-looking, he hadn't got a posh accent, he hadn't got an academic education – which he always felt a tremendous asset. He would always say that the important thing is simply being able to convey to people that you are genuinely interested, and he *was* interested, and I think this was the key. He wasn't just another interviewer coming up – of course, men in prison would have been interviewed hundreds of times – and he was a man who really wanted to listen to them; and he *could* listen.[9]

Over the years, Parker's interviewing technique was honed into an art. It was part of the whole process that he thoroughly enjoyed and would speak with delight of the 'astonishing things' he heard, and many surprises.[10] But it was an arduous stage: the sheer amount of

9   Margery Parker, interview with Lyn Smith, 11/12 June 1998.
10 Tony Parker in conversation with Lyn Smith.

interviews done for any one book meant a huge cost in terms of travel, time and money. He would spend fifteen hours, spread over several weeks, with some of his informants. The interviews for *Russian Voices* involved five visits to the Soviet Union and involved 141 people and 230 hours of tape. When interviewing for *The Frying Pan*, he lived in Grendon Underwood Prison for three months, gathering 200 hours of taped conversation. Yet this, he maintained, was the *easy* part. The really hard work was ahead.

The first stage in writing the books was transcribing the tapes. Over the course of twenty-two books the system varied. Parker transcribed all the early books dealing with offenders. From *The People of Providence* onwards this task was passed to his wife and associate, Margery, who was involved henceforth, sometimes for part of a collection with Parker transcribing anything he deemed ultra-confidential, and other times – *Bird*, for instance – the entire range. Most original transcripts, like the tapes, have been destroyed, but one sample transcript shows every 'um' and 'ah' has been faithfully recorded together with signs for short or long pauses. Parker would then select from the full transcripts, listening all the while to the tapes reminding himself of little characteristics of behaviour, and redraft. At one point he experimented with a very laborious method of reading off his selection from the original interview onto tape which Margery would then transcribe. He would then work through it, listening again to the original tape, annotating where necessary, and writing up another draft. Whatever the system, the final version was the result of numerous journeys through the original interview. It was a very time-consuming stage to which he had 'a down-to-earth, workmanlike approach but from which he gained great satisfaction and enjoyment'.[11]

Getting the voice right was crucial. Parker strove always to be faithful to the language of the informant being well aware of the distortion which can occur when the spoken word is constrained in forms of written prose. He'd edit things out, and change the order but he was always concerned to keep the original integrity of the voice, never overshaping or inventing things that had not been said for the sake of flow. He would speak as he wrote, using italics to indicate unexpected emphasis. Punctuation was almost sacred to him and many an inexperienced editor has been taken to task for daring to alter one comma: a comma, after all, meant just that – a pause. He

11 Margery Parker, interview with Lyn Smith 11/12 June 1998.

249

was particularly concerned with getting accents correct, resorting sometimes to phonetic spellings. Over the course of his twenty-two books he was challenged with Scottish, Irish, various English dialects, American and the halting English of an English-speaking Russian. His artistry was conveying in words not only the integrity of the original speech but the deep emotions – anguish, regret, loss – that he had shared during the intimacy of an interview.

One of Parker's most cherished skills was that of editing: of selecting and of shaping his oral material into something readable and of just the right length that it left the reader wanting more. It has to be remembered that throughout the whole process of interviewing, it was the *written* result which was his goal. It was a pattern, a structure, not a storyline he was after and given the variety of projects he worked on there were few rules to follow. Parker had no role model; his style was entirely his own invention.[12]

Each book presented a fresh challenge. *The Unknown Citizen* was regarded by Parker as his greatest challenge because Charlie Smith was uneducated and uncommunicative with hardly any insight into himself: '...repeatedly in trouble...they go over and over again to prison, come out, get into trouble and back again'.[13] Parker set out to present him to the public, not as a wicked offender, but someone who was victim of his own upbringing and circumstances. Because Smith was so inarticulate, there is more of Tony Parker in this book than any other.

With books dealing with a range of people, he gave a deal of thought to juxtaposing people and grouping them into a shape and structure. If he got this right, he felt, then readers would not only be kept fully engaged, but they could make their own judgements on the basis of what was being said, without any analysis or commentary. He always maintained that the shape would grow out of the material itself, but it sometimes took a great struggle to get his 'pattern', as he called it, worked out. Often a few voices would have to be discarded because they did not fit the pattern which had emerged. He called this process 'composing'. Music and writing were inextricably linked

---

12 In his work with offenders Tony Parker was, however, influenced by: the psychiatrist Anthony Storr, the criminologists Terry Morris and Trevor Gibbens, and Douglas Gibson, a prison governor. Paul Stephenson, a BBC producer, was an early influence on his interviewing style. George Ewart Evans and Studs Terkel were 'inspirational rather than influential' (Margery Parker) on the oral history dimension.

13 Tony Parker, *The Unknown Citizen*, London: Penguin, 1966, p. 11.

for Parker and symphonies – Brahms and Beethoven, in particular; Shostakovich for *Russian Voices* – very often would give him the dynamics of a book. As Margery Parker explained:

> You always knew when something had gone right – that he'd found what he had been groping for because you'd hear a great yell. He'd emerge looking completely wrung out at times, but if it had gone well, then he was on a high and ready to have a drink and relax.[14]

Tony Parker always strove to put the reader in the picture, and became a very skilled pen-portraitist describing the informant in his or her setting. Because of his promise of confidentiality, he would change the height, hair and eye colour, but always tried faithfully to reproduce body language and behavioural characteristics. I have seen a few of his resource books which contain some very detailed observations of people and places which were later used. Parker obviously gave a deal of thought to these: determined to be faithful to the person and setting, yet at the same time adhering to his principle of confidentiality. If one looks through his range of books, it is apparent how, with experience, he hones these pen-portraits to economic perfection.

'Writing's got nothing to do with talent or gift, and everything to do with loneliness, determination, application and sheer graft', he wrote to Mary Loudon.[15] Although tributes have been paid for his 'elegant prose',[16] Parker was not a confident writer. Although he had been writing poetry and prose since his youth, and could turn out a first-rate article, radio or TV play at will, he preferred to describe himself as 'a channel of communication'.[17] But over the years he became a very accomplished writer, increasingly confident about allowing his informants to speak for themselves with the minimum description, intrusion or commentary. Just as he shunned commentary or judgement during the interviews, so he resisted putting his views into the books. His aim was to introduce readers to his people, listen to them and let readers make their own judgements.

On the whole, Tony Parker's books have received critical renown

---

14 Margery Parker, interview with Lyn Smith, 11/12 June 1998.
15 Mary Loudon, 'A Rare Gift' in *The Author*, Spring 1997.
16 Margery Parker, interview with Lyn Smith, 11/12 June 1998.
17 Tony Parker in conversation with Lyn Smith.

and popular success. But he does have his critics. One criticism concerns the lack of commentary or viewpoint in his books. As many see the strength of his work in the quality of the raw voices which are presented, so other critics have criticised him for his 'open-minded journalism...his refusal to pre-judge all too often means a refusal to have an opinion on anything...'[18] Anyone who knew Tony Parker will vouch for his strong opinions. He was a convinced socialist, atheist and pacifist who never shirked making his views plain in discussions, on platforms and in the alternative press. It is surely all the more remarkable that he sought the role of silent witness – 'a *real* agent of epiphany' as he was once described.[19] True, he does make great demands on his readers who are forced to think for themselves about sex offenders, murderers, thieves and con-men, very often having to come to terms with themselves and their prejudices in disturbing ways. Also, although he is more *obviously* present in his early books such as *The Unknown Citizen* and *A Man of Good Abilities*, his presence *is* there in all his books. John Banville was spot on when, reviewing *Life After Life*, he wrote:

> ...but he is a very cunning writer. By means of arrangements and pattern, rhythm and tone, even of punctuation, he achieves an extraordinary narrative tension. He knows exactly how to place things, so the reader is carried along from one sly revelation to the next...he is as little present in this book as is possible to be, but that does not mean he is off paring his fingernails.[20]

As we have seen, once the book is finished, in keeping with his pact of confidentiality with his informants, Parker wipes all the tapes and the original transcripts are shredded. This has dismayed oral historians. As Margaret Brooks, at the Imperial War Museum, has explained: 'Historians who erase their oral history recordings are equivalent to those who might find some unique written documentary sources only to destroy them after taking notes exclusively for themselves.'[21]

---

18 Catherine Porter, *Independent on Sunday*, 21 June 1996.
19 Boyd Tonkin, *New Statesman*, 18 October 1996.
20 John Banville, *Independent on Sunday*, 11 March 1990.
21 Margaret Brooks (Keeper of the Sound Archives Department, Imperial War Museum) 'Methodology for Oral Archives', in A. Seldon and J. Pappworth (eds), *By Word of Mouth*, London: Methuen, 1983.

Peter Hart's concern is that 'where no checks could be made on the original tapes, material could be construed as works of fiction.'[22] In our several discussions on this topic, Parker would vigorously defend his stance and would not hear of an alternative such as placing the tapes, under restriction, in a safe archive. Secure anonymity and confidentiality, he felt, were the key to people trusting him. Without this guarantee, he strongly felt that people would not be so open and revealing of themselves. He therefore had no compunction in wiping the tapes and destroying the original word-for-word transcripts. As for criticisms of not working in the interests of oral history, he would reply: 'This is what I do and what I want to do, and if it doesn't fit in with any neat methodology – no problem for me.'

Although Parker's work was greatly respected by members of criminological research establishments and academe, he did receive some criticism from these institutions, as Margery Parker explained:

> Some of them thought he had a very unscientific way of going about things. I know some people criticised him for not adding graphs, which made him fall about laughing. Others would argue that he should organise his interviewees in a really scientific manner with scientific sampling. He would say 'I'm not writing a scientific paper. If I worked for the Department of Criminology, yes, I would, but I'm not doing that. I'm not appealing to scientists and academics. I'm trying to get through to your ordinary everyday reader who doesn't know anything about statistics and doesn't want to know.'

> Tony saw himself as the man in the street, presenting another man in the street, to the man in the street. To judge him from the viewpoint of academic research is just to miss the point completely. His dream was that he would open up perception, that if people listened to these offenders and saw them as real human beings and not stereotypes, it would somehow help a more liberal and understanding attitude develop towards them. Later, he felt that this was too optimistic, that his books had no effect at all on the general population. But when he died, I received many letters in which people said that they had changed their views through contact with his work.[23]

---

22 Peter Hart (writer and interviewer for Sound Archives, Imperial War Museum) in conversation with Lyn Smith.

23 Op. cit. (Margery Parker, interview with Lyn Smith, 11/12 June 1998).

Finally, it is the genre itself which has come under attack: find an interesting topic, get people talking into a tape recorder, copy out what they say – there's your book! 'OK, do it!' was always Parker's response. It was his total dedication to his project and informants, the perfectionism in all stages of his idiosyncratic methodology which made his work so outstanding. Tony Parker's legacy is as guide, exemplar and inspiration to all of us working in the field of oral history. As a respected and successful writer, he was genuinely mystified why more people weren't working in the same genre and would often throw out the challenge: 'If I can do it, anybody can. There's no mystique, just hard graft and application.' Is anyone listening?